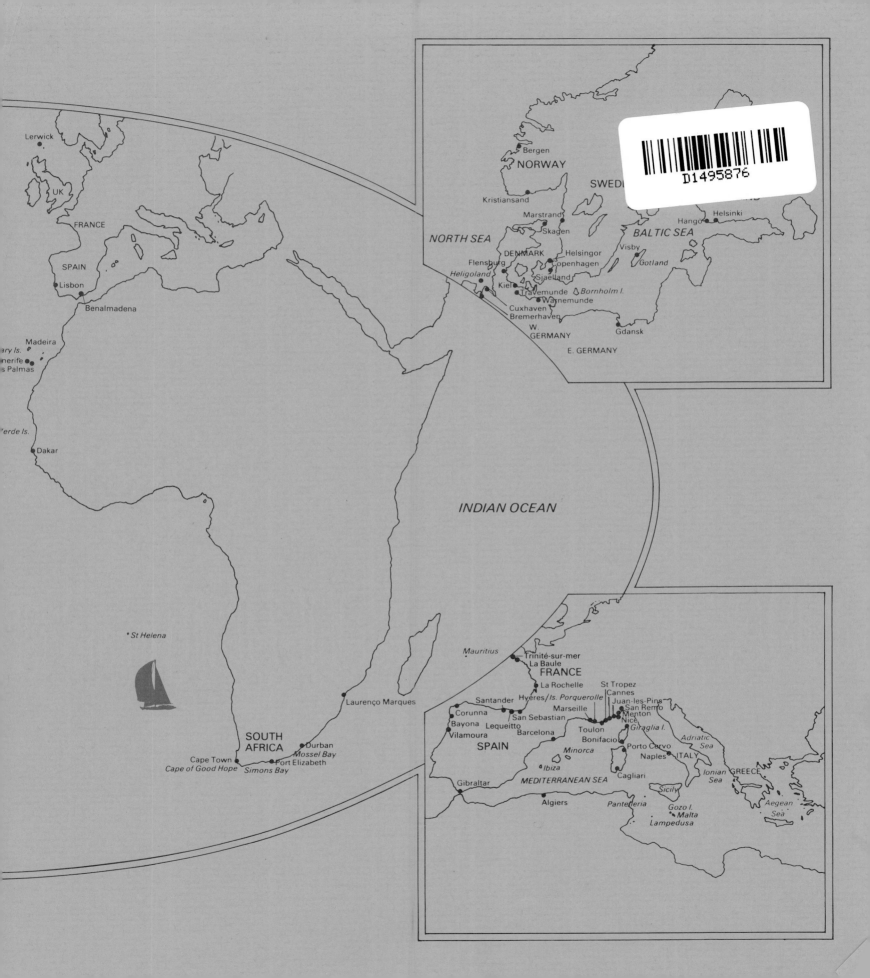

Lerwick

UK

FRANCE

SPAIN

Lisbon

Benalmadena

Madeira

ary Is.
nerife
s Palmas

'erde Is.

Dakar

NORTH SEA

DENMARK
Flensburg
Heligoland
Kiel
Cuxhaven
Bremerhaven
W.
GERMANY

E. GERMANY

Bergen

NORWAY

Kristiansand

Marstrand

Skagen

Helsingor
Copenhagen
Sjaelland
Travemunde
Warnemunde

SWEDE

BALTIC SEA

Hango

Helsinki

Visby

Gotland

Bornholm I.

Gdansk

INDIAN OCEAN

St Helena

Laurenço Marques

SOUTH
AFRICA

Cape Town
Cape of Good Hope
Simons Bay

Durban
Mossel Bay
Port Elizabeth

Mauritius

Trinité-sur-mer
La Baule
FRANCE

La Rochelle

St Tropez
Cannes
Juan-les-Pins
San Remo
Menton
Nice
Giraglia I.

Santander

Hyères/Is. Porquerolle

Marseille

Corunna
Bayona
Vilamoura

Lequeitto
Barcelona

San Sebastian

Toulon
Bonifacio

SPAIN

Minorca

Ibiza

Porto Cervo
Naples
ITALY

Adriatic
Sea

Gibraltar

Cagliari

MEDITERRANEAN SEA

Algiers

Pantelleria

Sicily

Gozo I.
Malta
Lampedusa

Ionian
Sea

GREECE

Aegean
Sea

THE
CHAMPAGNE MUMM
BOOK OF
OCEAN RACING

THE CHAMPAGNE MUMM BOOK OF

OCEAN RACING

AN ILLUSTRATED HISTORY

IAN DEAR

HEARST MARINE BOOKS
NEW YORK 1985

Library of Congress Catalog Card Number: 84-62749

ISBN: 0-688-05822-1

Printed in England

First Edition

1 2 3 4 5 6 7 8 9 10

CONTENTS

One treasures that story of the diminutive yacht in the Channel Race of, I think, 1928, which reached the finishing line after two long days and two even longer nights of wet, windward driving. As the finishing gun was fired the drenched and weary but indomitable paid hand turned to his owner and, in all good faith, shouted, 'twice round, sir?'

from *Little Ships*, by John Scott Hughes

AUTHOR'S NOTE

WITH THE HISTORY of ocean racing stretching back well over a century it is impossible – and perhaps not even desirable – to cover each event, or anything like it. I have therefore concentrated on those races, yachts, designers and owners who, in their various ways, have contributed to the development of this exciting sport, while at the same time recording the regular long distance fixtures that are its backbone.

Before proceeding I had to ask myself: what exactly is an ocean race? When the Fastnet was first sailed in 1925 some of its critics refused to allow that it was a true ocean race. Such a race, they said, had to be 'off soundings', away from any coast, and involving substantial distances across an ocean or sea. The Transpac and Bermuda races, both of which had been run many years before the Fastnet had ever been thought of, certainly qualified under this definition. However, others thought that if it was not eligible to be called an ocean race then nothing was, for the Fastnet – which had been likened by the American yachting journalist Alfred Loomis to the Grand National – had all the ingredients of an ocean race. So, despite its setting, it certainly qualifies as one as far as this history is concerned.

This classic aside, I have spent limited space on offshore events, particularly those that are less than 300 miles long, and have concentrated on the races which take place over great tracts of ocean or open sea, but not across fresh-water lakes.

Lest anyone feel I have taken, by excluding this last category, an altogether too narrow a view of the sport, I can do no better than to quote from an article on the history of ocean racing which Alfred Loomis wrote in the 1950s: 'A benign providence has not yet filled the Lakes with salt water. We therefore skip lightly over the famous long distance events of Lake Ontario, Erie, Huron and Michigan, merely pausing to remark that the Chicago-Mackinas, which was first sailed in 1898, is the oldest regularly scheduled long distance event in the world.'

So there we have it. For the purposes of this book an ocean race is a yacht race between two or more boats in salt water that generally exceeds 300 miles. With this definition in mind I have striven to record the past accurately and to bring to life a sport which is not only full of excitement, glamour and danger, but is totally international. And that can only be good.

Blow High or Low

1866–1912

THE BEGINNINGS of ocean racing are rooted deep in the history of yachting. The Yacht Club, later the Royal Yacht Squadron, was founded in 1815, the Royal Swedish Yacht Club in 1830, *La Societé des Regates du Havre* in 1837, the New York Yacht Club in 1844 and the Royal Netherlands Yacht Club in 1847. These dates show the foundation of yachting in just some of the countries which are now at the forefront of ocean racing and they approximate fairly closely to the dates of some of the first known 'ocean races'. In 1834, Lord Belfast's *Waterwitch* beat C.R.M. Talbot's *Galatea* in a two-day, 224-mile race around the Eddystone lighthouse, and in 1858 four schooners and four sloops belonging to the New York Yacht Club took part in the first American ocean race around Long Island Sound. The following year the Royal Cork Yacht Club organised a race from Dublin to Cork and received a surprisingly large entry of nine cutters, seven schooners, and a yawl. And when in 1863 The Royal Victoria Yacht Club sponsored a race from Ryde, Isle of Wight, to Cherbourg there were twenty entries.

In the US, there was a suspension of yachting during the Civil War, but in 1865 the 212-mile course from Sandy Hook to the Cape May Lightship and back was raced twice, with another long-distance race also taking place around Long Island. These races were matches between schooners belonging to members of the New York Yacht Club, and large wagers were laid on the results. Gambling amongst gentlemen was, after all, practically obligatory on both sides of the Atlantic at that time.

Another ocean race which became established early on was the 298-mile course for the Brenton Reef Cup, which was sailed from the Lightship off Newport, around the Lightship off Sandy Hook and outside of Long Island, and back. This Cup was donated in 1871 by James Gordon Bennett Jr, who had taken part in the first ocean race in 1858 in his 77-ton sloop, *Rebecca*. It was first raced in 1872 when it was won by *Madeleine*, the 1876 defender of the America's Cup.

The first Transatlantic race 1866
James Gordon Bennett Jr was, by all accounts, a rather wild young man who enjoyed indulging in these ocean races and gambling on the result, but after the 1865 season he proposed something altogether grander. A rich fellow — he was later to inherit the *New York Herald*

from his father — Bennett liked nothing more than to wager large sums on his horses and on his deep keeled, 107-foot schooner, *Henrietta*, which had taken part in the Cape May races in 1865. So when the question arose at a friendly dinner the following year as to which type of yacht, a centreboarder or a vessel with a fixed keel, was the better Bennett was quick to take up the challenge of a Transatlantic race which would resolve the question. Two other members of his club entered their schooners, one of which had a centreboard the other a deep keel and the stake was $30 000 each, winner take all. It was also agreed that no channel pilots were to be allowed on board and that the race would start at 1pm on 11th December, 'blow high or low.'

The announcement of the race caused a tremendous stir and, as the day of the start approached, excitement reached fever pitch. Millions of dollars were bet on the result. Large sums were also spent on crews. Bennett offered Samuel 'Bully' Samuels, the most experienced sailing master in the United States at the time, $10 000 to leave the ship he was commanding to skipper the *Henrietta*. Samuels accepted, and promptly put $7500 on himself to win. He must have died a rich man.

Finding good crews was not easy for it was generally acknowledged that the men were sailing to certain death. Unhappily, the presentiments of those who held this opinion

▲ *James Gordon Bennett Jr, the owner of* Henrietta *in 1866 and* Dauntless *in 1870, became Commodore of the New York Yacht Club at the early age of 26 in 1871.*

were not entirely based on fear or ignorance.

The day of the start dawned fine and cold. The wind blew neither high not low, but fresh from the west. The public turned out in their thousands to watch the start and the atmosphere was festive. The three schooners had had their rigs cut down for the crossing and two of them, *Henrietta* and the centreboarder, *Vesta,* had had their cockpits boarded over to avoid being swamped. Significantly, the third boat, *Fleetwing,* which had beaten *Henrietta* the previous year in the first Cape May race, was not given the same protection.

The start was a close one – 'you could have tossed a biscuit from one to the other,' commented Samuels afterwards – and was accompanied by loud cheers and the popping of champagne corks. The skippers of *Henrietta* and *Vesta* decided on a modified Great Circle route that took them across the Grand Banks. *Fleetwing's* skipper took a slightly more southerly course in the hope of finding easier weather and a boost from the Gulf Stream. They were to be the first of many ocean racers to ponder upon the vagaries of a Transatlantic crossing.

The three schooners soon lost sight of one another and each was left on its own to face the rain, snow and high winds and huge seas which is the usual mixture offered by the North Atlantic during December. For a week they plunged eastwards suffering only minor gear damage, but on the 18th the wind began to rise alarmingly. By 1600 it was blowing a full gale.

Up to that time *Henrietta* had, in the words of her skipper, been 'fairly burying herself', and this Samuels had found entirely to his liking. 'This is yachting in earnest,' he noted exultantly. But the onslaught of the gale was too much even for the *Henrietta* and that evening she was knocked on her beam ends. In the ensuing shambles the carpenter rushed aft and announced that the schooner had opened up forwards. This proved to be nonsense, but the carpenter's panic could well have influenced even the normally stoic Samuels, for around midnight he hove to and then waited far too long before making sail again, a mistake that could have cost him the race.

The storm hit the other two competitors with equal ferocity, but instead of heaving to they ran before the wind and the mountainous waves. *Fleetwing* was driven almost to the same latitude as *Henrietta,* while *Vesta* ran far further north. *Vesta,* until then well behind the other two, behaved magnificently, and once more became a con-

tender to win the race. When the gale blew itself out she was just a few miles behind *Henrietta. Fleetwing,* too, was well up with *Henrietta,* but was then struck by a huge wave which flooded her unprotected cockpit. The force of it swept all eight members of the crew on watch overboard. Two managed to hold on to the trysail which had come adrift, and were eventually hauled back on board. *Fleetwing* searched the area for five hours but the others were never seen again. It must have been a crushing blow not only to the morale of the decimated crew but to any remaining hope of winning the race. Yet in the following days *Fleetwing* clocked up some remarkable runs, covering as much as 260 miles in one 24-hour period.

In the meantime *Vesta* had managed to creep ahead of *Henrietta* and take the lead, and she too was going like a train. During one 24-hour period she covered 277 miles, at times touching 15 knots. 'She fairly flew,' noted one of those aboard, 'and considering the fact that the breeze lightened during the last few hours, this may be called an asto-

▲ *The 123-foot schooner,* Dauntless, *and the 108-foot schooner,* Cambria, *at the start of the second Transatlantic race.* Cambria *won but later failed to win back the America's Cup.*

nishing run. Had it continued strong, we would have made a good 300 miles. And she did it easily, too, in the same style that Kentucky wins his races, with his ears pricked!'

However, it is a good deal easier to navigate a horse to the finishing post than it is to sail a schooner on the most direct course through a series of mid-winter gales. *Vesta* had, in fact, been driven too far to the north and was eventually forced to beat into a south-easterly in order to weather the Bishop Rock which guards the entrance to the English Channel. While she was doing this *Henrietta* to the south of her passed ahead and had the Bishop Light abeam at 2200 on 23rd December, some two hours before *Vesta*.

Though *Fleetwing* was closing fast the centreboard schooner should have taken second place behind *Henrietta* which crossed the finishing line on Christmas Day at 1545.

But after picking up a pilot, and hearing that *Henrietta* had won, everyone on board *Vesta* retired below instead of making sure the pilot knew his job. By the time they had found out that he did not, and that he had mistaken the light at St Catherine's Point for the one at the Needles, it was too late and *Fleetwing* had passed them in the dark and finished at midnight on Christmas Day.

The second Transatlantic race 1870

Henrietta's phenomenally fast time of 13d,21hrs,45mins was not bettered until 1905. Although this first Transatlantic race had proved to be a memorable one, and had been received with tremendous acclaim on both sides of the ocean, it did not inspire similar races, much less promote the sport which we now call ocean racing. Its influence on the next Transatlantic race, which took

place three and a half years later, was probably small indeed for this second race was a very different affair. To start with it was an international match; secondly, the race was east to west; and thirdly it was a race for a prize not a race to settle a wager.

An English businessman, James Ashbury, decided to try to retrieve the Queen's Cup, as it was then called, which the schooner *America* had won nearly twenty years before. His challenge was accepted but as *Cambria*, his challenger, had to cross the Atlantic it seemed to Ashbury a sensible idea to race her across.

Ashbury was an inveterate haggler. It

took him over a year to come to some agreement with the New York Yacht Club over his challenge and his correspondence with James Gordon Bennett Jr over the proposed match across the Atlantic was equally protracted. *Hunt's Yachting Magazine* commented that it was 'so long and so tedious as at one time to make it appear likely to be interminable', but in the end the two schooners, *Cambria* and Bennett's new *Dauntless*, did start, off Daunts Rock on the Southern Irish coast. Afterwards, however, no one seemed certain as to the exact time of their departure. *Cambria* took a slightly more northerly course than *Dauntless* and covered 2994 miles to get to the finish at Sandy Hook in an estimated 23d,5hrs,17mins. *Dauntless* lost two of her crew who were washed off her bowsprit during a storm and finished only 1hr,43mins behind the English schooner. *Cambria's* triumph was short-lived however, for she failed to recapture the Queen's Cup, but she is the only instance where the two most exotic branches of yachting – America's Cup matches and ocean racing – came briefly together before going their very separate ways.[1]

There was a lapse of seventeen years before another Transatlantic race took place showing that, while the previous matches had generated a good deal of enthusiasm amongst the general public, this fervour had not rubbed off on yachtsmen who were generally more cautious. With a casualty rate of eight dead in the two Transatlantic fixtures which had taken place no one could blame them. But when Lt Henn, the 1886 challenger for the America's Cup, failed to find any opponents when he suggested a race to Bermuda[2] newspapers lambasted American yachtsmen for being so faint-hearted.

The third Transatlantic race 1887
Perhaps it was this lack of response from his countrymen that inspired Rufus T. Bush, the owner of the brand new schooner *Coronet* to issue a general challenge for a match across the Atlantic giving as his reason that the hon-

our of the New York Yacht Club had to be upheld. The stake was $10 000. It must be added, however, that Bush himself had no intention of actually taking part.

Bush found a worthy opponent in Caldwell H. 'Colly' Colt, the son of the inventor of the Colt revolver. Colt now owned the ageing *Dauntless*.

For the historian the most memorable aspect of this next race is that it threw up a character like 'Colly'. 'It seems,' wrote Alfred Loomis in his book, *Ocean Racing*, 'that "Colly" Colt, although a boaster and an exhibitionist of sorts, was a nearer approach to the genus of ocean racing man than anybody who had yet flashed across the scene. He raced, not as Bush did, vicariously from his cloistered home on the Heights, nor yet as Bennett had done, for the glory and prize at stake, but because he knew he would have a hell of a good time. There is a revealing glimpse of him midway in the race when *Dauntless* burst her water tank and "Colly" led a tour of inspection around his floating castle, triumphantly producing from each unsuspected cache a bottle of champagne to ward off the horrors of thirst!'

Determined to win the match, Colt dug 'Bully' Samuels out of retirement and persuaded him to skipper his schooner, reckoning that the experience and hard-driving tactics of the old sea dog would be an effective counter to his opponent's newer and faster vessel. There is no doubt that Samuels drove his vessel hard for at one point, despite being plagued by a leak that could not be detected, *Dauntless* overtook a steamer travelling in the same direction! *Coronet's* skipper, on the other hand, took the race at a much easier pace. This is confirmed by one reporter on board who noted that after one particularly squally evening, 'the vessel was, as usual, got under easy canvas for the night.'

But though *Coronet* was not driven as hard as *Dauntless* she maintained a higher average speed, so that despite *Dauntless* making some remarkable runs, her best was 328 miles in one 24-hour period, a record which stood till 1905, it was *Coronet* which arrived first off the finishing line at Cork some thirty hours ahead of her rival.

However, of all the stories of this epic race which appeared in the press the oddest of them was not printed until some years later when *Dauntless* had her copper bottom stripped off and it was found that two auger holes had been neatly drilled each side of the

stem. When interviewed, Samuels made it clear that he thought it was sabotage. 'There is not a doubt now in my mind that those holes were bored with the intention of disabling the *Dauntless*,' he was quoted as saying, 'for had they been made for the purpose of rebolting we could easily have seen them from the outside. Whoever committed the dastardly act must have concealed himself in the forepeak while we were on the dry dock and worked from in out. Moreover, he must have been a very skilful man, for the distance from the waterline was calculated to such a degree of delicacy that the hole being invisible on the copper surface caused no leak as long as we remained at anchor or sailed in smooth water. The moment we drove her, however, and her head was at all buried in the sea, the pumps had to be worked every fifteen minutes in order to keep afloat.' When asked if this was the reason *Dauntless* lost the old man replied stoutly: 'Most assuredly I do.'

Jubilee races 1887
In the same year as *Dauntless* and *Coronet* battled it out across the Atlantic the precursor of one of the most interesting modern events, the Round Britain race, took place. Who exactly came up with the idea of sending yachts on a 1500-mile jaunt round the British Isles to celebrate Queen Victoria's Golden Jubilee is not known, but it was certainly greeted with a great deal of enthusiasm. It was intimated that the Americans would come in large numbers, and the Prince of Wales, Commodore of the organising club, the Royal Thames, agreed to enter his beautiful schooner, *Aline*, and to start the race. Soon the rumour spread that over 80 yachts were entered to compete for the £1000 prize money.

Ocean racing may still have been no more than a twinkle in old Father Neptune's eye in 1887 but even in those far-off days everyone knew the importance of good publicity and they played up the event for all it was worth. Inevitably, therefore, the actual race was something of a let down. No Americans appeared – British yachtsmen's continued stubborn refusal to accept the unrestricted use of the centreboard may have been the reason for this, as by now nearly all top American racing yachts were constructed with one – and there were only twelve starters. But the Prince of Wales did turn up at Southend to send the yachts, including *Aline*, on their way northwards, and a mass of spec-

---

[1] It is interesting to note that after the Second World War John Illingworth when Commodore of the Royal Ocean Racing Club, had some lengthy but abortive discussions with the New York Yacht club about reviving the America's Cup by racing for it with a new breed of ocean racer.

[2] Perhaps Henn should be best remembered as the first man to propose a race which has now become one of the great classics in ocean racing. He certainly can't be remembered for his challenge in his cruising cutter *Galatea* which was a disaster.

tators saw them go. The fleet was a pretty mixed bunch, ranging from the brand new *Atlantis*, a 52-ton yawl specially constructed for the race, to some rather ancient craft which had obviously been entered for the hell of it. But the two favourites were Lord Francis Cecil's 43-ton cutter, *Sleuthhound*, and the 1885 America's Cup challenger, *Genesta*, an 85-ton cutter owned by Sir Richard Sutton, which had won the Brenton Reef Cup two years previously.

Genesta took the lead early on and never seemed to lose it. Apart from nearly drifting onto some rocks when becalmed, and meeting a 'moderate gale' off Stornaway, she had an uneventful passage and reached the finishing line at Dover at dawn on 27th June having covered the 1590 miles in 12d, 16hrs, 59mins. *Sleuthhound* was second in 13d, 11hrs, 59mins, *Gwendoline* third, *Selene*

fourth, and the Prince of Wales' *Aline* fifth. None of the others finished. As no damage or accidents were reported it must be assumed that their owners simply gave up, having run out of provisions, water, time, or simply the will to carry on. It was the first taste British yachtsmen had had of long distance ocean racing, and for some of them it had been too gruelling. Afterwards *The Times* commented sniffily that 'the course, if not ill advised was altogether unnecessary in length and too risky in character for a fair racing trial.' Later the same year the Royal Yacht Squadron held its own Jubilee race. It was open to all yachts over 30 tons, with £500 going to the winner.

The course took the 14 starters from Cowes, across the Channel to the Cherbourg breakwater, around the Eddystone Light, and back to Cowes, a distance of 330 miles, and was won by *Irex*, the most successful racing

cutter of the period.

Single-handed Transatlantic 1891
In short, the idea of ocean racing was given the thumbs down by both critics and participants and it was another ten years before British yachtsmen again ventured to race a long distance in open water. During this period the Americans were equally coastbound, with the quite extraordinary exception of two Boston men who challenged each other to a single-handed race across the Atlantic in the summer of 1891 in tiny 15-foot sailing boats, with the winner taking £1000 and a silver cup.

Amazingly, these two were by no means the first to make the Transatlantic

voyage in such cockleshells – a man called Johnson had done it in 1876 – but they were undoubtedly the first to race across in such small boats, and both men had already completed one such trip separately.

For the race William Andrews built a 15-foot centre-boarder called *Mermaid*. His rival, Si Lawlor, was the son of a well-known boatbuilder who constructed for him a boat of similar length called *Sea Serpent*. 'More like a maggot,' was the general opinion of the tiny craft. But Lawlor knew what he was doing when the two of them set off from Boston on the evening of 21st June. He took the shorter, more dangerous northerly route, while Andrews decided to cross via the easier but longer Azores route. Their proposed courses were known to the large crowd which saw them off, and few had put their money on Lawlor.

Nevertheless, it was Lawlor who turned up first, on 5th August, off the Cornish coast, having made the voyage in the very creditable time of 45 days. On landing he shrugged off the voyage as being 'without incident', but a keen reporter was eventually able to draw from the young man that he had fallen overboard, his tiny craft knocked over, and that he had been attacked by a 'monster' which he had driven away by firing a flare at it.

While Lawlor was being fêted, Andrews was still at sea. After 55 days of light southerlies he was still 700 miles from land and was running low on provisions. On 18th August a storm blew up and for the seventh time *Mermaid* capsized. After a struggle, Andrews righted her, only to find he had lost what remained of his food and water. Miles from any shipping route his prospects looked, to say the least, grim. However, by sheer chance

▲ *Freda, designed by Dixon Kemp, won the first Dover-Heligoland race, though she had been built purely as a cruising boat.*

a steamer found the tiny craft four days later with Andrews still alive in the bottom of it. Both were taken to Antwerp where Andrews sold *Mermaid* for a handsome sum to a syndicate of showmen.

Single-handed Transatlantic 1892
Undeterred by his narrow escape, Andrews travelled to Britain and met Lawlor, wagering him he would cross in 30 days, an impossible feat as even he must have known. But Lawlor had decided to try and lower his own record so he accepted Andrews' challenge and they both set about constructing new boats. Andrews built a collapsible 14-foot dinghy carrying 30 square feet of sail. This time he

fitted a lead keel rather than a centreboard, and called her *Flying Dutchman*. Lawlor called his vessel *Christopher Columbus* to coincide with the 400th anniversary of Columbus' discovery of the new world.

As early as 1892 sponsorship made itself felt in ocean racing. 'While my vessel was being built,' Andrews told a *Strand* magazine reporter some years later, 'I was commissioned by the manufacturers of a well-known domestic commodity to name the vessel the *Sapolio* and to undertake the trip on their behalf.'

Lawlor started first and was never heard of again. Andrews left on 2nd July 1892, and in favourable weather conditions reached the Azores on 26th August where he received a hero's welcome. After a short stay he carried on to Spain where he had chosen to land to take part in Columbus' anniversary celebra-

tions. He arrived at Fuzetta on 24th September and went on to Palos where again he received a great welcome which included an audience with the Queen of Spain.

Andrews continued his Transatlantic voyages, making two unsuccessful attempts to cross before challenging Captain Blackburn to another race in 1901. Blackburn crossed but Andrews failed to do so, and when, with his wife, he later tried yet again both of them were lost.

So, before the century had closed there had been various kinds of races across courses well known to us today. But they were isolated incidents, and though part of the pre-history, as it were, of the sport, no one felt inclined to make them the starting point of ocean racing as we know it today.

Dover-Heligoland races 1892-1908

A glimmer of what was to come did emerge before the end of the century when the German Kaiser donated a cup in celebration of Queen Victoria's Diamond Jubilee to be raced for by British yachts exceeding 40 tons over a 300-mile course from Dover to Heligoland. A keen yachtsman himself, the Kaiser, a great-nephew of Queen Victoria, had for long been envious of the sea power displayed by his British relations. He watched the increasing popularity of yachting on the other side of the North Sea and perhaps calculated that an injection of the sport into his own countrymen might increase their enthusiasm for the sea. In those days the Germans were not much interested in sailing.

▼ *An artist's drawing published in* The Illustrated London News *of the Prince of Wales starting the 1887 Round-Britain Jubilee race in which his schooner,* Aline, *took part.*

'The Germans are not a yachting nation,' remarked the Kaiser's brother to a friend. 'Our people race yachts to please my brother. I daresay they get very seasick.'

In spite of this reluctance the Kaiser founded the Imperial Yacht Club at Kiel in 1891 and thereafter annually held a regatta. One of the Kaiser's motives for suggesting the race to Heligoland was to make sure there were British yachts in this regatta. What better way of luring them over than to offer a handsome cup for the winner, with plenty of lesser prizes for the other competing yachts? The idea seemed to appeal and 21 entries were received for the race which was to begin on 23rd June 1897, though eventually only 13 started.

As the Emperor's Cup was to be raced for only by yachts over 40 tons, a Mr Gordon Hodgkinson put up another trophy, the North Sea Cup, to be competed for by yachts under that tonnage. Again, though there was a lot of initial interest there were only four starters, and two of these soon gave up. This race began on 29th June and was won by Mr Hodgkinson in his 35-ton cutter, *Wave Queen*, in an elapsed time of 54 hours. The rudimentary handicapping system, based purely on length, gave him the race by a large margin from his one remaining rival.

In the official race, a head breeze and a foul tide made the going slow at first, but later the wind freshened and *Anemone*, a 96-ton yawl, took the lead and passed both the South Sand and Goodwin lightships first. She would probably have won if she had not gone the wrong side of the Terschillenger Bank lightship and been forced to retrace her steps. As it was, Lord Iveagh's 203-ton schooner, *Cetonia*, took line honours after covering the course in 42hrs, 29mins, but she was subsequently disqualified for fouling another competitor, *Jullanar*, off the South Foreland. On corrected time the Dixon Kemp-designed yawl, *Freda*, was declared the winner of the Cup, with the schooner *Ariadne*, at 380 tons the largest yacht in the fleet, second, and *Jullanar* third.

The result rather surprised the yachting press as *Freda* had never been designed for racing and was then 12 years old. However, the method of handicapping by length only afterwards resulted in haphazard ratings and unexpected results.

Although the Jubilee race had not been conceived as an annual event, it proved such a success that the Kaiser offered another cup

the following year when seven yachts started.

Again it attracted some of the finest yachts of the day, but also some of the slowest. When one Squadron member became intent on participating in his 80-ton cutter which belonged firmly with the latter category, his son, when wishing him luck, said, 'I'm sorry you're going – we've always had such happy Christmasses together!' First home was the 317-ton schooner, *Rainbow*, in an elapsed time of 36hrs, 12mins, but on corrected time the 73-ton yawl, *Merrythought*,

▶   A sketch of Mermaid, *the 15-foot centre-boarder in which William Andrews raced solo across the Atlantic in 1891.*

▼   *Lawlor was Andrews' only rival in the 1891 Transatlantic race. He took his 15-foot* Sea Serpent *by the more northerly route and won easily.*

▲ *William Andrews and his 14-foot collapsible boat, Sapolio, in harbour after winning the 1892 solo Transatlantic race.*

claimed the cup. That year the North Sea Cup attracted a larger entry, six, and was won by the 31-ton *May Morn,* but after 1899 this event for the smaller yachts fades from the newspaper records. The Emperor's Cup race, as it came to be called, continued however, and was raced every year until 1908 with the exception of 1901, the year of Queen Victoria's death. After the 1908 race the Kaiser announced he wished the fixture to be a triennial one, but there is no record of any race over the same course until 1933. This is a great pity. The First World war would, of course, have put an end to it, but a regularly held ocean race in those early years might have helped to encourage the sport. As it was, European yachtsmen had to wait until 1925, the year ocean racing really started in their waters.

Looking at the records, one can see what might have been, for the early years of this century saw an upsurge in interest in ocean racing in Europe. The Germans began

running their own feeder races for the Dover-Heligoland fixture, which in 1904 became open to yachts of any nation. That year there were entries from the US, Germany, and France, as well as Britain, making it the first-ever regularly run international race.

The Dover-Heligoland race was well patronised the following year as well, and included entries from the Transatlantic race which had been held earlier that year. The German-owned, American-built *Navahoe,* with the well-known English professional skipper, Edward Sycamore, at the helm. finished first, but on corrected time the race was won by Herr Holdschinsky's schooner, *Susanne II,* a feat she was to repeat in 1907 and 1908.

Other early European ocean races

The Dover-Heligoland fixture was the only regularly held ocean race during the early part of the century, but there were other 'one-off' fixtures which showed that ocean

racing was not confined to those interested in attending the Kiel Regatta.

The most unusual event held during this period was undoubtably one organised by the Royal Yacht Squadron and held in 1902 to celebrate the accession to the throne of their Commodore, the Prince of Wales. A Coronation Cup was donated by one of the Squadron's members, the Earl of Crawford, who stipulated that the cup should only be raced for by 'auxiliary steam vessels' of 340 tons TM, or above. Engines, however, could only be used to arrive at the starting line, between St Helen's Fort and the Nab light-ship, and propellers had to be feathered at least 30 minutes before the start. Entries had to race in sea-going trim with all boats carried, though steam-launches were optional. Only the normal crew – Lord Crawford's huge full-rigged ship, *Valhalla,* carried 120! – could be shipped and the course was to be the same as that used for the 1887 Jubilee Cup: across to Cherbourg, round the Eddystone Light, and back to Cowes.

This extraordinary fixture attracted five starters: Lord Crawford's 1490-ton *Valhalla*; Lord Brassey's 532-ton schooner, *Sunbeam*; Mr Albert Brassey's 564-ton schooner, *Czarina*; Mr John Fergusson's 439-ton schooner, *Rosabelle*; and the 560-ton schooner, *Utowana*, owned by a member of the New York Yacht Club, Mr Allison Armour. *Utowana* was the only fore-and-aft rigged vessel in the race and she won it easily, thereby becoming the first American yacht to win a British organised ocean race, albeit a rather unusual one.

An altogether less eccentric race was the one held from Cowes to the Clyde in 1905 for the North Cup which was organised by the Royal London Yacht Club. It was won by *White Heather*, a 147-ton yawl owned by Mr Myles Kennedy from a fleet of five others.

A return race, this time organised by the Clyde Clubs, was arranged the following month so that the five entries could arrive at Cowes in time for the regatta. *White Heather* again won first prize. King Edward VII was present to present the cups and it is apparent that it was hoped that the races would become regular fixtures. However, there is no further record of any races taking place, the only other fixtures being ones from Bremerhaven to Felixstowe (1908) and Heligoland to Deal (1910).

Although the North Sea saw most of the European long-distance racing in 1905, a race from Cowes to the Clyde was also organised, with another running in the reverse direction later the same year. A similar event took place the following year.

Racing on the Eastern US seaboard

In the US, also, the first years of the new century saw a revival of racing over open water. The Atlantic Yacht Club, which at the time rivalled the New York Yacht Club in importance and prestige, had organised a short-distance event in 1899, from Montauk Point to Coney Island, and this had attracted six starters. Encouraged, the club organised similar fixtures in the following years, and in 1903 two ocean races were organised by the Club: one around the Nantucket Shoal lightship, from the Brenton Reef lightship and back to the Scotland lightship, a distance of 295 miles, which was won by Morton F. Plant's *Ingomar* from a fleet of three; and a much longer one from Scotland lightship, around Nantucket Shoal lightship and Northeast End lightship (off Cape May), and back to

the Scotland lightship, a distance of 524 miles. This was also won by *Ingomar* from a fleet of six which included three entries for the 1905 Transatlantic race, *Fleur de Lys*, *Endymion*, and *Thistle*.

The 1905 Transatlantic race was first proposed by the Atlantic Yacht Club's Commodore, Robert E. Tod, in 1903, who wanted it run the following year. The idea of such a race was taken up with great enthusiasm. Sir Thomas Lipton came forward with the offer of a cup; the number of entries mounted rapidly; and it looked as if the race was on. But then the Kaiser heard about the forthcoming event, and asserted that he had been about to offer a cup for an identical race, and everyone had to go back to square one, delaying the race until 1905.

Thomas Fleming Day and the first New York-Marblehead race, 1904

Meanwhile, the editor of the American yachting magazine, *Rudder*, Thomas Fleming Day, proposed a race for cruising yachts between New York and Marblehead, a distance of about 330 miles and turned over the organisation of it to the Brooklyn Yacht Club. Again, Sir Thomas Lipton stepped forward, offering a hundred guinea cup for the first boat home. Adverse comment from armchair critics and the sinking of a fishing boat in dense fog off the Nantucket Shoals just before the race probably scared off a number of entries, but nine of the 18 crossed the line off the Brooklyn Yacht Club station on Gravesend Bay on 2nd July 1904, and in a rising north-west breeze began to make their way north. The weather held up well, and though there were one or two minor incidents — one yacht sprung her mast and broke her centreboard; another lost a man overboard but recovered him — nearly all the entries covered the course. First across the finishing line, and first on corrected time, was the brand new 35-foot keel sloop, *Little Rhody*, in an elapsed time of 58hrs, 48mins. Day, taking part in the smallest yacht in the race, the 25-foot *Sea Bird*, came a bad last. But unlike one competitor who promptly and unsuccessfully lodged a protest because he considered the winner 'a racing machine', Day saved his ire for the critics of the race.

'It was astonishing and disgusting what a lot of rot was printed in the newspapers about the dangers of this race,' he wrote afterwards. 'Newspapermen ought to know better than to consult a lot of grey-headed, rum-

soaked piazza scows about such racing. What do those miserable old hulks, who spend their days swigging booze on the front stoop of a clubhouse, know about the dangers of the deep? If they ever make a voyage from Larchmont to Cow Bay in a ten knot breeze it is the event of their lives, an experience they never forget and never want to repeat. What does the average yachtsman know about sea sailing? Absolutely nothing! Then let him hold his tongue.'

First Marblehead-Halifax race, 1905

The Marblehead race proved such a success that the Eastern Yacht Club ran a similar race over the same course a few days later and then organised another the following year, this time to Halifax, Nova Scotia. This first international race between Canada and the US attracted six starters – all American – and was won by the 125-foot steel schooner, *Elmina II*, which in the following seasons went on to win the Astor Cup, one of the most prestigious US short-distance ocean racing prizes, no less than five times, an unbeaten record. *Elmina II* covered the 357 miles in 45hrs, 53mins. The Marblehead-Halifax is now a popular biennial but after the first race was not run again until the 1930s.

First Brooklyn-Hampton Roads race 1905
Manned by a crew of 30 professionals, *Elmina II* was not the kind of yacht Day had in mind for the races he wanted to promote, and the 250-mile race from Brooklyn to Hampton Roads which he organised in 1905 could only be entered by cruising yachts helmed by amateurs. The Brooklyn Yacht Club offered a perpetual challenge cup as the chief trophy and it was won by *Tamerlane*, a yawl built specially for the race by her owner Frank Maier, who then sold her to Day. The race certainly whetted the appetite of the starters for an even more adventurous undertaking. 'After the finish of the race last year to Hampton Roads,' wrote Day, 'the boys came to me and said they wanted a real ocean race, one that would take them well offshore and into blue water, and I promised they should have it.'

The Transatlantic race 1905
Day kept his promise, but before the first historic Bermuda race was sailed in 1906 the fourth crewed Transatlantic race took place amidst a flurry of publicity and excitement. The 11 starters were now racing for the honour to receive a gold cup donated by the Kaiser, Sir Thomas Lipton having gracefully bowed out of what had become an embarrassing situation. The Atlantic Yacht Club had also been obliged to relinquish all interest in the race, but this snub did not deter Commodore Tod from entering it in his 110-foot schooner, *Thistle* – the only yacht to be skippered by its owner. The other starters consisted of the German schooner *Hamburg* (ex-*Rainbow*), owned by a syndicate headed by Herr Adolf Tietjens; two British yachts, *Sunbeam* and *Valhalla*; and seven miscellaneous American entries which included the current holder of the fastest crossing, the

137-foot schooner, *Endymion*, and Wilson Marshall's two-year-old 187-foot schooner, *Atlantic*.

The weather on the day of the start, 17th May 1905, was unsettled, with an easterly wind. For the first few days the fleet stayed together moving south-east until they were all south of the fortieth parallel. Then it split up, a few taking the northerly route via the foggy Newfoundland Banks while the rest stayed south of them. Charlie Barr, the professional skipper of *Atlantic*, took the most northerly course of this second group and it proved to be a wise move. Barr, a Scotsman who had settled in the US, was a hard-driving skipper just like 'Bully' Samuels before him, and he was at the top of his tough profession. When a gale sprang up on 26th May he did not flinch from driving his ship and crew to their utmost until *Atlantic*, her decks awash, oil bags over the weather rail, and two men

lashed to the kicking wheel, was running before the storm under just a squaresail and her foretrysail. At this point with the wind still rising, Barr had a difference of opinion with the owner.

'One night we had a good beam wind,' Barr later told his friend Nat Herreshoff with true Scottish understatement, 'and *Atlantic* was reeling off the knots, when the owner came aft to me at the wheel and requested me to take in some sail. I said to him, "Mr Marshall, sir, you hired me to try to win this race and that is what I am trying to do." After that he went to his stateroom.'

Rumour had it, however, that the confrontation was a good deal more dramatic than that. One version of it was that Barr locked Marshall in his stateroom and that Marshall fell on his knees and led his guests in prayers that they be saved from drowning. It is a rather unlikely tale. Still, the rougher the

race the wilder the stories after it has always been one of the sport's maxims. What matters is that *Atlantic*, from that moment until within 50 miles of the finish, reeled off 24-hour runs of 282, 279, 243, 309 and 282 miles, which is phenomenally fast sailing by any standards, and finished in 12d, 4hrs, 1min, a record which remained unbroken until 1980.

As with the 1887 Transatlantic race the best story concerning 1905 one did not break until some years later. When Marshall's son died in the First World War Marshall donated the Kaiser's gold cup that he had won to the Red Cross. The cup was auctioned several times, always being returned by the highest bidder. In this way $125 000 was raised. As a final gesture to raise money, an audience, which included the President, filled the Grand Met at $5 a time to watch Marshall smash the cup with a sledgehammer before it was

melted down and sold. But when Marshall hit the cup it shattered! It hadn't been made of gold at all, but of pewter covered with gold plating. At the most it was worth $35!

The first Bermuda race 1906

The 1905 race was one that caught the public's imagination, and indeed Transatlantic races continue to do so. And there are, of course the modern equivalents of Charlie Barr. But the yachts that raced in 1905 have gone forever, with only the giant square-riggers in the Tall Ships races to remind us what some of them were like. They were magnificent, but they and their large professional crews had little connection with ocean racing as we know it today. Far more relevant was Day's enthusiasm for small cruising yachts, owned and sailed by amateurs, and

▼   *The start of the 1908 Dover-Heligoland race.*

◄ The 24-foot yawl Sea Bird was partly designed by Thomas Fleming Day who sailed her in the 1904 race. He described her as 'heavily built, ugly, and very slow.' She came last.

raced on the open sea. He set out to show that a small boat, properly sailed, could be perfectly safe. It was partly to prove the 'rum-soaked piazza scows' wrong again that Day organised the first Bermuda race.

Like the British Fastnet race, from Cowes to a rock off the south-west coast of Ireland and back to Plymouth, which was inaugurated in 1925, the Bermuda race is not, by today's standards, a long ocean race. Both are about six hundred miles. What makes them the blue ribband fixtures in their respective countries is that they are both courses which test the skills of the crews to the utmost. The Fastnet, a course where the wind has a habit of heading you whatever the direction you happen to be steering, is bede-villed by currents and headlands where races form at certain states of the tide. The Bermuda race is equally challenging, for it is sailed over the Gulf Stream, 'a river in the sea'. Fine judgement is required if its current is to be exploited to the full, and many a yacht has missed Bermuda altogether because of it.

However, it was not the Gulf Stream which worried critics of the race which Day proposed, but the fact that yachts would be racing miles from any shelter in an area noted for its hurricanes. Day countered by pointing out that there were no hurricanes in May or June, and proceeded with his plans.

As it happened, the race did not turn out as much of an advertisement for Day's beliefs. Only three yachts – all of which had been specially built the previous year to race to Hampton Roads – started on 26th May, and one of them, Lila, was dismasted soon after the start. She was escorted back to Gravesend Bay by Day in his 38-foot Tamerlane, while the third yacht, Gauntlet, which did not see the accident, continued.

Tamerlane did not get under way for another 65 hours and Lila followed her a few hours after that. By this time Gauntlet was well out in the Gulf Stream and seemed a certain winner. But she then got caught in a south-east gale which forced her to run off to the north-west for more than 48 hours. Day, on the other hand, found the going perfect, made a fast passage of 5d, 6hrs, 9mins to Hamilton Harbour and beat Gauntlet by over 25 hours. Lila, hit by a series of squalls, turned back, her skipper probably distrustful of his hastily re-rigged mast.

The Bermuda race: 1907-1910

It was an anticlimactic beginning to what has now become one of the world's top ocean races. But Day proved that it could be done, and the following year no less than 12 yachts came to the line in Gravesend Bay, their num-

bers swelled by yachts crewed by professionals – though skippered by an amateur afterguard – who had been barred from the previous race.

The fleet for this second race was split into two classes. The small class included *Lila* and *Zena*, which was Bermudan-rigged, the first yacht so rigged to engage in ocean racing. Day thought *Zena's* marconi rig – as it was then more commonly called after the new Marconi radio masts – completely inappropriate for the new sport, and when *Zena* performed poorly in the race he felt vindicated. Well, even the best of us cannot be right all the time, and *Zena's* tall mast with its complicated rigging must have looked fragile indeed compared with the sturdy gaff rigs of the other competitors.

Dervish won the large class in the excellent corrected time of 3d, 17hrs, and *Lila*, proving that she could not only finish the race but do it in style, won the small class.

The Bermuda race now seemed set to be an annual affair attracting a respectable number of entries, but there were only five starters in 1908 and 1909, and these dwindled to two in 1910. It is worth recording that in 1908, the two yachts in the small class beat the three in the large class not only on corrected time but boat for boat, an event which perhaps began the trend towards a smaller type of ocean racer.

▲ *The start of the 1905 Transatlantic race just after the gun has been fired.* Atlantic *is second on the left.*

▼ *Charlie Barr concentrates on sailing* Atlantic *while her owner, Wilson Marshall, and a guest, pose for the camera.*

Sadly, however, owners of small yachts and large ones did not seem to take to any kind of ocean racing, and despite the enthusiasm of Day and a few others it simply petered out. There was talk of a race in 1911, but nothing came of it, and it was not held again until 1923. The same fate overtook the races organised by the Eastern and Brooklyn Yacht Clubs. The latter club attracted only five starters for its 400-miler round the North East End lightship in 1906 and though this rose to 19 when it was run to Cape May and back in 1907, the numbers then dwindled again until in 1911 there was only one entry and the race ceased.

The first Transpac 1906

While attempts were being made to establish the sport on the East Coast, ocean racing was also taking its first hesitant steps on the West.

The man who started what was to become known as the Transpac race was a Los Angeles yachtsman called Sinclair. In 1905, he sailed his 72-foot schooner, Lurline, to Honolulu where he met a local yachtsman, Clarence MacFarlane. Together they hatched up the idea of a race from San Francisco Bay to Honolulu. Subsequently, MacFarlane wrote to several yacht clubs in the bay about the idea. But while American yachtsmen were only too willing to race to the Hawaiian Islands they were not at all keen on the idea of the

passage back against the prevailing trade winds. To show them that there was nothing to it MacFarlane sailed his 47-foot schooner, La Paloma, to San Francisco.

While MacFarlane was making this passage there occurred the earthquake which devastated San Francisco, making it virtually impossible for any yachtsman from the area to take part in the proposed race. MacFarlane wrote to Sinclair, who was Commodore of the South Coast Yacht Club at San Pedro (just south of Los Angeles), to tell him he had

▼ *The Gardner-designed, 187-foot schooner, Atlantic, was one of the great yachts of all time. She established a record time across the Atlantic which was not beaten until 1980.*

arrived, and challenged him to a return race. Sinclair suggested it was easier for MacFarlane to sail down to him than *vice versa*, and so it was agreed that the start should be from the southern port.

Sinclair managed to rope in a third entry, the 91-foot ketch, *Anemone*, owned by Charles L. Tutt from Colorado, and the three yachts set off on the 2225-mile race on 11th June 1906. Despite having only a ballooner to carry her through the Trades, *Lurline* won easily in an elapsed time of 12d, 9hrs, 59mins, with *Anemone* second and *La Paloma* third.

There is no doubt that Sinclair won the first Transpac because he had done his homework and planned on a route which made the best of the summer weather pattern. 'At this season of the year the Northeast Trades are usually met with from 200 to 400 miles offshore and extend to about 30°,' wrote one of Sinclair's afterguard some years later. 'Consequently, it was the object of all the yachts to make them as soon as possible. With this end in view, the *Lurline* and *La Paloma* took a SSW course and ran on the starboard tack with wind abeam. The *Anemone*, however, kept close to the wind and shaped her course directly for the Hawaiian Islands, and this latter proved to be a mistake; when the Trades were finally encountered they proved to be a little east of northeast, generally NE by E, and the *Anemone* was forced to run before them with headsails flapping. The *Lurline*, however, took the most southerly course of all, steering SSW until noon on the 13th, when she had gotten as far south as 28° 08'N. She the held up to SW, and early in the morning of June 15th the wind, which up to that time had been from the NW, gradually began to haul to the east, and by 4am was blowing from NE by E, and we knew we had reached the Trades.'

Lurline's tactics were followed by all competitors in the subsequent Transpacs and were not challenged until the 1923 race.

The Transpac Race: 1908-1912

The first Transpac did not cause much of a stir on the mainland, but it was greeted with enormous enthusiasm in Hawaii, and a $25,000 fund was immediately raised to build an Hawaiian yacht for the next race, scheduled for 1908. The Boston architect B.B.

▶ *Designed by L D Huntingdon Jr, 38-foot* Tamerlane *won both the 1905 ocean race from Sandy Hook to Hampton Roads and the first Bermuda race.*

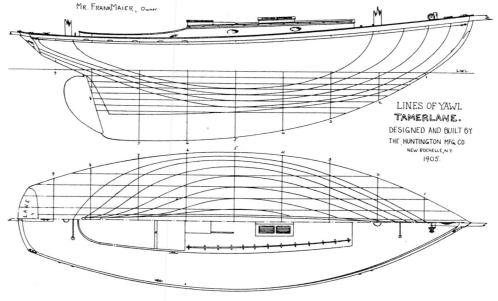

MR. FRANK MAIER, Owner.

LINES OF YAWL
TAMERLANE.
DESIGNED AND BUILT BY
THE HUNTINGTON MFG. CO.
NEW ROCHELLE, N.Y.
1905.

23

▲ Start of the first Transpac race. From left to right: 112-foot ketch, Anemone; 86-foot schooner, Lurline; and 48-foot schooner, La Paloma. Lurline won. She also won in 1908 and 1912.

◄ The 70-foot schooner, Hawaii, was built of Hawaiian wood and from a fund raised by local subscription. She came last in the 1908 Transpac but won in 1910.

► La Paloma (left), Lurline (centre), and Anemone (right) at Honolulu after the first Transpac.

heard of in those days — paid handsome dividends and Davis won in an elapsed time of 13d, 17hrs, 3mins, arriving a good day ahead of his closest rival, Hawaii.

Outbreak of the First World War

The 1912 Transpac was the last ocean race to be sailed on either side of the Atlantic before the First World War broke out in 1914. In Europe there had been one or two races across the North Sea in addition to the Dover-Heligoland fixture. The German Empress's Iduna won the race from Bremerhaven to Felixstowe in 1908 and there was also a race from Heligoland to Deal in 1910, but after that latter date there are no records of any long-distance ocean races, though it is worth noting that one to Dinard, established in 1909, was revived many years later.

Up until the First World War the interest in ocean racing, on both sides of the Atlantic, was limited, but the seed had been sown, and though the sport was dormant for a long time, once it sprouted it grew with amazing speed.

Crowninshield — who had been responsible for the freakish America's Cup contender, Independence, at the turn of the century — was commissioned to design her, and the result was the 70-foot schooner, Hawaii. Built in Honolulu entirely of native wood, Hawaii was entered for the second Transpac which started on America's Independence Day, 4th July.

She did not come up to expectations and finished last of four yachts. Lurline repeated her win in an elapsed time of 13d, 21hrs, 31mins, a longer time than for the previous race due to lighter trade winds. Hawaii was entered again in 1910 and this time she won against two other starters, though it took her over two weeks to complete the course. In 1912 the number of entries increased to four and included Lurline, now under the ownership of A.E. Davis of the San Diego Yacht Club who went about winning in a very organised manner. First of all he put Cap Harris, a professional sailor of formidable reputation, in command, and then sailed his yacht on a series of trial cruises to pick the best crew available. This planned approach — quite un-

The King of Sports

1923–41

A DECADE PASSED after the 1912 Transpac before anyone talked seriously again about an ocean race. The yachtsmen who did the talking on this occasion were members of the Cruising Club of America (CCA), recently founded to emulate the well-established Royal Cruising Club (RCC) in Britain. But while the RCC would have nothing to do with the new sport when it eventually arrived in British waters in its modern form, several members of the CCA, led by Herbert Stone, then editor of the magazine, *Yachting,* saw no reason why they shouldn't encourage some sporting competition amongst themselves. As the yachting journalist Loomis pointed out, when two cruising men sail in company it's only natural for one to see if he can go faster than his companion, and it was in that spirit that 22 yachts crossed the start line at New London for the first race to Bermuda since 1910.

Bermuda race 1923

Almost every member of the CCA turned out for the race, but strong objections from the remaining members prevented the club being officially involved – a curious occurrence in the light of the CCA's future role as *the* American authority for ocean racing.

The race circular also reflected this antipathy, for it emphasised that the motives for the race were to encourage cruising. Indeed, readers had to look closely to spot that the passage to Bermuda was a race at all. 'In order to encourage the designing, building, and sailing of small, seaworthy yachts, to make popular cruising upon deep water, and to develop in the amateur sailor a love of true seamanship and to give the opportunity to become proficient in the art of navigation, an ocean race has been planned for this year from New London* Conn., to Bermuda.'

The 1923 Bermuda race was won by an American yacht designer called John Alden who sailed his schooner *Malabar IV* through strong south-west winds in the Gulf Stream to a historic victory which in many ways marked the beginning of modern ocean racing. Based on the New England fishing schooners, Alden's designs had, by 1923, become refined into fast, good sea-keeping yachts which had no equivalent in Britain. As a consequence, the schooner rig dominated

the American yachting scene for many years, giving way only gradually to yawls and then to the modern cutter and sloop rig. In that first postwar Bermuda race, 17 out of the fleet of 22 were schooners. In 1934 the percentage had dropped from 77 per cent to 55 per cent, and by 1938 there were only a handful in the fleet of 43, and none of them did well.

The rough weather caused some gear damage – and a classic comment from the skipper of *Seafarer,* which was second overall. 'The next time I come to Bermuda,' he commented, removing an evil smelling pipe which he had smoked throughout the race, 'it will be in a submarine. Then I can be under water all the time, instead of half under all the time.'

Although the fleet was handicapped under the rudimentary system Day had used in 1906, where a time allowance was calculated on a flat figure of 60 minutes per foot of length for the course of 660 nautical miles, the race proved to be a close one. The first six yachts, on corrected time, were all grouped together within a five-hour timespan while on elapsed time seven competitors finished within 87 minutes of one another, *Black Hawk, Bagheera* and *Sunbeam* crossing the line within the space of a minute. But despite the closeness of the racing and the CCA's partial involvement the number of starters dropped to 14 when the race was repeated in 1924 and thereafter it became biennial.

The 1923 Transpac

By a curious coincidence the Transpac race was also revived in 1923 when Commodore Pedder of the Santa Barbara Yacht Club issued a challenge to Pacific coast yachtsmen to race against his yawl, *Viva,* to Honolulu. The start of this proposed fixture was to be the finale of the Southern Californian regatta. The initial response was so enthusiastic – at one time there were 12 entries – that Pedder got cold feet. But it was not his ability to race that worried Pedder but the ability of his yacht to beat the rest of the fleet. So he hastily purchased the more suitably rigged Herreshoff-designed schooner, *Haswell,* which he renamed *Diablo,* and sailed to the start line on 21st July 1923 an altogether more confident man.

As it happened, only five others joined him at the Santa Barbara start line and two of them soon returned to port, one because she blew out her sails (they were rotten), the other because of a fire aboard.

---

* With the exception of 1932, the race was started off Sarah's Ledge, New London until 1936 when it was moved to Newport which is still the start line today. In 1932 the start was off Montauk Point.

In all the previous races to Honolulu the competitors had gone to leeward of the Catalina and San Clemente Islands, following *Lurline's* successful Transpac run in 1906. But on this occasion the skipper of the new 78-foot schooner, *Mariner,* seeing the other starters becalmed, decided instead to work his boat to windward of Santa Cruz Island. Within two hours he was clear of the land and speeding towards the Trade Belt which he reached in two days. This put *Mariner* in a strong position and she eventually crossed the line first in the record time of 11d, 14hrs, 46mins. But Pedder had done a wise thing to buy *Diablo,* as on corrected time she won the race by two and a half hours.

His appetite now thoroughly whetted, Pedder turned his schooner about and raced the three other remaining Transpac entries to San Francisco. He cleaned up in that race, too, and it was unanimously decided by all the participants that the Transpac should be held again in two years time. But when the 1925 season started someone came up with the bright idea of racing to Tahiti instead, something which had never been attempted before. The idea caught on and it was decided to postpone the Transpac until 1926.

The Tahiti race 1925
The Tahiti race started on 10th June 1925 from San Francisco and was timed so that the four starters would arrive at the French-owned island before the celebrations for Bastille Day, on 14th July, began. They all arrived before that date though one, the 64-foot schooner, *Eloise,* had centreboard trouble, chose the wrong course and took nearly 30 days to cover the 3660 miles. The winner, *Mariner,* took 20d, 11hrs, 3mins, having stuck to the great circle course which had the advantage of crossing the doldrums at their narrowest point. By contrast, the second boat home, *Idalia,* did not finish until a week later, having failed miserably to find a better method of avoiding them. The Tahiti race was not repeated for many years, and it did not become a regular fixture until the 1960s.

On the east coast another Halifax race was organised in 1924, this time from New Rochelle, but like the Tahiti event the race to Halifax failed to become a regular fixture until

▲ *The Bermuda race was revived in 1923 and attracted 22 starters. Note the preponderance of gaff rigs which within a few years had disappeared.*

much later. This left the Transpac and Bermuda races as the only two events planned on a regular basis. But it was a situation which did not last long for in 1925 the British organised the first Fastnet.

The first Fastnet race 1925
During the 1924 Bermuda race one of the entries, *Diablesse,* missed Bermuda altogether, sailed right round the island, and was heading in the opposite direction to the finishing line when she cam abeam of another entry, *Northern Light,* which had also been having navigation problems. Thinking that *Diablese* had won the race and was returning home the crew of *Northern Light* lined the deck of their yacht and cheered her! What comments subsequently passed between the two crews is not recorded, but aboard *Northern Light* was a young Englishman called Weston Martyr who was so impressed with the new sport of ocean racing, despite

formed to promote an English ocean race. It consisted of Martyr; E.G. Martin, who had recently acquired a converted Le Havre pilot cutter called *Jolie Brise;* and Malden Heckstall-Smith, the editor of the yachting magazine Martyr had written to. After some deliberation and debate the committee proposed a course from the Isle of Wight to the Fastnet rock off the south-west coast of Ireland and then back to Plymouth, a distance of about 615 miles.

In the early Fastnet races the yachts rounded the Isle of Wight either eastwards or westwards, depending on the state of the tide; and for many years the Scillies and the Fastnet Rock could be rounded in either direction. Nowadays both the Rock and the Bishop Lighthouse marking the Scillies have to be left to port on the homeward leg.

It is often supposed, quite wrongly, that the 1925 Fastnet was Britain's first ocean race. But it was new in one vital sense: it catered for a new breed of yachtsman, the amateur cruising man of moderate means who was looking for a challenge which cruising alone could not satisfy. He was in a quite different tradition to the pre-war yachtsman who had employed up to 30 men to sail his huge racing machine in the early long-distance races held around the turn of the century. The new breed may have employed a professional hand or two, but he sailed his yacht himself.

The committee had hoped the race would be started off Cowes, but the Royal Yacht Squadron would have nothing to do with the idea. So the Royal Victorian Yacht Club at Ryde agreed to be responsible for the start while the Royal Western Yacht Club organised the finish.

Seven British yachts came to the line on the morning of 15th August 1925. This was rather less than had been anticipated – at one time the entry list had grown to 20, including one American – but doubtless some yachtsmen had been put off by the vocal opposition which had been raised against the race. In an age where it was deemed good seamanship to shorten down at night, experienced and influential cruising men like Claud Worth openly doubted the wisdom of a race in open water especially over such a challenging course as the Fastnet.

Despite the opposition, the starting gun was fired and the first Fastnet got under way. It turned out to be, in many respects, a typical race for the course. The faster yachts made

▲ *The winner of the 1923 Bermuda race, Malabar IV. She was one in a long line of successful schooners designed and sailed by John Alden from Boston.*

◀ *The 107-foot, Burgess-designed schooner* Mariner *took line honours in the 1923 Transpac. Two years later she won the inaugural race to Tahiti.*

the rather aimless wanderings of some of the participants, that he wrote a lyrical letter about it to an English yachting magazine.

'It is,' Martyr wrote, 'without question the very finest sport a man can possibly engage in: for to play this game at all it is necessary to possess in the very highest degree those hallmarks of a true sportsman: skill, courage and endurance. The name of this great game is ocean racing, and it is also known as the King of Sports by those who understand how high are the qualities demanded from its followers.'

Martyr's enthusiasm was catching and when he returned to Britain a committee was

good time with relatively little trouble and were safely anchored in Plymouth Sound when the slower entries were hit by high winds which raised an uncomfortable sea. Two retired and one made such a slow passage that the timekeepers had gone home by the time she arrived at the finishing line.

The small fleet which set out on this historic race really could not compare with that which took part in the Bermuda race the previous year. Although Martyr may have been right when he stated in his panegyric about the new sport that the British probably did have yachts capable of beating *Memory*, the 1924 Bermuda race winner, certainly none of them turned up off Ryde on that August morning in 1925. What did arrive was a mot-

ley collection of old cruising boats. With the exception of one, *Gull*, they had all been built as working boats. *Gull* was at least a proper yacht but she was at that time already 30 years old.

Of all the starters, the only one that looked as if she really meant business was the converted pilot cutter, *Jolie Brise*, on which her bachelor owner, George Martin, had lavished much care and attention; and though it was *Gull* which took the lead at the beginning, by the time they reached the Eddystone *Jolie Brise* had overtaken her. Nevertheless, *Gull's* Irish owner, H P F Donegan, hung on grimly and if his topsail halyards had not parted in the Irish Sea it is conceivable that *Jolie Brise* might not have had such a resound-

ing victory. As it was, by the time she turned the Rock she was 12 hours ahead of her rivals, a lead which she increased to 20 hours by the time she finished, crossing the line after 6d, 14hrs, 45mins at sea.

The last boat to finish was forced by a fierce ebb tide to kedge right on the finishing line. Her crew had just retired below for supper when they heard a loud cheer from the nearby clubhouse of the Royal Western. It was George Martin announcing that the Ocean Racing Club had been formed. Few if any of that small group of yachtsmen could have foreseen that evening how their new club would eventually grow into an organisa-

▼ *The 60-foot, Herreshoff-designed schooner,* Diablo, *won the 1923 Transpac and then the race back to San Francisco.*

tion which encouraged and promoted ocean racing on a world-wide basis. What they did know was that the race had been fun and that they proposed to hold it again the following year.

Establishing regular events

In 1926, three ocean races, all of which had been run before, were established on a more or less regular basis. It was the year that the ocean racing calendar really started. From this modest beginning the programme has become so full that hardly a day passes in the year when an ocean race is not underway somewhere in the world.

The Bermuda race 1926

The year also saw American and British yachts being sailed across the Atlantic to enter each other's races, with *Jolie Brise* crossing to take part in the Bermuda Race and the Alden schooner, *Primrose IV,* crossing to race in the second Fastnet.

Much to everyone's surprise — for by American standards she was already old-fashioned — *Jolie Brise* took the lead at the start of the Bermuda race and held it for 24 hours until the breeze dropped and a rather lumpy sea slowed her down. Even so, she came fifth (on elapsed and corrected time) out of a fleet of 16 very competitive yachts that included Bob Bavier's new marconi-rigged ketch, *Dragoon,* John Alden's latest *Malabar* (his seventh), and Paul Hammond's Seawanhaka schooner, *Cygnet,* complete with an experimental staysail rig which was to

become so popular over the next few years in American waters. A fierce south-westerly hit part of the fleet in the Gulf Stream and scattered it across a wide area. But there was no severe gear damage and, despite predictions to the contrary, *Dragoon's* 85-foot mast stayed in place and Bavier took line honours though he could not save his time on *Malabar VII* which took the new Bermuda Cup for the overall winner.

The 1926 Fastnet race

On the other side of the Atlantic, *Primrose IV* did not have the same calibre of competition. The line-up for a second Fastnet was marginally better than the previous year but it was to be some time yet before the British tackled the business of designing and building yachts to the new ORC rule that governed the 1926 race. This replaced the one drawn up for the first Fastnet which was a complicated formula and included measurement of a yacht's sail area, freeboard, length and displacement. The 1926 formula excluded displacement which meant that a yacht could be measured while afloat. It was the one the CCA used from 1928 until they devised their own in 1932.

These rating rules were devised, of course, not just for working out a yacht's time allowance, but to encourage a fast, seaworthy type of boat. *Primrose IV,* with her short overhangs and small sail plan, fitted the ORC rule very well and gave her a distinct advantage over her rivals. The 51-ton *Hallowe'en,* for example, was a beautiful new Fife design

which covered the course in the remarkable time of 3d, 19hrs, 5mins, a record which was not broken until 1939. Yet Fife had given no consideration to the rule with the consequence that on corrected time she dropped to third place behind the winner, *Ilex,* and *Primrose IV.* The American yacht, which had finished fourth, only missed winning the race on corrected time by less than 14 minutes.

The 1926 Transpac

During both the Fastnet and Bermuda races, competitors experienced rough conditions. By contrast, the 1926 Transpac was for the most part a drifting match with the winner, *Invader,* carrying her club topsail over the complete course. But the Transpac did have something in common with the other two events of that year. 'This year's Honolulu race,' wrote one of the crew of *Mariner* which was now owned by actor John Barrymore, 'proved, among other things, that the time has passed when the long jaunt can be won by boats of the comfortable cruising type, represented by the old *Lurline* and the modern *Mariner,* against such fine racing machines as the *Invader* and *Poinsettia.*'

The Transpac now settled down to being a biennial fixture taking place during even-numbered years — the same as the Bermuda race — with its start at San Pedro, except for 1928 when it started at Newport (California). The Fastnet continued to be held annually until 1931 — the year the Ocean Racing Club was allowed to use 'Royal' as a prefix — but thereafter it, too, became biennial.

The Gibson Island races 1927-1937

With yachtsmen on the east coast of the US becoming increasingly keen on the rigours of the new sport it did not take long for someone to come up with a long-distance race during odd-numbered years. This gap was filled in 1927 by a race from Cape May to Gibson Island, in Chesapeake Bay. The first race was only 270 miles but in 1929 the course was lengthened to 475 miles by its start being moved to New London. The first race attracted a modest number of starters, but the second brought 41 yachts to the line — a number, as one amazed columnist remarked, never dreamed of in a long-distance race.

This event marked the ocean racing debut of two brothers, Olin and Rod Stephens. They sailed Arthur Hatch's 30-foot *Kalmia*, one of the first designs of 21-year-old Olin. She was one of the smallest vessels in the race but she beat much bigger yachts boat-for-boat and came first in the special class for sloops and cutters. It was a notable start for two men who were to have a lasting influence on the sport. After 1929 the Gibson Island Race became quadrennial, but was only raced in 1933 and 1937.

Return of the Transatlantic

Between the first two Gibson Island races the oldest ocean racing fixture of all, the Transatlantic, was rerun in the summer of 1928. The idea for this was sparked off when two old friends, an American called Henry Howard and a Spanish diplomat, Mariano Amoeda, met again after first getting to know one another when racing in a pre-war Marblehead regatta. Their enthusiasm for reviving the Transatlantic race was transmitted to the King and Queen of Spain who each offered a cup for a race to Santander.

The large class attracted five entries. They were the dinosaurs of the sport, the huge vessels with professional crews which were soon to disappear off the oceans. The favourite to win this class was the 1905 winner, *Atlantic*, now owned by Gerard Lambert. The small class, limited to yachts between 35 feet and 55 feet waterline length, consisted of Paul Hammond's new staysail rigged schooner, *Nina*, two Alden-designed schooners, *Mohawk* and *Pinta*, and a Herreshoff-designed schooner called *Rofa*. *Pinta* was a proven boat for she had, when named *Nicanor*, taken part in the 1927 Fastnet. She had not finished what turned out to be one of the toughest races in that event's history — only two finished out of 15 — but she had weathered the extreme conditions well until a broken gaff had forced her to retire.

Nina had been designed by Edward Burgess — soon to make his name immortal in the 'J' Class era — and she was specially built for the Transatlantic race with no expense spared. Quite apart from the peculiarities of her rig — she was, strictly speaking, a double masted cutter — *Nina* possessed assets which put her far ahead of her time and enabled her to race in top class company, sometimes beating it, right into the 1960s*. By giving close attention to the handicap system, which was to govern a Transatlantic race for the first time, Burgess ensured that *Nina* entered the event with the lowest possible rating, so low that she rated lower than *Pinta*, a shorter yacht with a smaller sail area.

The small class, racing for the Queen of Spain's Cup, started on 30th June, with the large class, racing for the King's Cup, a week later. Strong westerlies greeted the small class and one soon retired, but *Pinta* revelled in these wet conditions though the crew didn't.

'When we get to Spain — if we ever do — I'm going to put up a cup for the King and Queen both,' said one disgruntled crew member, after two weeks of high winds and heavy seas. 'The race will be from Santander to New York, and it will start in January. They'll sail six metres. I haven't worked out the details yet, but the course will take them three times round Cape Horn.'

Eventually, the head winds which prevailed near the Spanish coast gave the advantage to the larger *Mohawk* and the closer winded *Nina*, and they both passed *Pinta*. Then the wind lightened and *Nina* slipped further ahead. She crossed the line after 23d, 22hrs, at sea, a phenomenally fast time which not only gave her line honours over the rest of the fleet but the Queen's Cup too.

---

* She won the Bermuda race in 1962 and took line honours in the Halifax race five times.

▼ *The first Fastnet race started off Ryde on 15th August 1925. From left to right:* Jessie L, North Star, Jolie Brise, Saladin, Gull, *and* Fulmar. *The seventh entry was* Banba IV.

In the large class everyone had been expecting *Atlantic* to repeat her 1905 triumph, but it was another schooner, *Elena*, which finished first – just half-an-hour after *Nina*, having covered the course in 16d, 19hrs, 49mins. This, too, was something of a feat for she beat the much larger *Atlantic* and *Guinevere* into second and third place respectively on corrected time to win the King's Cup.

The 1928 Fastnet race

Nina sealed her reputation that year by going on to win the Fastnet in mixed weather conditions against a fleet of 11 others which included the first French entry, *L'Oiseau Bleu*. The British had never seen anything quite like *Nina* and the general reaction to her victory was not one of unalloyed pleasure. There were dark mutterings about 'racing machines' and suggestions that foreign yachts should be banned. But the Ocean Racing Club elected Sherman Hoyt, who had raced *Nina* to victory, rear-commodore of the club and stated that the adverse opinions of *Nina* expressed by some were 'ill-informed, prejudiced, and even unsportsmanlike', and they hoped more boats would be built for ocean racing – the term 'ocean racer' had not yet come in – in both Britain and the US.

The 1929 Santander race

The controversy over *Nina's* Fastnet win seems to have soured relations for a while for there were no American entries in the 1929 Fastnet. Instead, it was left to that summer's inaugural race to Santander to show just how international the sport had become. It also showed that the large class was not quite dead for four of them came to the starting line: the German Kaiser's old yacht, *Meteor IV*, renamed *Maria del Carmen*; the Nicholson-designed *Ailee*, owned by the well-known French yachtswoman, Virginie Heriot; Lord Stalbridge's massive three-masted schooner, *Cetonia*; and the Spanish owned *Serva la Bara*. The small class was equally international, with the British entering six yachts, the French two, and the Germans and Spaniards one each.

The race to Santander was the first the infant Ocean Racing Club had organised to a foreign country. It was held again the following year with the same success (though there

◄ *The 56-foot Le Havre pilot cutter,* Jolie Brise, *won the first Fastnet race and then won it again in 1929 and 1930. She is still sailing.*

▲ *The 136-foot, Lawley-designed schooner,* Invader, *won the 1926 Transpac. She set a course record which was to stand for 23 years.*

was no large class) and the fleet included yachts from the US, France, Colombia, and Britain. But then politics intervened and the fixture was not repeated until 1948.

New events in Europe

By the early 1930s ocean racing had become established in both Europe and the US, and the gaff rig was slowly but surely being superceded by the Bermudan. The Depression did cause some hiccups – in 1933 only six yachts raced in the Fastnet, only two took part in the 1932 Transpac, and the number of Bermuda entries levelled off – but on the whole there was a steady increase in both the number of races and in the numbers taking part in them, and this was maintained throughout the decade.

In Britain, a number of shorter races were established, with the Channel and Dinard fixtures being run in conjunction with the Fastnet. In Scotland, the Clyde Cruising Club started the Blue Water Trophy in 1933 after running local short-distance fixtures for some eight years. This first race was from Rothesay, round the Isle of Man, and back to the Clyde, a distance of 310 miles. It was won by a 30-ton Bermudan yawl called *Sulara*. The following year the course was round the Kish light vessel, a distance of 350 miles, but in the following three years it was held over shorter courses. It ceased to be run between 1939 and 1966, but was then resurrected to celebrate the centenary of the Royal Ulster Yacht Club, with the finish in Belfast Lough. It was won by *Siolta*, an Excalibur class sloop, which had further victories over shorter Blue Water Trophy courses in 1968 and 1969. In the 1970s races for the Trophy went further and further afield. The 1972 race was a 350-miler from Inverness to Bergen as part of the *Bergens Seilforeng* centenary celebrations, and it was won in severe weather by a Nicholson 32 called *Killegray*. Since that date there have been races to Port la Foret (1974), Benodet (1977), and La Trinité-sur-mer (1981), all of which were won by the Irish Admiral's cupper, *Tritsch Tratsch*, which also scooped the pool in the shorter races in the intervening years. The course for the Golden Jubilee race in 1983 took the 30-strong fleet round the Kish light vessel with the finish at Hunters Quay in the Clyde, a distance of 350 miles. First in the IOR class was *Starry Night II* which also took first in the overall CCC handicap. Apart from the Fair Isle race which is organised by the Forth Corinthian YC the Blue Water Trophy is the only regularly held long-distance race in Scottish waters.

In 1933 the Heligoland race was reintroduced. It was run every year until 1938 when it was replaced by one from Burnham to Weser in 1939.

The revival of the Heligoland fixture encouraged the re-entry of German yachts into international long-distance racing, and by the end of the decade they nearly outnumbered all yachts from other countries in this event. The race also encouraged the Dutch, and the 1934 race saw the inclusion of *Goodewind*, a ketch owned by Kees Bruynzeel. Bruynzeel was later to win the 1937 Fastnet in *Zeearend* and then to achieve a phenomenal record of successes after the war in his yachts, *Stormvogel* and *Stormy*. The number of races to France also increased, some of which were organised jointly by the RORC and the French *Union Nationale des Croiseurs (UNC)* and these stimulated interest in the sport amongst French yachtsmen living along the Atlantic coast.

Racing in the Mediterranean

In the Mediterranean, the first ocean race, from Toulon, round the Isle of Giraglia via Cape Corse, and back to Juan-les-Pins, a distance of 260 miles, took place in 1927. It was the direct forebear of the famous Giraglia race which takes place annually. This first race was open to yachts between nine and 20 metres, with entries being measured and handicapped by a local formula. Eight yachts started, all of them French. They were mostly old cruising boats though one of the schooners, *Velella*, had been built only the previous year. Line honours were taken by a very elderly (1903) Fife-designed yawl, *Eblis*, in 76hrs, 40mins, but on corrected time the race was won by an only slightly less elderly (1910) yawl called *Le Ramier*, owned by Raymond Recouly.

During the years up to the start of the Second World War, short races were regularly run between different resorts on the French Riviera and sometimes down the coast to Italy, or occasionally to Sardinia. In 1930 local yachtsmen tried something more ambitious when they entered a race of 600 miles between Cannes and Algiers. An unusual feature of this race was that it was run in four legs, with stops at Marseille, Barcelona, and Ibiza, surely the first race ever to be run in several legs. There were 14 starters, ten of which were French, Italian or Spanish entries. But there were also two American yachts and one English. Line honours went to a Spanish boat, *Slec*, while on corrected time the race was won by Jean Lefranc's *La Railleuse*.

Racing in the Baltic

Races had been held in Europe's other large enclosed sea, the Baltic, since the beginning of the century with the Germans organising events from Kiel to Travemunde, and from

▼ *The 106-foot yawl,* Contender, *took line honours in the 1939 Transpac which, for the first time, was started from San Francisco. As* Poinsettia *she came second in the 1926 Transpac.*

Travemunde to Warnemunde. However, the first modern long-distance race did not take place until 1937 when the first Round-Gotland race was established. This 300-mile event attracted a fleet of 42, with representatives from the US, Sweden, Germany, Poland, Lithuania, Finland, Estonia, Britain, and Danzig. They were split into those who raced under the Bermuda rule and those who raced under two different Swedish rules. The race was – and still is – organised by the Royal Swedish Yacht Club (KSSS) and the course started and finished at Visby. The German yacht *Schwanenweiss* took line honours, but on corrected time the Gotland Challenge Cup was won by the Swedish yawl, *Mosca*. The class racing under the Bermuda rule was also won by a Swedish yacht, *Havsorneen*, sailed by Sven Salen, a great innovator who is credited with inventing the genoa. The race was a success and was repeated in 1939.

Between these first two events there was an ambitious series of races in the Baltic which included a feeder race from Dover to Kristiansand – in which French and Dutch yachts as well as British took part – and then one from Kristiansand to Copenhagen, and then another to Warnemunde, which was the start of a 387-mile race round Bornholm, finishing at Kiel. This latter event attracted a huge fleet of 87 which ranged from an old 19-metre down to a 25-footer. It was an unusually run race with the fleet being split into a number of groups, according to size and ability, and each group having its own prizes. But it was also divided into three classes. *Zeearend* won the large class; the British *Ortac* the middle class; and the German *Westwind* the small class.

New events in the US and Canada

On the other side of the Atlantic the Depression did not prevent new races being started, events like the Swiftsure and the Stamford Vineyard which are now classics. The 135-mile Swiftsure, run in the Strait of Juan de Fuca between Vancouver Island and Washington State, was raced only three times pre-war, before becoming one of the West Coast's most prestigious annual fixtures when it was started again in 1947. The Stamford Yacht Club's Vineyard race takes competitors over a 238-mile course along Long Island Sound to Buzzards Bay and back to Stamford. Tricky currents make it a challenging course which has always attracted competitive fleets. Started in 1932 it has been run annually ex-

cept for the war years.

But perhaps the best known event started during this period, and run for nearly 30 years, was the 284-mile St Petersburg-Havana fixture inaugurated in 1930. It rapidly became a popular annual event for Florida yachtsmen – and for others, too. It came into being, as have so many other ocean races, over a drink in a bar and the reason for its instant success, according to American yachting writer, Jeff Hammond, was not hard to find.

'In the 1930s Havana was the gayest and wildest city in that part of the world. Word quickly spread through yacht club bars far and wide of the beautiful and fun-loving women of Havana and of the gambling casinos and

▶   *The 30-foot* Kalmia *was one of Olin Stephens' first designs. He raced her in the 1929 Gibson Island race in which she won her class.*

▼   *The 136-foot, Herreshoff-designed schooner,* Elena, *winner of the King's Cup in the 1928 Transatlantic race. She was owned by a member of the New York Yacht Club, William Bell.*

boisterous waterfront saloons that welcomed the warring yachtsmen.'

It established itself quickly as one of the most popular events on the American calendar until politics finally interrupted the fun after the 1959 fixture. By then it had become established as the long-distance race in America's most prestigious series, the Southern Ocean Racing Conference (SORC).

The SORC started life in 1941, when it was more popularly known as the 'Southern' or 'winter' circuit. It was the first of its kind in the world and, in addition to the Havana race, consisted of the 184-mile Miami-Nassau fixture, started in 1934, and three much shorter events. Each had its own prizes but a points system for yachts competing in all five (now six) races gave an overall winner in the series, which is now held annually.

In 1935, the Royal Nova Scotia Yacht Squadron organised a race from Portland to Halifax. Rather grandly called 'the Portland to Halifax International Yacht Classic', it nevertheless attracted only six starters, and was won by the 68-foot American schooner, Sayonara, with the Canadian Nomad second. Both club and sailing conditions impressed the Americans. One of the winning crew described the Squadron as a 'quiet, hard-sailing outfit. It likes to race over hard water in its own hard conditions. Nine times out of ten there is a breeze to blow your wig off before you can get a bottle of beer open.'

However, it was another four years before American yachts raced to Halifax again. This time the start was at Marblehead, as it had been in 1905, and it was from this event that the popular biennial run today developed. It was won by a Class B yawl, Tioga Too, one of the few pre-war Alden designs which was not a schooner, though another, Estrella, won the inaugural New London to Annapolis the same year. This, too, is still a biennial favourite though it is now run from Annapolis to Newport.

Besides showing that the yawl rig had by now superseded the schooner, these two long-distance races showed that ocean racing in the US had reached a peak just at the time

◄ Under the American Universal Rule, Nina, one of the most successful ocean racers ever, was a 'two-masted cutter'. She was still winning races in the 1960s.

► L'Oiseau Bleu, the first French entry into the Fastnet race. She started well but developed a bad leak and had to retire.

that war broke out in Europe. Needless to say, the war had an immediate effect on the sport on the East Coast with the 1940 Bermuda race being diverted to a safer course. Perhaps with the Fastnet in mind, the CCA found a rock off the Maine coast called Mount Desert and ran the race round that. With the start at Block Island it ended at Gloucester, Mass., a distance of 460 miles.

It proved to be a cold, wet, and miserable race with Rudy Schaeffer's Edlu II burning a coal fire in her cabin fireplace the whole distance.* The scratch boat, Baruna, which had distinguished herself in a number of Bermuda races, added another victory to her long list of successes, beating Blitzen, the 1939 Transpac winner, by eight and a half hours. Although the race had not been to Bermuda, Baruna was nevertheless awarded the Bermuda Trophy.

Although the Transpac was held in 1941, the last long-distance race before the

*As can be imagined it was not a popular race, but in the early 1950s the Storm Trysail Club attempted to establish a biennial event over more or less the same course. It was run a few times but then ceased.

US entered the war was organised by the Storm Trysail Club over Day's 1905 course from New London to Hampton Roads. Cups were won by Blitzen and the Class B Revonoc, but the most unusual prize – though now in various forms it is a standard award in many races – was an engraved stainless steel stewpot, which, as the Forgotten Man Trophy, was awarded to the cook on the last boat!

This brief survey of the shorter ocean races on both sides of the Atlantic during the 1930s illustrates how the sport established itself firmly in just one decade. But the ocean racing calendar during this period was dominated by the Bermuda and Fastnet fixtures – and on three occasions by Transatlantic races which fed yachts from one to the other.

Dorade and Olin Stephens

Of these three, the 1931 race was the most significant so far as the development of ocean racing was concerned. For this event, and the Fastnet that followed it, brought to promin-

ence a small yawl called *Dorade* and her designer, Olin Stephens. Two years previously Olin and his younger brother Rod had done well in the Gibson Island race, and their success persuaded their father, Rod Senior, to back another of his elder son's designs by building *Dorade*.

Olin, a junior partner in the firm of Sparkman & Stephens, was, by 1931, beginning to establish himself as a talented designer, while Rod was learning all the tricks of the trade at Nevins yard. Later, Rod joined his elder brother to help run what was to become one of the most successful firms of yacht architects ever.

But Olin's success was not instantaneous, and nor was *Dorade*'s. After being built under Rod's supervision she was launched from Minneford's yard in May 1930. At 37 feet on the waterline, *Dorade* was, by the standards of the day, a small boat. She was also a revolutionary one in a way which the successful Burgess-designed staysail schooner, *Nina*, was not. *Nina*, with her staysail rig and lavish fittings had exploited an existing type to the full. But *Dorade* broke away from the traditional American schooner rig and wide beam. Instead, Stephens went for a yawl rig*, a narrow beam and an interior and deck layout which emphasised lightness and sparseness.

By concentrating on these aspects Stephens went against many people's preconceived notions of yacht design. To start with there were still many who thought that the sea-worthy schooner rig, as exemplified and refined by Alden's series of *Malabars*, was the only safe and speedy means of tackling ocean races. Then there were those who sniffed at *Dorade*'s excessively narrow beam. 'Just a six metre,' they said, and condemned her as being 'too narrow, so therefore too tender'. Finally, there were those who were still rooted in the idea that racing yachts should be designed for cruising, and they found *Dorade*'s weight-saving interior far too spartan.

The 1931 Transatlantic

Perhaps *Dorade*'s critics felt themselves justified when she failed to sweep the board in that year's Bermuda race, managing only a very respectable second in her class and third

*It is interesting to note, however, that the influence of the schooner rig was still so strong that Olin Stephens published – but never installed – a schooner rig for *Dorade*.

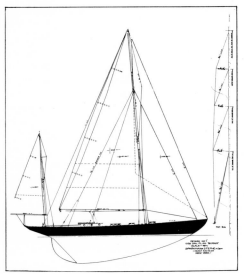

▲ Dorade. *Her dimensions were: LOA 52 feet; LWL 37 feet, 3 inches; beam 10 feet, 3 inches; draught 7 feet, 8 inches.*

overall. But they were soon silenced when the following year the Stephens brothers won with her in the Transatlantic race and the Fastnet which followed it. By calculating that the more northerly Great Circle route would benefit them, and by racing every yard of the way, *Dorade* and her young all-amateur crew made the 2838-mile crossing from Newport to Plymouth in 17d,1hr,14mins. On corrected time she won by a massive margin of three days and nearly six hours, a staggering achievement against a fleet of nine other yachts, all of modern design, three of them specially built for the race. Nothing had been seen like it before and it set the pattern for the sport on both sides of the Atlantic for the rest of the decade.

The Fastnet In the 1930s

Six of the American Transatlantic entries went on to compete in the Fastnet race, by far the largest number of Americans ever to enter. There were also two French yachts; both the British Transatlantic entries; and seven other British starters including the old timer *Jolie Brise* which had won the race in 1929 and 1930, as well as the first one in 1925. With the French and American yachts swelling the number of starters to 17 it looked as if the Fastnet, after six years of fluctuating numbers, had at last become established.

But it was not the low number of starters in the Fastnet up to that time which had

caused comment but the high proportion of yachts which had failed to complete the course. No less than 28 out of a total of 61 yachts which had entered the race between 1925 and 1930 had not finished, and another two were so slow they were never timed. The toughness of the course must take some of the blame for this high casualty rate, as must the crews of the yachts, many of whom were inexperienced or simply not determined enough to stay the course. The yachts, too, were not up to it. They were too old, or too ill-equipped, or too slow, and quite often all three. Design lagged badly behind the US, for the British clung more strongly to their traditional craft and it was just this type of inadequate design that the new generation of designers like Jack Laurent Giles was trying to eliminate and which he summarised neatly in a heartfelt prayer:

From lack of freeboard, sterns too long,
From lean bows and narrow beam,
From reefing bowsprits, sluicing seas,
From fo'c'sle cooking and from long booms,
Libera nos Domine

In addition, the weather was especially bad during the earlier Fastnets. The 1927 race took place in a constant gale and the 1930 race had hardly been any better with five out of the nine starters retiring. Perhaps it was these early fixtures which established the Fastnet's reputation as a foul-weather race, a reputation which only began to fade in the early and middle 1970s when a succession of light-weather races lulled many yachtsmen, unfortunately as it turned out, into a false sense of security.

It certainly seemed on that brilliantly sunny day of 11th August 1931 that the weather pattern had at last changed, for there was not a breath of wind at the start and some of the competitors took over an hour to get away from the line. But before some of them had even cleared Lands End the weather broke and the wind rose quickly to gale force. Gear began to break and at least one yacht ran for shelter. By the time some of the slower yachts reached the Rock there was a wild sea running. *Amberjack II*, an American entry, was almost swamped and then nearly driven on to the Rock; and another American yacht, *Water Gypsy*, was within an ace of being driven aground near Lands End. *Ariel*, a French entry, was hove to for 32 hours. *Viking*, an old cruising cutter, fared even worse, for she was forced to heave to twice, once near the Rock for over 48 hours and then again off the Lizard for 24 hours on the way back. By this time two of the entries had retired and *Viking* would have joined them if one of the crew, a young British naval officer, hadn't managed to persuade her elderly owner to continue. His name was John Illingworth and in the years to come he was to dominate the ocean racing scene in Britain as the Stephens brothers were to do in the US.

But of all the starters in the 1931 Fastnet, *Maitenes II*, a new yacht designed and built for the 1929 Fastnet (though not designed to the ORC rule), suffered the worst. After rounding the Rock she was forced to heave to on the Saturday afternoon. By 1000 the next morning the wind had risen to force 10, and at 1145 the boat was almost laid on her beam ends by a particularly vicious gust. Fearing that she might be overwhelmed it was decided to tow warps and run before the storm under bare poles. This was successfully accomplished after some difficulty, but *Maitenes II* was now over the Labadie Bank, an area of shallow water which the yacht's skipper later described as 'notorious' because of the confused seas it created. Many of the yachts in trouble in the 1979 Fastnet were in the same area. Oceanographic experts have stated that the bank is too far down to have anything but a minimal effect on the wave patterns, but to the crew on *Maitenes II* it certainly seemed as if the steepness of the seas had increased and that they were breaking with greater frequency. Oil bags were put out, and then at about 1245 Colonel Hudson, the co-owner of the yacht, was lost overboard.

It was later reported that the Colonel had been clearing an oil bag when the boat lurched and he was catapulted overboard. But years later Charles A. Nicholson, the nephew of the yacht designer Charles E. Nicholson, corrected this story. He was at the helm and the Colonel was sitting in the cockpit when the yacht lurched violently, pitching the Colonel into the sea. 'He must have dozed off,' said Nicholson.

'The sheets jammed so we could not round up. I doubt if we could have saved him anyway as he was wearing seaboots and he would have sunk at once.'

The loss of Colonel Hudson was the first death in modern ocean racing, though another was to occur during the 1932 Bermuda race when one of the crew of *Adriana*, which had caught fire, missed his foothold while jumping from the burning yacht, and

▲   The Dutch sloop, Zeearend (202), at the start of the 1937 Fastnet race which she won.

▶   Dorade kedged at the start of the 1931 Fastnet race which she won. She won it again in 1933.

drowned.

The tragedy marred what otherwise would have been a classic Fastnet, for the leading four yachts raced the last miles in close company and finished within minutes of one another. The scratch boat, the Nicholson-designed *Patience*, beat an American entry, *Highland Light*, across the line by just 1min,18s. Twenty minutes later *Water Gypsy* appeared; and then, to everyone's amazement, the much smaller *Dorade* finished, having saved 19 of her 20 hour allowance. *Jolie Brise* could do no better than seventh for she had been outclassed. It was the end of an era and she did not take part in another Fastnet, though she did enter the

1932 Bermuda race and was responsible for rescuing the crew of *Adriana*.

Dorade's victory, and her repeat of it in the 1933 Fastnet, persuaded the British that if fast new designs were not forthcoming the Fastnet Cup would be lost permanently. So by 1935, when the next Transatlantic race took place, several new yachts had been built to meet the American challenge. One, *Trenchemer*, was the first yacht to be specifically built to the RORC rule, but it was the Nicholson-designed cutter, *Foxhound*, which showed the most promise of success. However, the Americans had a hand even in her, for it was an American living in London who gave Nicholson the order.

Like Stephens, Nicholson took his inspiration from the metre boats which were governed by the IYRU rule and *Foxhound*, and her later sisterships, *Bloodhound* – the 1939 Fastnet winner – and *Stiarna*, rated as 12-metres. But unlike any 12-metre of that period they were beautiful seagoing yachts capable of high speeds. Although not built to the RORC rule they conformed to its requirements and rated well under it.

But though the British produced some competitive yachts for the 1935 Fastnet they were just not good enough to beat the latest Stephens design, *Stormy Weather*. This re-

▼ *The 59-foot schooner, Water Gypsy, was one of the six American entries in the 1931 Fastnet race. She was the first to round the rock and finished second overall behind Dorade.*

40

markable yacht – among other successes she won the Miami-Nassau race every year between 1937 and 1941 – was really a development of *Dorade*. Longer and beamier than the earlier boat, *Stormy Weather* was built for Philip Le Boutillier who persuaded Rod Stephens to skipper her in the 1935 Transatlantic race which was sponsored by the Royal Norwegian Yacht Club.

The 1935 Transatlantic race

Despite the increasing popularity of ocean racing, the race to Bergen attracted only six starters; *Vamarie*, a wishbone ketch that had taken line honours in the previous year's Bermuda Race; *Stormy Weather* and *Mistress*, both of which had conventional Bermudian rigs; and three gaff-rigged entries: *Vagabond*, *Hamrah*, and the only German entry, the cutter, *Stoertebeker*.

The 3050-mile course took the yachts to the north of the British Isles and only the German cutter dropped below the 40th parallel at the start – which could have been one of the reasons why she took nearly 35 days to finish! None, however, was bold enough to sail as far north as *Stormy Weather*, up the coast of Nova Scotia and then through a foggy 50-mile wide lane between the ice which led to the most direct course to the finish. It was a remarkable feat of seamanship, and on corrected time it won her the race by a huge margin of nearly two days.

This race, too, was marred by tragedy when Robert Ames, the owner of *Hamrah*, was washed overboard on the tenth day out. Both his sons tried to save him but all three were drowned, and after being hove to for 50 hours the yacht returned to Nova Scotia.

The single German entry in the 1935 Transatlantic race had struggled in last but her participation was noted by the German yachting community, which up to that time had been somewhat lukewarm about racing long distances. The skipper of *Stoertebeker*, Captain Schlimbach, had been trying for years to encourage his countrymen to participate in the longer races. 'Europe is slow,' he wrote. 'The men of European nations can see the Atlantic rollers breaking at their front doors and never – or at least rarely – take any part in Transatlantic racing under sail.'

Schlimbach himself had tried to set an example and though he failed to reach Newport in time to start in the 1931 race he subsequently circumnavigated the British Isles and sailed from Hamburg to Brazil. But until

the 1935 Transatlantic race his achievements had been disregarded and though the Heligoland race had always attracted German entries it was not until 1936 that they exceeded the number of British entries. By then a great deal of enthusiasm had been generated by Schlimbach's adventures and a Transatlantic race from Bermuda was proposed with the finish at Cuxhaven, in time for the crews to attend the Olympic Games being held that year in Berlin.

Three new German yachts were built for the race, and four others re-rigged. Altogether, eight German entries were shipped, and six took part in that year's Bermuda race.

The 1936 Bermuda and Transpac races

It was a hard-weather race in 1936, but the German yachts that participated all finished though they were not among the prize winners. *Vamarie* continued her run of successes to take line honours; but the Class B *Kirawan* put up a remarkable performance to finish third overall and take the Bermuda Trophy on corrected time, even beating the Class A winner, *Stormy Weather*, across the finishing line by seven minutes.

Dorade was not in contention that year as she had been sold to a West Coast owner

who entered her for the 1936 Transpac. She performed just as well in the very different conditions of the Pacific as she had in the Atlantic, taking line honours and winning overall with ease.

After the 1936 Transpac it was decided to co-ordinate the fixture with the Bermuda race so that in future yachtsmen from either coast would be able to enter both. The next Transpac was therefore postponed until 1939. This policy of co-ordinating events became increasingly important in the post-war era as the ocean racing calendar became more crowded. In the case of the Transpac it showed immediate dividends. In 1938 the Californian yachtsman, J.L. Stewart Jr, took his schooner, *Santana*, which had come second in the 1936 Transpac, to the East Coast. He showed the eastern schooner fleet how to race by capturing the Schaeffer prize for the first schooner to finish in the Bermuda race, ending up a very respectable ninth overall.

The 1936 Transatlantic race

The eight German yachts and one Dutch one, *Zeearend*, crossed the start line of the 1936 Transatlantic race on 5th July. *Roland von*

Bremen took an early lead and held it all the way across the Atlantic to finish first in 21d,10hrs,45mins, winning on corrected time from the Rasmussen-designed Brema.

Captain Schlimbach, skippering Brema's sistership, Hamburg, could manage no better than fifth place on corrected time. It may have been that Schlimbach's performance was affected by his sleeping habits at sea. 'We stood six-hour watches,' wrote one of his crew after the race, 'six on and six off, which gave us more unbroken sleep, we thought. That is, all but Skipper Schlimbach who has a way of never sleeping at sea. When it was impossible for him to stay on his feet any longer, he would lie on the cabin floor with his feet stretched across the passageway so that anyone passing would stumble over him and he would be on deck again.'

Racing in the southern hemisphere: the Bass Strait races

While ocean racing developed around and between the coasts of the US and Europe, the sport was struggling to come alive off the far more isolated – and hazardous – coasts of Australia and New Zealand.

The first Australian ocean race had taken place at the beginning of the century. Early in 1906 Thomas Fleming Day, the Editor of Rudder magazine and the instigator of the Bermuda race, wrote to a Mr T.A. Dickson of Geelong, a supporter of the magazine, and offered to donate a cup for an ocean race in Australian waters. Dickson took up the idea enthusiastically and suggested the cup be deposited with the Geelong Yacht Club. They agreed that the cup should be a perpetual challenge trophy and that the course should be across the Bass Strait, from Melbourne to Devonport, a distance of 200 miles. The race was to be for cruising yachts sailed by amateurs.

Dickson had a yacht specially built for the race and named her Shamrock. Unfortunately for him she was only finished a few days before the start on Boxing Day, 1907. She did not perform as well as she might have and the race was won by Thistle, a 48-foot yawl. It was a rough race – it usually still is – and when the trophy was handed to Mrs Newland, the wife of Thistle's owner, she stated that no yachtsman should ever be

◀   Another phenomenally successful S&S-design was the 53-foot yawl, Stormy Weather. In her first season, 1935, she won the Transatlantic and the Fastnet races.

▲ *In 1936* Dorade *sailed in her first Transpac. She not only took line honours, but won her class and the race on corrected time. She is seen here approaching the finishing line.*

▶ *The 59-foot cutter,* Circe, *finished only 13 minutes behind* Dorade *in the 1936 Transpac, but had to allow her over 30 hours. She was credited with the best 24-hour run in the race – 254 miles.*

tempted again to sail such a hazardous course, and she flatly refused to hand it back!

Whether it was Mrs Newland or, more likely, the stories that filtered back of the perils encountered, that delayed the next race till 1929 will never be known. One thing is quite certain, however, which is that the second race was every bit as bad as the first. *Phyllis* was forced to take shelter; *Wanderer* was blown so far to the north-east that she ended up off Wilson's Promontary with her sails in tatters, and was forced to motor home; *Shamrock* hove to for eight hours; and the 42-foot ketch *Oimara*, the eventual winner, came within an ace of losing two of her crew.

But the worst disaster was reserved for the 10-ton cutter, *Maysie*. After a rough night in which the crew had unsuccessfully tried to ride out the storm to a sea anchor, a squall hit them with great ferocity. 'We went off like a shot for a few hundred yards,' one of the crew wrote later, 'and were then forced to jibe. Jock put her over and I was getting in the sheet when the sail came over with a bang; away went the main block shackle and "whack" went the boom against the runner. Finish boom; the broken half swung forward

and at the same minute away went our number three jib, literally shredded to ribbons. We were then in trouble with our peak halliards, for the gaff holding up the broken boom was swinging about dangerously. We yelled below for an axe to cut loose, but the gaff solved the question by parting against the crosstrees, bringing down the topmast, which went overside, with all its wire shrouds, and completely tangled around the propeller, tearing the tail shaft out of the clutch, making a thorough job of our mess.'

Leaking so badly that the water was up to the top of the settees, and being pooped by every tenth wave, *Maysie* was driven north towards the mainland. More by luck than anything else the crew managed to get her into Westernport Bay, practically the only place on a hundred miles of coastline that they could have got ashore alive in a south-west gale.

'Not a man who dared the straits this year,' wrote the crewman, 'was anything but lucky to get through with his life.'*

The first TransTasman race 1931
Though the 1929 race had obviously put the fear of God into some of the crews it did not deter the owner of the winning yacht, F.J. 'Doc' Bennell, from issuing a challenge in 1930 through the newspapers to Australian and New Zealand yachtsmen to race across the Tasman Sea the following year. This created quite a stir – and the open hostility of the local yacht clubs who considered the idea foolhardy – but as it did not produce any takers Bennell decided to sail *Oimara* across to New Zealand and issue the challenge again once he arrived.

The passage across would have deterred most men for the Tasman Sea is as noto-

*Despite dire predictions that the race would not be held again 'for many a long year' Melbourne's centenary was celebrated in 1934 with another Bass Strait race, and was again won by *Oimara*. Races across the Strait have been held ever since.

▲   Dorade *at* Honolulu *after the 1936 Transpac.*

◄   *When the Bass Strait race was resurrected in 1929 it was won by the 42-foot ketch,* Oimara, *seen here at the start of the first TransTasman race.*

▶   *The German yawl,* Roland von Bremen, *won the Fownes Cup for the first foreign boat home in the 1936 Bermuda race. She is seen here at the start of that year's Transatlantic race from Bermuda to Cuxhaven, which she won.*

rious as the Bass Strait, and during one storm Bennell broke a rib. This forced him to put into Wellington, and while there he again tried to find some competiton. One local enthusiast got as far as procuring uniforms for his crew and a band to play him out of harbour, but unfortunately he did not have a yacht!

Refusing to give up, Bennell set sail for Auckland, then, as now, New Zealand's yachting centre. No one seemed very keen to race there either. Then, a Norwegian yachtsman called Erling Tambs, on a round-the-world cruise in his 40-foot cutter, *Teddy*, took up Bennell's challenge, and later the New Zealand cutter, *Rangi*, also joined in.

As an impromptu affair the first Trans-Tasman race beat even the first Fastnet or Transpac. *Oimara* was allowed by the rules of the race, which was organised by the Royal New Zealand Yacht Squadron, to use her engine, and all three entries were at liberty to carry as many extra sails as they chose to. The course was from Auckland to Sydney, a dis-

▲ Oimara*'s crew for the first TransTasman race. 'Doc' Bennell, her owner, is second on the left.*

▶ Oimara *making quick progress during the Trans-Tasman.*

tance of 1280 miles.

Tambs took aboard a New Zealand crew, thus being one of the first to start the now long-established custom that an ocean racer can be sailed by a multi-national crew, and often is. Competiton amongst the locals to get aboard *Teddy* was so keen that those chosen were offered £10 to give up their berths, an offer that was loftily refused. The Akarana (now Royal) Yacht Club donated a perpetual challenge trophy, the TransTasman Cup, and at 1400 on 31st March 1931, two of the yachts crossed the start line. The third, *Rangi*, in less of a hurry, did not cross for another half an hour.

Teddy led the way towards North Head, but *Oimara*, all sails hoisted and engine full ahead, soon caught up with her. Then

46

behind them they saw *Rangi*, with a huge spread of racing canvas on her, coming up astern, travelling, as Tambs put it, 'like a witch.'

After a crossing which was rough enough to break another part of the unfortunate Bennell's anatomy – this time his nose – *Oimara* arrived in Sydney having covered the course in 11d,20hrs, finishing just over two days ahead of the Norwegian. But Tambs won as his old cruiser had been given a time allowance of 96 hours.

Rangi, in the meantime, had been dogged by long periods of calm as well as by the usual gales and head winds, and she took 19d,16mins, having called in at Lord Howe Island on the way.

◄ Teddy, a *Colin Archer*-designed, 40-foot pilot cutter, was the winner of the first TransTasman race. Here she is seen arriving in Sydney Harbour after the race.

▼ Te Rapunga *(nearest the camera) and* Ngataki, *at the start of the second TransTasman in 1934. The weather was described as 'boisterous'.*

▲ *The 38-foot cutter,* Rangi, *was the only New Zealand entry in the first TransTasman race. She was originally built as a fishing boat.*

▶ *The 56-foot, S & S-designed sloop,* Blitzen, *was second overall in the 1938 Bermuda race and the following year won the Transpac, the first single-sticker to date that had done so.*

The 1934 TransTasman

Three years passed before any yachtsman volunteered to race again for the TransTasman Cup, but in 1934 another round-the-world cruising man, the German, George Dibbern, raced a young New Zealander called Johnny Wray from Auckland to Melbourne, a distance of 1630 miles. Like Tambs, Dibbern created something of a precedent with his crew, for it consisted entirely of girls. This did not prove to be in any way a distraction for him as he covered the course in his 33-foot yawl *Te Rapunga,* in 18d,23hrs, 58mins, and won the race by three days from Wray who'd built his 34-foot hard-chine cutter, *Ngataki,* in his backyard.

The 1938 TransTasman

The third pre-war TransTasman was no more popular than the second, with only two competitors prepared to risk their necks: H.E. Terry in his 40-foot schooner, *Aurora Star,* and K.G. Reid in *Wayfarer,* a 36-foot canoe sterned, gaff cutter. The course was from Auckland to Hobart, a distance of 1530 miles. But neither were to complete it. Both yachts were so badly buffeted by a cyclone that *Wayfarer,* leaking badly and with a damaged rudder, turned for home, while *Aurora*

Star, blown 400 miles off course, had to abandon the race and shelter at Lord Howe Island. She eventually reached Sydney, where her owner promptly sold her and returned home by steamer!

These *ad hoc* long-distance races in ancient cruising boats did not really compare with the more sophisticated events in Europe and the US that occurred during the same period. But they formed a basis on which to build the sport in what are some of the toughest conditions in the world and after the war yachtsmen 'Down Under' were quick to catch up with their northern rivals.

Cotton Sails, Iron Men

1945–59

NO SOONER HAD the Second World War ended in Europe than British yachtsmen had their boats back in the water. Miraculously, the RORC managed to arrange a race to Dinard that year, and on 13th September 1945 eight yachts, escorted by a destroyer to see they did not wander into any minefields, set off across the Channel.

The first Sydney-Hobart race 1945

Although the British were back into ocean racing first, it was the Australians who were responsible for initiating that year what was to become one of the great ocean racing classics in the post-war period: the Sydney-Hobart race. It came about because John Illingworth found himself in Sydney at the end of the war, and while going about his job of overseeing the dismantling of the repair yard at Woolloomooloo he bought himself a canoe-sterned 30-footer which he renamed *Rani*. Soon afterwards, he was asked to give a talk to the members of the Royal Prince Alfred Yacht Club about ocean racing. When he had finished, the chairman proposed that Illingworth should sail *Rani* in company with several other yachts on a cruise to Hobart during the Christmas holidays. Illingworth said that he would be glad to – provided they made a race of it. This was agreed, and it was decided to start on Boxing Day, although, as Illingworth said, 'to keep oneself completely sober over Christmas is, to be honest, a bit of a bind'. However, this date has always been adhered to.

At that time of year, a 'southerly buster', as it is known locally, often springs up off Australia's south-east coast. For those on land it comes as a welcome relief from the heat. But to yachtsmen it can spell trouble as it often blows at gale force or more for anything from 12 to 24 hours. It can cause big seas and a dangerous lee shore.

Without warning one of these 'southerly busters' hit the fleet of nine. Illingworth's competitors kept plugging into it for as long as was possible and then either hove to or, as was considered prudent in those days, ran for shelter. One yacht anchored in the lee of Gabo Island and while waiting for the storm to blow itself out the crew went ashore to shoot rabbits!

Illingworth, however, took a long seaward tack and back again and kept going. *Rani* nearly foundered off Montagu Island, but when one of the crew prudently suggested they reduce sail, Illingworth said, 'No. We'll only have to put it all up again.'

▲ *Captain John Illingworth RN, the man who started one of the classic ocean races, the Sydney-Hobart.*

▶ Rani, *one of the nine entries in the first Sydney-Hobart race. She nearly foundered in a storm but went on to win.*

Illingworth's tactic of riding the storm instead of trying to bash his way through it paid dividends, and afterwards it was found that the others had eventually sailed greater distances than *Rani*. But though she was kept sailing it must have been touch-and-go whether she would ever reach Hobart. 'Trying to keep the old girl afloat,' wrote the mate, Norman Hudson afterwards, 'was a nightmare indeed. The pumps broke down. At times the water came over the level of the bunks and we bailed with plates, pots and pans – in fact, with everything that would shovel that wet stuff back to its rightful place. We bailed till we dropped. Somehow we licked it.'

The aircraft keeping an eye on the race could not identify *Rani* amongst the stormy wind-lashed seas, and the pilot reported her missing. So when *Rani* appeared out of the squalls and mists off Tasman Island to cross the line first in an elapsed time of 6d,14hrs,22mins, the local Tasmanian newspaper ran the biblical but appropriate headline '*Rani* Not Lost but Gone Before!' She arrived 17 hours ahead of the next yacht, and on corrected time won by a day and five hours.

The first Sydney-Hobart underlined, just as the Fastnet and the Bermuda races had, that a small yacht can be kept going in the most extreme conditions provided the crew can take it. The Australians have always been hard-weather sailors so that was not much of a lesson for them to absorb, but it was also realised that while speed is of the essence, tactics also count. It was something the Australians were quick to learn when they entered the international arena, but their affection for pure speed is still reflected in the local headlines where line honours are always more prominently displayed than they are in other parts of the world.

Revival after the war
Of course, no one knew how the Sydney-Hobart was going to develop, so all eyes in 1946 were on the ocean races that had become established before the war. It had been hoped that the Transpac could be run that year. But Pearl Harbor was still closed to civilian vessels, and ships crowded the docks at Honolulu three and four deep. It was decided, reluctantly, to postpone the race until 1947. However, the Bermuda race got under way once more and attracted 15 yachts to Class A and 19 to Class B. It proved one of

the slowest races on record and *Baruna*, the first yacht to finish, took 119hrs, 3mins to complete the course. Only *Tamerlane*, the line honours winner in 1906, had taken longer. The RORC entry, *Latifa*, which had failed to finish in 1938, could manage no better than sixth in Class A even though the hard-driving Illingworth was at her helm. The overall winner on corrected time was Howard Fuller's sloop, *Gesture*.

A revolution in design
While on a transport ship to the US to take part in the Bermuda race, Illingworth began putting on paper his idea for a revolutionary ocean racer. In 1937 he had launched his first cruiser/racer, as the yachts which raced during the middle and late 1930s were often called. The hull of *Maid of Malham* had been designed by Jack Laurent Giles. He had never designed a cruiser/racer before but Illingworth had chosen him over such venerable names as Fife and Mylne because they understood one another. Giles knew Illingworth wanted something radical, and in some ways he got it, and *Maid*, with her sawn off counter and cutaway keel was much nearer to being the progenitor of the post-war ocean racer than, for instance, the long-keeled *Bloodhound* with her classic lines.

On this radical hull Illingworth had

▼ *Designed by Laurent Giles for John Illingworth in 1937, Maid of Malham, 35-feet LWL, was one of the first yachts to carry a masthead rig.*

added an even more radical rig. The single stick of the Bermudian rig had become infinitely stronger than the solid, tapered mast of the old gaff rig. The hollow mast that had succeeded it did not need to be tapered to save weight and could therefore sustain a much wider radius right up to the truck. This increased load bearing, a factor which was further enhanced after the war by the wider use of metal masts. Yet designers were still making the joining point of the forestay where the main upper cap of the main mast of the gaff-rigged vessel had been, though this joining point was now quite meaningless. Illingworth had changed all this by making a masthead rig for Maid, so that her powerful jib could be hoisted right up to the truck.

Now he wanted to advance beyond Maid with an even more revolutionary design. Myth of Malham was to be a short-ended, light displacement boat with a straight sheer that not only exploited the Rule but drove a hole right through it. Again, Illingworth took his ideas to Giles and between them they produced a yacht which proved to be as much a milestone in yacht design as Dorade. With her chopped off ends and rounded bow she was no beauty, and Illingworth's sail plan horrified Giles. 'I don't call that a mainsail,' he said, 'it's just a flag abaft the mast.'

But Illingworth knew what he was doing. 'At that time,' he explained later, 'the foretriangle rated at only 85 per cent of its actual area, and the staysails could have a foot length of up to 150 per cent base of foretriangle. In other words, foretriangle area was excessively cheap compared with mainsail area, and I was determined to take advantage of this small defect in the RORC rule.'

The move towards larger foresails, encouraged by men like Sven Salen, had started in the 1930s, but linking them with smaller mainsails was the start of an entirely new trend. Logically, the result was a mast stepped much further aft than normal and an extremely short boom. This in turn produced a very high aspect ratio rig that performed well to windward.

Having produced a yacht that was years ahead of the opposition, Illingworth proceeded to race her as perhaps no other owner up to that time had ever raced before. He was utterly relentless in his pursuit of saving weight and achieving the optimum from both boat and crew.

Myth got into her stride quickly, for she won her first two races in 1947, one from Rosneath to Portsmouth and the Channel race. But the event that Illingworth had his eye on was, of course, the Fastnet. It was a light-weather race that year, but Myth covered the distance at an average speed of just over six knots – most of it to windward – and romped home the overall winner by over six hours on corrected time. Hardly had the Fastnet finished than Illingworth and 18 others started on the 355-mile ace from Plymouth to La Rochelle which had proved so popular when it had been first run in 1939, and which remained a biennial fixture up to 1979. Myth very nearly won again, but this time was pipped at the post by the Dutch yacht, Olivier van Noort. For the first time the fleet was split into three classes, with the new Class III being for yachts with a minimum waterline length of 24 feet.

▼ The 39-foot cutter, Olivier van Noort, was designed by G. De Vries Lentsch in 1939. She sailed successfully for many years after the war and was a member of the first Dutch Admiral's Cup team in 1959.

Blyth to Kristiansand 1947
The other major event in the RORC calendar in 1947 was a race from Blyth on the Northumberland coast to Kristiansand in Norway, a distance of 360 miles. Two Norwegian yachts – Oregon, a quay punt, and a Colin Archer ketch, Stavanger – crossed the North Sea to join six British entries. It was a close fought race with four of the starters, including the winner, Mindy, finishing within 17 minutes of one another. Despite the event's success, the next long-distance race from this coast was not run until 1975 when the veteran Zeevalk, under British ownership, won a race organised by the Royal Northumberland Yacht Club from Blyth to Stavanger.

New events in the southern hemisphere
In the southern hemisphere, two new fixtures were inaugurated in 1947. Off the South American coast, eight Argentinian and two Brazilian yachts raced the 1200 miles from Buenos Aires to Rio de Janeiro to establish what has become one of the best known races in the world. Held triennially, until the 1983 fixture was postponed for two years, the BA-Rio has always attracted international competition though the Argentinians have always dominated it. Line honours in the first race was won by the Argentinian yawl, Alfard, which overhauled the Brazilian yawl, Vendaval, 400 yards from the finish. She also won on corrected time.

The other new fixture was the 350-mile Montagu Island race, which now opens the Australian ocean racing season. The course, from Sydney, round Montagu Island and back, was described by one writer as being sailed in either 'a succession of exasperating calms which breaks the hearts of lesser helmsmen on the long beat back against the southerly setting current, or in screaming gales which spread-eagle the lightly geared bravos gambling on only light stuff.'

The 1947 Sydney-Hobart race
The third Sydney-Hobart was started under a cloudless sky and watched by a huge crowd of spectators. At first, a good steady breeze sent the fleet of 28 scudding southwards, but as the yachts entered Bass Strait they were savaged by a 65-knot storm. The first boat in, the cutter Morna, had five feet of brass track stripped from her mast and her mainsail slashed to ribbons. This forced her to finish the last 85 miles under trysail and headsails, but she still managed to finish only ten mi-

nutes behind her 1946 time when she had also won the Illingworth Trophy for the first boat home. On corrected time the home-built Tasmanian cutter, *Westward*, was declared the winner.

The 1948 TransTasman

The Hobart race finished, two of the participants, from it, the 57-foot ketch *Kurrewa III*, belonging to the Livingston brothers, and the 36-foot cutter, *Peer Gynt*, owned by the Halvorsen brothers, sailed across to Auckland to take part in the third TransTasman race.

An attempt had been made the previous year to resurrect the race when Ken Pragnall, the owner of the 33-foot cutter, *Drifter*, had challenged George Dibbern, the holder of the Challenge Cup. Dibbern accepted the challenge but failed to turn up at the start line. It was decided that if Pragnall sailed the course he would be entitled to the Cup. But 300 miles out of Auckland a crew member fell seriously ill and Pragnall was forced to return. The failure of this race prompted the Royal Akarana Yacht Club to declare that the TransTasman Cup was no longer a challenge trophy, but could now be raced for in open competition.

This spurred no less than eight yachts — four from New Zealand, three from Australia and one, *Pagan*, skippered by Bill Weld, from the US — to come to the start line. For the first six days the Tasman was unusually kind. Then, inevitably, the weather detoriated and a passing cyclone hit the yachts with devastating effect.

The Livingston brothers tried to keep their yacht sailing as long as possible but even under reefed trysails *Kurrewa III* was exceeding her designed speed, and eventually they were forced to round up. While she was hove to a freak roller — some reports say it was a tidal wave — hit her, throwing her on her beam ends and injuring two of her crew. About 50 miles away, *Peer Gynt* was knocked down by the same wave. *Kurrewa III* went on to make a record breaking run of 9d,23hrs,24mins but on corrected time, however, she dropped to third place behind the eventual winner, *Peer Gynt*, and Peter Luke's *Wayfarer*.

The 1948 Bermuda race

The second post-war Bermuda race drew several foreign entries which included *Cangrejo*, designed by the Argentinian, German

▲ *Though she appeared in 1939, Mindy was a typical post-war Class III ocean racer. 28-feet, 3 inches LWL she had a sail area of 570 square feet and was designed by F.B.R. Brown, later her co-owner.*

Frers. During the next two decades Frers established himself as one of the world's top designers, a mantle which he passed on to his son, German Jr, in the 1970s. Another foreign yacht was the redoubtable *Myth of Malham* which had already won two shorter East Coast ocean races before she came to the start line at Newport. Unusually, it was a reaching race and not suited to *Myth's* windward abilities. Even so, she managed to finish fourth in Class B and took away the Thomas

Day Memorial Trophy for the fastest yacht under 40 feet as well as the prize given to the first foreign yacht on corrected time. The overall winner was *Baruna*. The Class B winner was John Alden's ketch, *Malabar XIII*, which he had designed and built in 1945. By

1948, schooners belonged to the past, and in the Bermuda race that year there were only two out of a fleet of 36. From the point of view of yacht construction, the most interesting yacht was *Nimrod IV*, designed by Sparkman & Stephens for she was the first ocean racer to be built of aluminium.

Santander race reintroduced

After the resurgence of the sport in 1947, the following season in Europe was a quiet one, but it did include the reintroduction of the Santander race, last sailed in 1930, and another race to Kristiansand, this time from Harwich. The Santander race tested the stamina of both boat and crew when a force 10 scattered the fleet and sent several running for shelter. Among the starters was *St Barbara*, one of the few new post-war British yachts: the French *Margelic*; and the Argentian sloop *Joanne*; but it was an old-timer, *Eilun*, that stood up best to the conditions and she won Class I, with the pre-war *Erivale* taking Class II, and *Mindy* Class III.

New rating rules

In Europe, shortage of materials had severely restricted any kind of yacht construction. Indeed, Illingworth had had the greatest difficulty in having *Myth* built at all. By 1948, the restrictions were beginning to ease, but yachtsmen were generally content to continue racing their pre-war craft until it became clear how the RORC would react to *Myth*. The club did not react immediately, but for the 1949 season it was decided that all yachts built after 1940 had to be re-rated to new criteria. These did something to plug the gaps *Myth* had driven through the Rule.

With the new Rule in force, 1949 and 1950 saw several new yachts, perhaps the most interesting being the aluminium *Gulvain* and the hard-chine *Zeewalk*. Both yachts, one British the other Dutch, were light displacement boats which were logical developments of *Myth*. *Zeewalk*, designed by E.G. Van de Stadt, displaced about one-third of a conventional vessel of the same length of 35-feet LWL, her plywood construction and narrow hull form making her both exceptionally fast and also strong. Kees Bruynzeel raced her with great success for a number of years. *Gulvain*, designed by Laurent Giles, started her career well with a win in the Cowes-Dinard race, but the exceptionally heavy weather in 1949 Fastnet caused her to retire and thereafter she never reached her full potential.

The 1949 Fastnet race

The 1949 Fastnet was one of the hardest ever. For the fleet of 29, the first night at sea brought a moderate westerly, but the dawn was an angry red. On board *Myth*, the barometer fell with such extraordinary swiftness that the navigator, Mary Blewitt, working below, had great difficulty in persuading Illingworth, who was on deck, of what was happening. The gale, when it came, was right on the nose, gusting force 9, and one by one nearly all *Myth's* opponents hove to, retired, or ran for shelter. But Illingworth kept driving his boat and, under a staysail and double reefed mainsail, followed *Bloodhound* through the gap between the Scillies and Lands End, and rounded the Rock less than three hours behind her. The run back under spinnaker soon had *Myth* notching up her theoretical maximum speed, and then exceeding it. Driven like that, it is not surprising that *Myth* arrived at Plymouth less than 12 hours after *Latifa*, the first boat home, and

won easily on corrected time from *Bloodhound*. Only six other boats finished.

First Wolf Rock race

On the same date as the Fastnet started, the first 305-mile Wolf Rock race was begun for the Class III yachts which were not eligible for the longer race. The fleet of 14 was plagued by the same weather as the Fastnet entries, but as they did not have to pass Lands End they fared better. The race was won by Dick Scholfield's *Blue Disa*, a RNSA '24' and a good example of the new breed of minimum length, light displacement ocean racer. The Wolf Rock ceased to be held after 1954 as Class III yachts were admitted to the Fastnet.

The 1949 Transpac race

Light displacement boats like *Blue Disa* which were being constructed in Europe at that time did not cut much ice with the yachting establishment on the East Coast of the US. They did, however, make an early impact on the West Coast when a light displacement 46-foot Kettenburg-designed sloop called *Kitten* first of all won that year's 135-mile Ensenada race, inaugurated in 1948, and then went on to scoop the pool in the 1949 Transpac, covering the course at an average speed of 7.9 knots. Steady trade winds also enabled the 98-foot schooner, *Morning Star*, to break the course record which had been held by *Invader* since 1926. She finished in an elapsed

▶ *The 98-foot schooner,* Morning Star, *well furnished with 'baggy wrinkle', took line honours in the 1949 Transpac and broke the course record which had been held by* Invader *since 1926.*

▼ *Start of the 440-mile Brixham-Santander race in 1948. Among the 35 starters are* Maid of Malham *(199),* St Barbara *(401), and* Myth of Malham *(352).* Theodora *(347) trails the fleet.*

time of 10d,10hrs,13mins,9.5secs. But her success in breaking the record which had stood for 24 years was also due to the use to which her crew put a carefully analysed weather chart which the Transpacific Yacht Club distributed for the first time that year to all competitors.

Revised CCA Rule
The 1950 season in the US brought a revision of the CCA Rule which took into account the appearance of light displacement yachts. But it was also found necessary to rewrite the Rule to make it more comprehensive, the Chairman of the Cruising Club Year Book Committee having deemed the 1940 version 'unintelligible to everyone except the Measurement Rule Committee, a few naval architects and God Almighty. In recasting the rule, the Committee laid stress on the fact that it had been revised to make it more adaptable to a wider variety of yacht than was normally found in the Bermuda race, the first hint perhaps towards actively finding a common international rating.

The 1950 Bermuda race
It was under this revised Rule that the largest ever contingent of British yachts raced in the 1950 Bermuda race, and failed miserably to make any impact. However, it was not the Rule which was responsible for this, but the wind, or at least the direction in which it blew.

It was a reaching race in strong breezes which occasionally reached force 6, not the kind of weather the British, bred as they were for beating to windward, relished. The Americans took all three prizes in all three classes.

The British yachts stirred up a lot of comment as there had been much speculation about their light displacement types. 'None of them finished in the money,' wrote one columnist afterwards, 'which confounds the extremists who have been preaching that all other yachts are obsolete. But none of them came apart, dove under and disappeared, or killed her crew, which confounds the equally extreme conservatives who predicted such disasters.'

It was the fastest race since 1932 and brought prizes and glory to two yachts which were both to feature prominently in ocean racing in the seasons ahead. John Nicholas Brown's Class A yawl, *Bolero*, was first to finish but failed to save her time on the S & S-designed *Argyll*, the lowest rated yacht in Class A.

▶ *The 73-foot, S & S-designed* Bolero *was built shortly after the war. She set a new course record for the Bermuda race in 1950, and again in 1956 when under the ownership of Sven Salen.*

▼ *The 46-foot* Kitten, *one of the early light displacement yachts built for the Transpac weather conditions. She won it in 1949.*

The 1950 Transatlantic race

When the Bermuda race was completed, five British yachts raced back to Plymouth, without any competition from the Americans who had yet to cross the Atlantic in the post-war period to race in European waters. Though the small fleet ran into one storm in mid-Atlantic the gentle weather favoured the smaller entries, and one of the features of the race was the close duel that developed between a RNSA '24', *Samuel Pepys*, skippered by Errol Bruce, and Adlard Coles' *Cohoe*. In the Bermuda race they had finished 23 seconds apart, and in the 2780-mile Transatlantic race five hours separated them.

Samuel Pepys arrived first but on corrected time *Cohoe* won by two hours, a remarkable performance by a yacht a mere 32-feet overall. It was, in fact, the size of these two and a third competitor, another '24' called *Galway Blazer*, that attracted press attention.

'The 1950 Transatlantic,' wrote one journalist, 'will go down in history not on account of one particular ship, but because of the splendid passage of three relatively tiny yachts. Their overall length was about the same as the after overhang of *Atlantic* (the crack American schooner, winner of the Transatlantic race 1905) and their waterline length several feet less than her beam! Their

displacement was about a third of that of *Dorade* (winner in 1931) – herself reckoned small to race the Atlantic.'

The 1951 Transatlantic race
The next year another Transatlantic race was organized, this time from Havana to San Sebastian, a distance of 4080 miles, and at that time the longest ocean race ever held. It attracted four entries: two Americans, the schooner, *Sunbeam*, and Alden's yawl, *Malabar XIII*, now owned by Kennon Jewett; an Argentinian cruising boat called *Gaucho*; and a Cuban yacht called *Cubana*. It wasn't much of a race, but it did bring the first American yacht to race in European waters since the end of the war. In due course, *Malabar XIII* sailed for Cowes and started in the 1951 Fastnet, but she was dismasted near the start in very heavy weather.

Consolidation in the early 1950s
The pattern of ocean racing in these years

was not particularly adventurous, yachtsmen preferring to stick to the pre-war ocean racing programme. For several seasons no new ocean race of any consequence was started. In Europe, a variety of races were run across the North Sea, and acted as feeder races for shorter events in the Baltic; and some were organised to ports in France and Spain, but none of these developed into fixtures of international stature.

In the US it was the same. The Transpac and the Bermuda were well attended, as were the shorter races, but it was not until 1953 that an important new long-distance event, the 1431 mile San Diego-Acapulco classic, was inaugurated.

In the waters around Australia and New Zealand, yachtsmen were a bit more adventurous. The 307-mile race from Brisbane to Gladstone was inaugurated in 1949 and later became an annual event; and in 1951 the White Island race was introduced in New Zealand. At 326 miles it was long enough to

test the inexperienced before they ventured further offshore – which was why it was started – and its course was an unusual one in that White Island, the turning mark, is an active volcano which often splatters yachts with ash. Nevertheless, it has proved to be a popular race and has been an annual fixture since 1967.

Though this period in the early 1950s was not an expansive one it was a time when the bonds between the US and Europe were strengthened by the presence of each other's yachts in the main long-distance races. In 1952, the Bermuda race, for instance, had entries from Britain again, and one from France, as well as the usual ones from Canada, Bermuda and Cuba. The French entry, *Janabel*, came 14th in Class B, while the British boat, *Samuel Pepys*, came third in Class C and

▼ *The start of the Dover-Kristiansand race, 1950, with* Benbow (151) *just in the lead from* Erivale (236).

fifth overall, and *Bloodhound* second in Class A and sixth overall. The US Naval Academy's yawl, *Royono*, won line honours and the Class A prize, but on corrected time it was one of the smallest yachts in Class C, Dick Nye's *Carina*, which took the Bermuda Trophy, the first time it had ever been won by a Class C boat. Rod Stephens won Class B in *Mustang*, acknowledged as being probably the best equipped and best raced yacht in the world at that time.

Following the Bermuda race the Royal Canadian Naval Sailing Association arranged its first race from Bermuda to Halifax – won by the Canadian schooner, *Wanderer IX* – and another Transatlantic race was run which was won by the phenomenal *Samuel Pepys*, skippered by Errol Bruce.

In 1952, past wounds were healed when the Permanent Committee of the International Yacht Racing Union (IYRU) approved applications from West Germany and Japan to be allotted the sail letters G and J, which meant both countries were free to enter any event organised within the framework of the IYRU. It was some years before the Japanese entered the international arena, but the Germans were quick to use the facility and in July 1953 organised their first post-war long-distance race, a 780-miler from Bremerhaven to Bell Rock and back, which was won by the 1936 Transatlantic winner, *Roland von Bremen*, in an elapsed time of 145hrs,13mins.

The Giraglia race 1953

On 14th January 1953 the International Committee of the *Course Croisère de Haute Mer* in the Mediterranean met at the Yacht Club de France in Paris. Present at this meeting were René Levainville, President of UNC, Fernand Rouf, President of the Royal Naval Club of Barcelona, and Beppe Croce, General Secretary of the Yacht Club Italiano. The meeting was to discuss the inauguration of a regular annual long-distance race which could be the focus for those sailing in the area, just as the Fastnet and the Bermuda were in Britain and the US. Up to that time a number of events had been held post-war in the Mediterranean – Illingworth had won the first Cannes-Cagliari race in 1951 – but it was felt more was needed. After some discussion a similar course to the 1927 race was chosen, with the start at Cannes and the finish at San Remo after rounding the Isle of Giraglia. The start of this first race – which soon became to be known as the Giraglia or the 'Fastnet du

Soleil' – was on 11th July though later races always began on 14th July, Bastille Day.

The first Giraglia attracted 22 starters, and they made a fast run to the turning mark, but then the fresh Mistral petered out into calms. Later, the wind came in from the west forcing those still in the race – seven retired – to reef when within 20 miles of San Remo. It was a sensational finish with the Class I Italian yacht, *Ea*, sharing line honours with the Class I French yacht, *Amity*, both being timed across the line at 30hrs,26mins,15secs. However, on corrected time Class I was won by the French yacht, *Enchanteur II*, with another French entry, *Jalina*, taking the Class II prize. Illingworth, in the hard-worked *Samuel Pepys*, was the only non-Italian or French entry, and he took the Class III prize.

The Giraglia was declared a great success and the next year it was started from San Remo and finished at St Tropez, a distance of 208 miles. These two places alternated as the start and the finish until 1959 when the course was lengthened to 243 miles, with the start at Toulon and the finish at San Remo. These two places have alternated as the start and the finish of the race ever since.

Now run jointly by the French and the Italians, the Giraglia is a race which attracts yachts from several nations, mostly the Mediterranean ones, and while it does not have the stature of the Fastnet or the Bermuda, it is a very popular fixture.

One of the most outstanding entries in the race's history has been *Susanna II*, owned and sailed by Italian Giuseppe Brainovich. She is the only yacht to have won Class I three times, in 1964, 1965, and 1966. Another remarkable competitor was the Italian, Franco Mazzucchelli, who had some remarkable wins between 1953 and 1974 in his succession of *Ninas*.

Racing in the Baltic

Further north, in the Baltic, the Round Gotland race, which had been revived in 1950 over a different course (the start and finish was now at Sandhamm), was joined in 1953 by a new race across the Skaggerak. Called the Skaw, it took place over a triangular course of 240 miles. Later races were increased to 290 miles, and, occasionally, to over 300 miles, with the start and the finish at either Skagen or Hankø.

The first Skaw race was organised by the Royal Danish Yacht Club (KDY), The Royal Gothenburg Yacht Club (GKSS), and

the RORC, but thereafter the Scandinavian clubs took it in turns to be the host club. It attracted 27 starters, nearly all of which were Scandinavian, though there was one Belgian entry and three British. Four of them were less than 24 feet LWL, a new class which had been started the previous year by UNC, and one which later developed into the RORC's Class IV. The participation of these smaller boats was to be dependent on the weather, but though a fresh south-west wind was knocking up a steep sea, which soon caused retirements, it was decided they could race. Despite being pooped twice in a fast and rough ride to the first mark, the overall and Class III winner was a Swedish sloop called *Honey*, which covered the course in 50hrs,27mins.

Apart from 1955, 1959, and 1961, the Skaw has been run every season since 1953, and, with the Round Gotland which became an annual race in 1969, attracts yachts from all over the world. Feeder races to both these classics were started from places like Dover and West Mersea throughout the 1950s, but they eventually petered out principally because of the dangers of racing through the congested Dover Straits.

▶ *The start of the first Giraglia race. The Class winner,* Enchanteur II *(960), trails the fleet.*

▼ *The overall winner of the first Skaw race was the Swedish Class III sloop,* Honey.

There were, and are, many other races which take place in the Baltic. The Germans, for instance, run a biennial Skaw race from Heligoland to Kiel, a distance of 550 miles, and a feeder race from Kiel to Sandhamn for the Skaw, as well as ones from Cuxhaven and Bremerhaven for 'North Sea Week' at Heligoland. There is also the famous 225-mile annual *Sjaelland Rund* which started in 1947 with 12 boats and which has now grown to over 1500 entries and tens of thousands of spectators. But none of these can really rival either the Skaw or the Round Gotland, and these remain the real Baltic classics.

Rising costs and changing attitudes

As the sport steadily expanded the question of cost loomed large. Even before the war yachting journalists had begun to question the cost of ocean racing. 'Is Ocean Racing Heading for a Lee Shore?' asked the editor of *Yachting* in 1938, before going on to list the formidable cost of designing, building and equipping an ocean racer. *Baruna*, for instance, was estimated to have cost in the region of $90 000, and she, and others like her, were disparagingly called 'gold-plated ocean racing

machines' by the old die-hards, and the name 'goldplater' has remained in the language of the sport ever since.

Part of the answer to keeping the cost of the sport under control could be seen in the trend towards smaller boats. By 1955 RORC Class III boats in Britain equalled those belonging to the other two classes; UNC, as had been mentioned, started the equivalent of Class IV; and in 1951 Illingworth founded the British Junior offshore Group (JOG), an organisation dedicated to racing offshore in really small yachts. Another aspect of the fight against rising costs was the advance in incorporating lightweight materials in the new light displacement yachts. In this Illingworth continued to lead the way by producing in 1955 the Class III *Mouse of Malham* – irreverently called *Bat of Balham* by some – which displaced half the weight of a normal 24-foot yacht.

In the US the question of economics was not as critical as in Europe, but though the light displacement yacht had been viewed critically, especially on the East Coast, their advantages were not totally ignored. *Hoot Mon*, for instance, which first appeared in

1952, was not much more than an enlarged racing dinghy, the first of many lightweight flyers to be so described. Her constuction and her phenomenally low rating made her much disliked by the old guard, but she did well in the SORC – which had been restarted in 1947 – in her first season, better in 1953, and won it in 1954 and 1955, the first post-war design to do so.

But the mainstream of American yacht design at that time was typified by the 57-foot yawl, *Caribbee*, in which a newcomer, Carleton Mitchell, campaigned with great success during the early 1950s. When he first raced her in 1952 he cleaned up the SORC so completely – winning the Ft Lauderdale-Cat Key, the Nassau and the Havana races – that he headed the list by the greatest margin then recorded. He won it again in 1953, but then *Hoot Mon* ousted him from the top spot and he decided it was time he built a new boat. He went to Sparkman & Stephens for his new design.

Finisterre

Finisterre has been called the most dramatically successful ocean racer in history, and her

feat of winning the Bermuda race three times in a row has never been equalled. The difference between Mitchell's two yachts was noted by Rod Stephens who felt that, while the arrangements on *Caribbee* had been somewhat casual, on *Finisterre* 'there was a clear place for everything and it was kept there most of the time', this close attention to detail having probably been picked up from Rod himself when Mitchell had raced in *Mustang*. Indeed, the yacht represented a perfect marriage between a superb design and top-flight handling and organisation, and it signal-

led to those still racing just for the hell of it in their pre-war yachts that ocean racing was about to enter a new, and more ruthlessly efficient, era.

Science and the 1954 Bermuda race

It was also the beginning of a more scientific era with the 1954 Bermuda fleet, for instance, being given a new aid for tackling the 635-mile course. It had been suspected for some time that the Gulf Stream, which dominated the race, had a loop in it, and that the Stream's direction and strength varied from year to year. In 1950 the Woods Hole Oceanographic Institute had started charting the Stream, and by 1954 a fairly accurate prediction could be made about its movements. This prediction was handed out to all competitors before the 1954 start, and though some navigators preferred to stick to their own judgement, the skipper of the winning yacht, *Malay*, followed the prediction exactly. It has not always proved to be so precise, but nowadays every competitor studies the information supplied by the Institute with great attention. It includes infra-red photographs of the Stream, the loop, and the eddies, while almost instantaneous updates of them can be received by radio while gauges built into the yachts' hulls give constant readings of the water temperature.

Man-made fibres

This new scientific era also introduced man-made fibres into the sport, with sails being made of both polyester and nylon. The more powerful, lightweight, synthetic spinnakers made a great deal of difference to a yacht's speed, especially for those racing in the Pacific where it was normal to run in the Trades for days at a time.

The effect that synthetic kites had on racing was demonstrated clearly when ten out of the 11 yachts in Class A in the 1955 Transpac beat the course record set by

Morning Star in 1949. It was described by one writer as a race of 'shattered records, shattered gear and wild, uncontrolled rides', and even the Class C winner, *Nalu II*, beat the time of the huge 1926 winner, *Invader*. The overall winner that year, *Staghound*, only 31 feet LWL, covered the course at the impressive average speed of 7.15 knots.

Transatlantic races 1955

After a lapse of two years, not one but two Transatlantic races were organised in 1955. The one from Newport to Marstrand attracted seven starters: four German, two American and one from Norway. The German yachts were *Peter von Danzig*, a runner in the 1936 Transatlantic race; Robert Clark's *Ortac*, one of Britain's most successful ocean racers from the pre-war period, and now owned by the Hamburg Ocean Racing Club; *Kormoran*, a yawl which had won line honours in the Dover-Hankø race the previous year; and another yawl, *Schlussel von Bremen*, at 44 feet LOA the smallest boat in the fleet. The Americans had two of their most competitive yachts at the start line: the 56-foot yawl, *Circe*, which, with Rod Stephens at

▲ *Carleton Mitchell's remarkable Rhodes-designed yawl,* Caribbee, *in which he campaigned so successfully during the early 1950s.*

◄ *No beauty to look at, the 39-foot yawl,* Hoot Mon, *nevertheless showed she was fast by ousting her great rival,* Caribbee, *and winning the 1954 and 1955 SORC.*

► *The 38-foot, S & S-designed yawl,* Finisterre, *won just about every American East Coast ocean race going in the middle and late 1950s.*

the helm had taken line honours in the 1951 Fastnet; and Dick Nye's second *Carina*, the eventual winner, which was finished just in time to compete. It was a competitive and modern fleet and only the Norwegian entry, the 54-year-old *Stavanger*, represented a bygone era. She had a four-day time allowance and she needed every minute of it.

The Spanish race was less popular and produced only four starters: the Spanish yawl, *Mare Nostrum*, which later that year took line honours in the Fastnet; the huge American *Ticonderoga*; the Argentinian ketch, *Gaucho*, a veteran of the 1951 Transatlantic race; and the Cuban yawl, *Siboney*, which was dismasted early in the race and was towed back to the mainland. It was sailed in fine but overcast conditions with a high barometer for the whole 4200-mile course. *Mare Nostrum* took both line honours and the corrected time prize, breaking the record set by *Malabar XIII* in 1951 by covering the course in 24d,2hrs,50mins.

Summer storms 1956
If the weather was mild in the northern hemisphere in 1955, it certainly made up for it in 1956 with the Bermuda race being sailed in heavy weather and the British season being ruined by some of the worst storms on record.

'Some of the old webfoots of the Bermuda rhumb line have been demanding a hard, fast race,' Loomis opened his article on the 1956 Bermuda race in his inimitable way, 'and boy, did they get it!'

Each year the numbers of starters had been increasing for all the major races. The 1956 Bermuda race attracted 89 and they all had a swift, rough ride to the Onion Patch, as Bermuda is called by Americans. After some light winds at the start, Class A reached all the way in strong south-west winds to Northeast Breaker before beating up to the finish in squalls heavy with rain. The smaller boats, however, had the benefit of a shift of wind after they had passed through the Gulf Stream and they had a fair breeze to the finish.

And what a finish it was for the leaders, with *Bolero*, now sailing under the Swedish flag and skippered by Sven Salen, covering the course in 70hrs,11mins, smashing the record set by *Highland Light* in 1932. Another Class A yawl, *Venturer*, also broke the old record. This was despite the fact that both yachts suffered damage near the finish and

had to cover the last miles under shortened sail. But fast as they were neither could save their time against the smaller, but speedy, yachts which were now beginning to dominate the east coast racing calendar. *Finisterre* won the Bermuda Cup, with Bill Snaith's *Figaro* coming second and winning Class C, and *Carina II*, the Class B winner, taking third place. Only in Class A did veterans like *Highland Light*, *Royono* and *Nina* continue to hold their own.

Though the weather was rough for the Bermuda race it was nothing to what hit the 23 starters in the 1956 Channel race. The storm gusted to force 10 and it wreaked havoc amongst the fleet. It was at its worst near the Owers – where, nearly 20 years later, Edward Heath's *Morning Cloud* sunk with tragic consequences in a similar storm – and both *Bloodhound* and *Tilly Twin* were driven helplessly towards the lee shore. *Bloodhound's* anchor held just before she was driven on to the rocks at Selsey Bill, but *Tilly Twin* was not so fortunate and she ended up on the beach at Bognor Regis. Both crews were rescued. Selwyn Slater's *Uomie* was also abandoned by her crew in favour of safety aboard a warship after a rigging failure, but the yacht was later salvaged. The rest of the fleet were not in the area when the worst of the storm struck, but only five finished the race.

Much of the RORC programme that year suffered from the bad weather. The race from Marstrand to Copenhagen - won by the Class III German yawl, *Inschallah* – had to be postponed for 24 hours because of high winds; the Cowes-Plymouth race was hit by a south-west gale which forced all but three of the 21 starters to retire; and the start of the 540-mile Cowes-San Sebàstian race was also delayed by bad weather. Seven of the 16 entries retired before they even crossed the line when the race eventually got going. So much damage had been caused to yachts by the weather that the numbers in the Plymouth-Belle Isle race, the last of the season, were severely reduced, and that started in a force seven. Even the Mediterranean produced bad conditions for the Giraglia that year, and there were many retirements.

But the bad weather was not confined to the northern hemisphere. Gales caused retirements in the BA-Rio at the beginning of 1956, more retirements in the inaugural Auckland-Suva race in the middle of the year, and then caused havoc amongst the Sydney-

Hobart fleet at the end.

The BA-Rio race 1956
By 1956 the BA-Rio fleet had grown to 28 and the generous shipping facilities offered by the organisers had already lured boats from as far away as the US and Portugal. However, the entries were still predominantly South American and in 1953 the race had been won by the Brazilian sloop, *Cairu II*. The 1956 race attracted strong competition again, for the event was beginning to be regarded as one of the classic ocean races. Also, yachtsmen were just starting to figure out how best to navigate the 1200-mile course and were learning to capitalise on the experience of others. The race fell into three distinct parts: the 200-mile sail out of the River Plate where the greatest hazards were some sunken wrecks and nasty quick squalls known locally as Pamperos. With the River Plate astern, yachts passed Punte del Este and turned northwards before having to beat the next 900 miles or so into the prevailing north-east winds which fluctuated in strength from calms inshore to gales offshore. Finally the last 60–100 miles to the finish where beating into the fluky winds had to be avoided. The key to the race was to ignore the rhumb line and pick an arbitary point a few hundred miles south-east of Rio from where it was possible to sail to the finishing line without beating. If a yacht did not do this, but chose the shorter inshore route it could be plagued by calms, counter-currents and adverse winds. The winning yacht in 1956, the Argentine Naval Academy's yawl, *Fortuna*, avoided all the pitfalls of the course and covered it in a record time of 8d,17hrs,47mins.

Auckland to Suva 1956
The inaugural race to Suva from Auckland was a rather different affair, attracting a mixed bag of 13 cruising boats, the largest of which was 34 feet LWL. As one commentator described them, 'winches were few, liferafts non-existent, synthetic sails and running gear unheard of, radios mainly war surplus models of dubious efficiency, indeed safety gear by today's standards was, to say the least, basic. Surely an era of cotton sails and iron men.'

Yet amongst the crews were men who later made New Zealand one of the top ocean racing countries in the world. John Lidgard was there skippering a yacht of his own design, *Matuku*, as was Cal Berriman who went on to compete in every single Auckland-Suva race held since.

The weather was perfect at the start, but within 24 hours the fleet was hit by the first of a succession of gales which scattered the yachts far and wide. Several were forced to return and two of them, *Aoma* and *Kehua*, were lucky to escape without loss of life. Eventually, however, the rest of the fleet found better weather with Tom Buchanan's *Wanderer* taking line honours in 11d,12hrs,26mins, for the 1150-mile course. *Wanderer* managed to save her time on *Nina* and *Matuku* which were second and third respectively. It must have been a rough ride because the race was not held again for another ten years, but is now a highly rated biennial, organised by the Royal Akarana Yacht Club.

Queenscliff- Sydney race 1956
In Australian waters, the 540-mile Queenscliff-Sydney race was inaugurated in 1956. The idea was to use it as a shakedown event for Victorian yachtsmen making their way to the start of the Sydney-Hobart, but it never attracted a sizeable fleet and was last raced in 1964.

The Sydney-Hobart race 1956
Though the Sydney-Hobart attracted the same number of entries in 1956 as in 1947, the quality of the 28 entrants had improved enormously. New yachts by such top designers as Olin Stephens did not take long to appear on the scene, and it was during this decade that a young Sydney naval architect called Alan Payne produced a 36-foot class called a Tasman Seabird, designed especially for the kind of conditions found during a Sydney-Hobart. It was one of these, *Cherana*, which won in 1959.

Payne's most famous design of the 1950s was a 57-foot steel cutter called *Solo*, owned by a Swiss-born engineer, Vic Meyer. Meyer was a well known ocean racing skipper of the period, the man who headed the 'rip or bust school', as it was called. These were the men who hoisted a spinnaker and kept it up until it blew out. Then they'd hoist a smaller one!

Solo won the overall prize in 1956 in another tough race where 40-knot winds left a trail of destruction through the fleet. One yacht was towed in with only three inches of freeboard remaining after the crew had been bailing for five days, and two other entries

▲ *The 57-foot steel cutter, Solo, designed by Alan Payne, was another enormously successful ocean racer in Australian waters during the 1950s and early 1960s.*

were beached. *Solo's* win was the first of several successes for her in the Hobart, for she took line honours in 1958 and 1959, and won again in 1962. She also won the Montagu Island race five times in a row, and set a new record for the TransTasman by covering the 1961 course from Auckland to Sydney in 7d,21hrs,12mins.

Line honours in the 1956 race went to the remarkable *Morna*, now owned by the Livingston brothers and renamed *Kurrewa IV*. She rated much too high to have any chance of the handicap prize, but between 1946 and 1960 she finished first a record seven times. In 1957 she established the course record of 3d,18hrs,39mins, a time not bettered until *Ondine's* run in 1962. She was still winning races in the late 1970s.

But the Australians did not confine themselves to racing in their own waters. In 1949, the Livingstons had taken their previous yacht, *Kurrewa III*, across the Pacific to race in the Transpac. Though she had not done well, it had encouraged the Halvorsen brothers to try as well and in 1951 they had shipped their 36-foot *Solveig*, in which they

had won the TransTasman race in 1949 and 1951, to California for the Transpac start. They took her again in 1955, and then tried with their 38-foot cutter, *Anitra V*, in which they had won the 1957 Sydney-Hobart. Both brothers were yacht builders by trade and they designed and built their own ocean racers. Both were vastly experienced yachtsmen and exceptionally good at racing over longer distances. Though they never managed to make much impression on the Transpac fleet – few foreign yachts ever have – they remained at the forefront of the sport in Australia for many years.

New rating rules
The 1956 Bermuda race had marked its 50th anniversary – and the anniversary of modern ocean racing, too. From an obscure 'ocean race' that had attracted a handful of cruising enthusiasts the sport had expanded to involve countries as far apart as Sweden and the Argentine, New Zealand and Canada. The yachts, too, had changed remarkably, as had the attitudes of the men who sailed them. Six hundred odd miles had seemed a long way in 1906, even in an 80-foot schooner. Yet, by 1956 yachts half that size were accustomed to covering six times that distance. Crews who had been used to shortening sail at night now kept a spinnaker flying till it blew out. It was all very different.

It was perhaps appropriate then that the RORC and the CCA each brought in a new Rule on 1st January 1957 that took proper account of these new advances.

In 1932, when the CCA Rule had first been formulated, most of the beamy vessels then constructed had been built with cruising in mind, not racing. Those that were specifically designed for ocean racing had been deep, relatively narrow keel boats. This meant that unless the cruising boat was awarded an increased time allowance for its broad beam, shoal draft and modest ballast it had very little chance of winning, so such an allowance was introduced. After the war, however, it had been realised that a beamy boat designed specifically for racing, and with a good-sized centreboard, could be swift and comfortable – and would attract a very low rating. While this type proved to be desirable as well as successful it was felt that it was wrong that a prospective owner had to accept this type of design in order to win. The rating was therefore adjusted so that the new type received less credit but nevertheless it still rated better than an similar boat with a deep, narrow hull. These changes increased *Finisterre's* rating, for instance, by 7.3 per cent and *Carina II's* by 3.6 per cent, but decreased that of a 12-metre like *Vim* by 2 per cent.

In Europe, there was some trepidation at the thought of changing the RORC Rule. By 1956, over 1000 yachts had been rated in Britain, 300 in Holland, 200 in France, 50 in Italy, 50 in Scandinavia, and 100 in Australia and New Zealand, and each one would have had to be remeasured. Nevertheless, it was felt that a new Rule was needed which would lessen the penalties for overhangs, alter the depth measurement which had produced yachts with straight or reverse sheers, and bring in penalties for freak rigs like the one on *Mouse of Malham*.

The Admiral's Cup introduced

However, 1957 is most likely to be remembered as the year when yet another Transatlantic race to Santander – won by *Carina II* – took three top American yachts across the Atlantic to take up a private challenge issued to them by five well-known British yachtsmen.

Myles Wyatt, then commodore of the RORC and the owner of *Bloodhound*; John Illingworth and Peter Green, co-owners of *Myth of Malham*; and Geoffrey Pattinson and Selwyn Slater, the owners of *Jocasta* and *Uomie*, had clubbed together to buy a cup to be raced for by a team of three British yachts (*Myth, Jocasta, Uomie*) and three American (*Figaro, Carina II, White Mist*) in a series of two inshore races, the 225-mile Channel race (double points), and the Fastnet (triple points). This was the trophy that soon came to be known as the Admiral's Cup, which is now the best known and most hotly competed ocean racing event in the world.

The British team entered that year's Fastnet with a lead small enough to be soon swallowed up if the Americans did well.

If the 1956 season had provided appalling weather the 1957 season was almost as bad, and the Fastnet took place in what one article later described as being 'a gale at the start, a gale at the end, with nothing much different in between.' It blew and it blew and it blew, and it ranked alongside the 1927, 1930 and 1949 races as one of the toughest Fastnets ever. There were 41 starters in a wind gusting to force nine and retirements started early. Gustav Plym, sailing the Swedish *Elseli IV*, described the conditions during

those first hours vividly. 'The wind blew the tops off the breakers, mixing the salt spray with the rain from quickly passing showers. It felt like needles hitting the skin to face the wind, and the breath was nearly taken away. The screaming sound in the rigging was like the shriek of a woman in despair.'

While the larger yachts were fighting it out ahead, the Class III yacht, *Elseli IV*, was having a remarkable match with Adlard Coles' *Cohoe III*. All round the course these two

kept close on each other's heels, first one drawing ahead and then the other taking over the lead. Much of the time they were in sight of one another, but eventually *Cohoe III* crossed the finishing line some 34 minutes before the Swede, and saved her time to win her class. They were the only two yachts to finish from their class, and altogether there were

▼ *The 65-foot, Fife-designed cutter, Kurrewa IV (ex Morna), was built as a 12-metre as long ago as 1913. She has an outstanding racing record in Australian waters.*

29 retirements from the fleet of 41. These included *Uomie* which left the other two British yachts to try and tie up the series. *Myth* did well by winning Class II, with *White Mist* and *Figaro* close on her heels in second and third place, and *Jocasta* managed to finish third on corrected time in Class I.

The Americans collected 33 points in the Fastnet to Britain's 27, nearly, but not quite, enough for them to snatch the cup which Britain won by the slim margin of two points.

Carina II and Dick Nye
What nearly brought the Americans victory was the performance of Dick Nye and his crew in *Carina II*. Early in the race, *Carina II* had fallen off a wave and had cracked several frames which had left her leaking badly. The whole way round the course the crew had had to keep pumping. To encourage them, Dick Nye had invented a war chant. 'Is every man a tiger?' he would roar. 'Grrr . . . grrr . . . grrr,' the crew roared back, and when eventually they crossed the finishing line Nye yelled out: 'OK, boys, we're over now. Let her sink!' But *Carina* stayed afloat and Nye found that not only had he finished first but that he had saved his time to win the Fastnet Cup

again, a memorable performance.

Admiral's Cup made international
Two years later, the Admiral's Cup was thrown open to teams from all nations. The Americans were not present as a team, but *Carina II* was back again to try and make it a hat-trick in the Fastnet. She was magnificently sailed once more to take first in her class, but overall she was placed third.

The French and Dutch sent a team each, and again the final result depended on the Fastnet. If the Swedes had entered a team they would probably have won for their new S & S-designed yawl, *Anitra*, sailed by Sven Hansen, won the Fastnet, while *Anna Marina*, another yawl from Sweden, took home the Erivale Cup for the first boat to finish. As it was, the British team, *Myth of Malham*, Selwyn Slater's new *Ramrod* and the RORC's *Griffin II* (ex-*Yeoman III* which had won the Fastnet in 1951), managed to hang on to the Admiral's cup by a margin of 12 points from a very competitive Dutch trio, the new Class I *Zwerver* and two veterans, *Olivier van Noort* and *Zeevalk*. From that date, the Admiral's Cup has never looked back, and nowadays it attracts many national teams from all over the world.

The last few seasons of the 1950s brought other innovations, too, and more signs of the sport's growing popularity. In Sydney, for instance, no less than 100 000 spectators saw the Sydney-Hobart fleet off through the Heads in 1959, while the Ensenada race of the same year attracted 288 yachts including a class of midget ocean racers (the American MORC had been started in the mid-1950s along the same lines as JOG) and one for multihulls.

Introduction of multihulls
The catamaran and the trimaran were still considered a fad by many yachtsmen and though they are now predominant in the major single- and short-handed events they have never caught on in conventional ocean racing in quite the way that some of their strongest supporters supposed they would. In 1957, however, the 46-foot catamaran, *Aikane*, the

▶ *The 48-foot, S & S-designed Swedish yawl,* Anitra, *denied* Carina II *a hat-trick by beating her in the 1959 Fastnet, by 51 minutes on corrected time.*

▼ *The 53-foot, Rhodes-designed yawl,* Carina II, *after she had won the 1962 race to Bermuda. She was also twice winner of the Transatlantic race and of the Fastnet.*

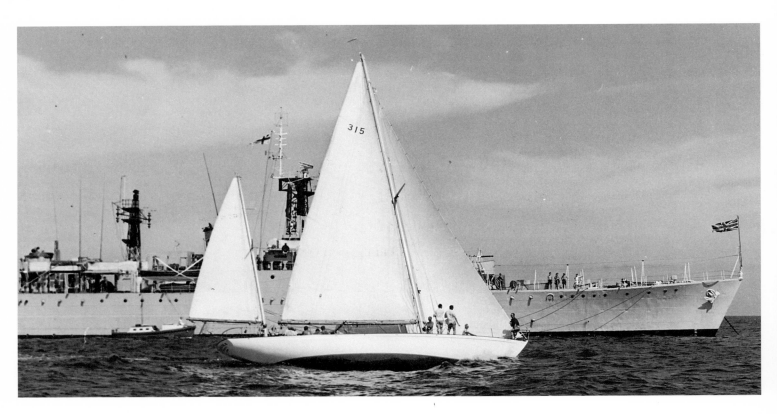

West Germany won both the 1983 Admiral's Cup and
the 1984 Sardinia Cup. Two members of the Sardinia
Cup team, *Container* (G89) and *Pinta* (G217), are seen
here at the start of the third inshore race. *Container*
was top boat in the series.

Ambrose Greenway

The Peterson-designed, British Admiral's Cupper,
Eclipse, having a spot of bother at the start of the 1979
Channel race. She was top boat in that year's Admiral's
Cup series after weathering the worst Fastnet race
ever, to come second overall to Ted Turner's
Tenacious.

Alastair Black

The Dubois-designed *Victory*, owned by Peter de Savary, was second-top scoring boat in the 1981 Admiral's Cup series, and helped Britain to victory that year by a substantial margin. Later, she was disqualified from the 1982 SORC because she had been wrongly rated.

The Joubert/Nivelt-designed *Diva* was the highest
scorer in both the 1983 Admiral's Cup series and the
1984 SORC. She was only the second French yacht to
top the list in the Admiral's Cup series. The other was
Pen Duick III which achieved this distinction in 1967.

The new Canadian maxi-multihull, *Formule TAG*, was sponsored by the same company that sponsored the 1984 TAG Transat. She was sailed by Mike Birch into fifth place and now holds the 24-hour speed record by covering 512.2 miles in 23 hours, 42 minutes. When averaged out, that's 524 miles in 24 hours which meant she maintained a mean speed of 21.8 knots!

Ambrose Greenway

The start of the 1981 Sydney-Hobart race. The photograph was taken from a member of the British Southern Cross team, *Yeoman XXIII*, sailed by Robin Aisher. The 1984 race was won by an Australian yacht, *Indian Pacific*, with the new New Zealand super-maxi, *Lion New Zealand*, taking line honours.

Pen Duick VI, sailed by Eric Tabarly, has taken part in ocean races all over the world. Here she is seen at the start of the 1975 Fastnet. She was second to finish but dropped to 59th place on corrected time.

Barry Pickthall

The new super-maxi, *Boomerang* (US 33700), seen
here at the start of the 1984 Bermuda race in which
she took line honours. She was also top boat in that
year's Pan-Am Clipper Cup series and winner of the
San Francisco Bay Maxi series.

Barry Pickthall

The Dutch Ketch, *Flyer*, the winner of the second Whitbread Round-the-World race, approaching the finishing line at Portsmouth in a Force 10 wind. The crew later agreed it was the worst weather they'd encountered during the whole circumnavigation.

Edward Heath's Holland-designed *Morning Cloud*, at the start of one of the Admiral's Cup inshore races.

Elf Aquitaine II was built to the maximum length for the 1984 OSTAR and had a revolutionary swing rig. She finished second and was then lengthened to 70 feet for the TAG Transat race later that year. She was unplaced in this and was lengthened again to 80 feet for the Benalmadena race, but suffered severe structural damage before the start and did not compete.

Credit Agricole at the start of the BOC 'Around Alone' race. She was sponsored by a French bank of the same name, designed by Guy Ribardeau Dumas, and sailed by Philippe Jeantot. She completed the course in just over 159 days and won by 11 days.

Barry Pickthall

Another of the new maxi-multihulls built for the 1984 TAG Transat was *Charente Maritime II*, seen here as she crossed the finishing line at St Malo. Sailed by Hubert Follenfant she finished second, just 15 minutes behind the winner, *Royale II*.

Tabarly's 54-foot multihull, *Paul Ricard II*, had large, adjustable-angle hydrofoils suspended from her pontoons to make her glide over the water more than slice through it. She was built of aluminium by *Constructions Mechaniques de Normandie*, Cherbourg, and launched just in time to compete in the 1979 *Transat en Double* in which she finished second.

The Holland 67, *Charley*, was launched just prior to the 1983 Transpac and was designed specially for the task of finishing first. This she managed to do after a series of magnificent runs of 300 miles or more in a day, but she could not beat the course record established by another Ultra Light Displacement Boat, *Merlin*, in 1977.

Phil Uhl

Jim Kilroy's highly successful 80-foot,
Holland-designed, super-maxi, *Kialoa IV*, seen here
competing in the 1984 Pan-Am Clipper Cup series.
Since her launch in 1980 she has become known as the
Million Dollar Machine and has raced all over the
world.

▲ *The age of the racing multihull arrived when the 46-foot catamaran* Aikane *broke the Ensenada course record in 1957.*

first true ocean racing catamaran, made a considerable impact. Designed by Rudy Choy for Ken Murphy, she broke the Ensenada record that year by covering the course in 13hrs,1min and then raced unofficially in the Transpac, beating that year's line honours winner, *Barlovento*, by 26 hours. The age of the multihull had begun.

Racing on the US East Coast

During the late 1950s there were one or two changes in the courses of long-distance races in the US. For a few years the biennial New London-Annapolis fixture had been losing its popularity, so in 1957 it was decided to reverse it. This made it mainly a reaching and running race, and the decision proved to be a popular one. It upped the entry list that year to 51, and it is still going strong.

That same year, the start of the race to Halifax was returned to Marblehead after a couple of experimental starts at Manchester, and in 1958 the classic Havana race had to be re-routed because of trouble in Cuba. As an alternative, the SORC fleet was sent on a 400-mile course from St Petersburg to Miami, leaving Rebecca Shoals to port. For the 29 starters it was a fast race in fine but cold weather. The Cuban yawl, *Criollo*, which still held the record for the Havana race, finished first, but on corrected time the race went to the Class C Texan yacht, *Ca Va*, which then went on to win the SORC.

In 1959, the course to Havana was – for the last time until 1983 – open again. But it was not that it marked the death of a great classic that made this particular race remembered but the participation in it of a new class of yacht known as Bounty IIs.

For the first time in 26 years it was a windward race all the way, and in these conditions the big boats thrived. Except for the winner, the Class B yawl, *Callooh*, sailed by Bus Mosbacher of America's Cup fame, the first eight yachts all came from Class A. Second to *Callooh* in her class was one of the new Bounty II class, *Celia II*.

Celia II and her sistership, *Glass Slipper*, were made of glassfibre (GRP), though otherwise they were of traditional design, with a large rudder hung from the keel, a wide beam, and the low graceful lines that the CCA Rule encouraged. GRP yachts had, of course, already been built, but they had proved expensive and yachtsmen, conservative by nature, had viewed them with some suspicion. The Bounty IIs were the first mass production GRP hulls to be produced, and they had sailed fast in a hard race without falling to bits. Economy, combined with speed and seaworthiness, was an equation no sensible ocean racing man could ignore. GRP was the breakthrough the sport needed to enable it to take its next quantum leap forward in popularity.

▶ *The enormous 161-foot schooner,* Goodwill. *She raced in the 1953 and '59 Transpacs but on both occasions failed to save her handicap time over smaller boats.*

Fibreglass Boats and Kids

1960–67

THE PREVIOUS ERA had truly been one of cotton sails and iron men. But by the mid-1950s, the introduction of synthetic fibres, and the increasing use of science and more sophisticated equipment began to bring about a change in the northern hemisphere, a change that percolated its way elsewhere during the next decade. It was also a period when the attitudes of yachtsmen began to alter. In the immediate post-war era, crews had been made up of friends or acquaintances. The idea was to race hard and have a good time amongst like-minded companions, and it was still the private pursuit of pleasure by a small minority.

The 1960s, however, saw the emergence of a more ruthless attitude to racing. Myles Wyatt had donated the Admiral's Cup to sharpen the competitive spirit of British owners but it was said that he later regretted the effect that it had had on the sport. Perhaps introducing direct rivalry between nations caused this change, or maybe it was made inevitable by the increasing competitiveness seen in other sports. Whatever the reason, winning mattered in the 1960s in a way it had not in the early days. During the decade, yachts like *Ondine* and *Stormvogel* emerged, racing worldwide with crews which consisted of dedicated professionals, men as far apart in thought and lifestyle from the week-end racing man as a boy catching minnows is from the deep-sea fisherman.

First OSTAR 1960

But while what could be called the traditional side of ocean racing underwent this critical metamorphosis the sport also spawned a new, and exciting, side to it.

The mainstream of ocean racing had, by 1960, become well established. All round the world, offshore events had virtually replaced the one-design regatta racing. Yet not everyone liked its predominance, nor the way in which it was developing. It was increasingly costly, it was bedevilled by rating rules that inhibited innovation, and it was generally becoming more and more regulated.

This, at least, was the opinion of an ex-Royal Marine officer, H.G. 'Blondie' Hasler, and on 21st September 1957 he put up a notice on the RORC noticeboard describing a proposed race which went right against all the accepted tenets of the sport. For Hasler was looking for challengers to race against him single-handed across the Atlantic, east to west.

A map publisher called Francis Chichester, whose offices were just around the corner from the RORC, read the notice and thought it an excellent idea. But as he was in the club for a farewell drink before a long stay in hospital there was little he could do about it, especially as the lung cancer from which he was suffering might prove fatal. However, he survived, and when he next went to the club the notice was still there, and this time Chichester acted on it.

While Chichester had been in hospital, Hasler had tried everywhere to find support for the race but without success, though the Joshua Slocum Society of New York had agreed to help organise it. But Hasler refused to give up, and while he kept looking for financial backing he refined the junk rig on his folkboat, *Jester*, along with the self-steering gear for which he has become so well known. When Chichester said he was interested, he and Hasler approached the editor of a British Sunday newspaper, *The Observer*, for support and, somewhat reluctantly, it was given. The committee of the Royal Western Yacht Club were equally hesitant when approached, and while their decision hung in the balance, Chichester remarked that if no one was willing to organise a proper race then he and Hasler would go it alone and race for half-a-crown.

It was not surprising that the idea for such a race was met with both reluctance and incredulity for, apart from it being a solo race, it was to take place against the prevailing wind and currents. Yet such a race had already taken place in 1957 when an Englishman, Edward Allcard, sailing a 36-footer called *Sea Wanderer*, had raced single-handed against a Norwegian called Tangvald for a $1 bet from Las Palmas to Antigua. Tangvald, sailing his 45-foot *Windflower*, won in 31 days with Allcard taking 33.*

In the end, the Royal Western Yacht Club agreed to help and when the word began to spread that the race was on, three other entries were received: Valentine Howells in his 26-foot Folkboat, *Eira*; David Lewis, a New Zealand doctor, in his 25-foot sloop, *Cardinal Vertue*; and Frenchman Jean Lacombe, who was sailing the smallest and lightest yacht in the race, a 21-foot centreboarder called *Cap Horn*. Hasler was to sail

*In 1966 there was a similar 'unofficial' race when six yachts, including Rene Hauwaert of Belgium raced from Las Palmas to Barbados. It was won by Rusty Webb of Britain who crossed in 28 days in his 29-footer, *Flyd*.

Jester and Chichester his 13-ton cutter, *Gipsy Moth III*, which had been designed by Robert Clark and built the previous year. At 40 feet overall she was the largest yacht to compete, and struck many people as being far too large to be sailed single-handed. After the race, Chichester was to agree with them, but right from the beginning he had grasped the crux of the problem that was to face all future competitors: since speed is a function of a yacht's length, the longer the boat, the better chance a skipper has of winning. It was an imperative that was to dominate every skipper and designer, and both had to subordinate themselves to it.

There were no handicaps for the race and the card describing the course was short and to the point: leave the Melampus buoy (a buoy close to the starting line at Plymouth) to starboard, and thence by any route to the Ambrose Light Vessel, New York. Such brevity and simplicity must have delighted Hasler, but it left wide open the problem of which route to choose. For cruising boats the conventional way was via the southern or Trade Wind route. This took a yacht east of the Azores and west of Madeira and the Canaries, after which it was best to follow the northern fringe of the Nort-east Trades at about a latitude of 23°N before curving up between the West Indies and Bermuda, approaching New York from the south-east.

Fair winds and warm weather made this the most comfortable way of crossing, but at 5000 miles it was also the longest. Shorter was the so-called Intermediate Route which passed just north-west of the Azores, then went along latitude 35°N until Bermuda was abeam when the course was altered to approach New York from a more easterly direction.

Shortest of all, but the most hazardous because of icebergs and fog around the Grand Banks, was the Great Circle route, which looped up from Lands End to a point at 51°N,25°W and then down past Cape Race and on to New York which was approached from the north-east.

Both Chichester, the eventual winner in 40 days, and Hasler, who arrived in second place eight days later, took the Great Circle route. Indeed, Hasler went even further north at one point, passing within 250 miles of Greenland. Both had comparatively uneventful passages, though Chichester, even then 59 years old, received several injuries sustained during the rough weather which he encoun-

▲ *Four of the five competitors in the first OSTAR. Left to right: Francis Chichester, 'Blondie' Hasler, Valentine Howells and David Lewis. The fifth competitor, Frenchman Jean Lacombe, started some days after the others.*

tered. He also suffered from the loneliness that all single-handed sailors must endure, but which was exacerbated for him because he could not make his radio transmitter work.

The third man to finish was David Lewis, who took more or less the same course as Chichester. However, he was delayed for several days because his yacht was dismasted, forcing him to return to Plymouth. Then off Cape Breton his rigging was damaged when a Canadian warship came too close, and later he nearly went aground off the rocky coast of Nova Scotia. Further south he encountered more trouble when he cut through Martha's Vineyard – which was not allowed in the later races – and accidentally sailed through a rip just south of Cape Cod. It was blowing force seven at the time, and he ran aground in the middle of the night. The main boom hit his head and fractured it, but he managed to refloat his yacht and eventually finished in 56 days. Such a succession of disasters would have kept most men ashore, but Lewis went on to become an outstanding single-handed yachtsman.

The other two competitors tried the more southerly route but neither did well. Howells was forced into Bermuda for five days and did not arrive in New York until 63 days after the start, while Lacombe, struggling against the Gulf Stream because he was in the wrong latitude, took 69 days.

Unlike the crew of *Dorade* after the 1931 Transatlantic race, Chichester received a subdued welcome. There were no spectator craft to cheer him in and no newspaper-

men clamouring for an interview. It was, to say the least, an unpretentious start to what has now become one of the classic ocean races. No one, least of all its instigator, 'Blondie' Hasler, could have predicted how it was to change the face of ocean racing; and maybe, like Myles Wyatt and the Admiral's Cup, he has some regrets about how it has developed. Yet it is now one of the supreme challenges for yachtsmen, and can be rated on the same level as climbing Everest or reaching the North Pole.

Racing during 1960

While five men were quietly making history, the traditional side of the sport was continuing to expand, though the Havana race was off the SORC programme again, this time for good, and its replacement, a 370-miler from Miami to St Petersburg was not well attended. But if yachtsmen found racing round Florida not as attractive as the prospects of Havana, they had no such inhibitions about crossing the Atlantic, and the 1960 Transatlantic race to Marstrand had a fleet of 17 from four countries. All of them had just taken part in a gale-ridden Bermuda race, now remembered as the race in which *Finisterre* scored her hat-trick by winning for the third time in a row, and the Atlantic weather was hardly any better. The race was won by

the Class B *Figaro*, the first of many major victories for Bill Snaith, and when Huey Long, the Class A winner in his brand new aluminium yawl, *Ondine*, was asked what it had been like, he just replied, 'cold, cold, cold.'

The race was to celebrate the centenary of the Royal Gothenburg Yacht Club, and many of the Transatlantic competitors went on to race in the Skaw where *Figaro* again performed well, finishing second in Class II to *Anitra*. The Swedish designer, Knud Reimers, who had crewed in *Figaro* across the Atlantic, won Class I in his pre-war Fife-designed yawl, *Bacchant III*, and Class III was won by *Honey* which at one time had been leading the entire fleet by half an hour on corrected time.

The La Rochelle Yacht Club also celebrated its centenary year in 1960 with a 360-miler from La Coruna to La Rochelle in which the combined top two classes was appropriately won by the French Admiral's cupper, *Marie Christine II*.

Racing in the US 1961

If interest in 1960 centred on European races, the following year the emphasis shifted to American waters where three new long distance races were inaugurated, the SORC saw the entry of a yacht which set an entirely new trend, and there were Pacific races to both Honolulu and Tahiti.

The success of the Bounty IIs in the 1959 'circuit' had caused a stir amongst American east coast yachtsmen, but the astonishing performance of a Class C production GRP yacht called *Paper Tiger* in 1961 created a minor sensation. The first ocean racing design of sailmaker Charley Morgan, *Paper Tiger* was a radical yacht not because of her design but because of her designer's revolutionary use of the new material. Although she only finished second to the Class A yawl, *Pipe Dream*, in the St Petersburg-Ft Lauderdale race (which replaced the one from Miami and is the course still sailed today), she showed her speed in the Miami-Nassau race by saving her time by a whopping 57 minutes, having sailed past all Class B and eight of Class A to finish tenth. In fact, she was so competitive and was rated so low that she was considered ineligible by some race committees that season. The same mutterings of 'rule cheater' that had been bandied about in the British

◄ *The winner of the first single-handed Transatlantic race, Gipsy Moth III, was a 40-foot cutter designed by Robert Clark.*

yachting press after the appearance of *Myth* were repeated in their American counterparts about *Paper Tiger*. Her owner, Jack Powell, entered her for the inaugural race of a new biennial, from Miami to Montego Bay, Jamaica, but to the disappointment of many, was forced to withdraw, and the 820-miler was won by *Escapade* which had taken line honours in the previous year's Transatlantic race.

Mexican races
The other two new long distance events started that year both finished in Mexico. The one from Corpus Christi to Tampico, a distance of 335 miles, was the first long distance race to be held in the Gulf of Mexico, and it was soon followed during the 1960s by others out of St Petersburg, Biloxi, Gulfport, Galveston, and New Orleans to places like Vera Cruz and Isla Mujeres. A return race from Can Cun to Naples was also started towards the end of the decade, but it was found that competing American yachts preferred to stay and cruise in Mexican waters so it ceased after 1972.

All these races, however, were much shorter than the long hauls that were organised down the West Coast to Mexican ports, and in 1961 the Acapulco race started in 1953 was joined by another biennial, from Los Angeles to Mazatlan, a distance of 1011 miles. By stopping short of the Gulf of California it was hoped that the worst of the calms that plagued the Acapulco event would be avoided. This first race attracted only a small fleet of nine, and was won by *Windspun*. But it later became much more popular and is still on the calender. It was raced again in 1962 and then became a biennial, alternating with the Acapulco fixture.

The 1961 Transpac
But by far the most important race in the Pacific that year was the Transpac whose fleet outnumbered the much longer but irregularly held Los Angeles-Tahiti event by 41 to seven. By now this unique fixture was regularly attracting top competitors from all over the US, and from overseas. In 1961 two representatives from the East Coast both acquitted themselves extremely well. Huey Long's *Ondine* took third prize in the fleet and second in Class B, while the huge *Ticonderoga* battled it out with the west coast M-Class sloop, *Sirius II*, for line honours, a tussle she lost by only 37 minutes. From Europe, Italy's

first Transpac entry, the 69-foot yawl, *Corsaro II*, did well to finish fourth in Class A, but neither of the Canadian entries, *Troubadour* in Class A and *Mary Bower* in Class C, distinguished themselves, finishing tenth and eighth in their respective classes. The winner on corrected time was the 66-foot cutter *Nam Sang*, the first Class A boat to win the race in 27 years.

Admiral's Cup 1961
The Americans also did well outside their own waters in 1961, their team of *Windrose*, *Figaro* and *Cyane* winning the Admiral's Cup from Britain by a margin of ten points, although the triple-point scoring Fastnet was won by the new Dutch yacht, *Zwerver*. Kees Bruynzeel's huge new South African-built ketch, *Stormvogel*, was the most impressive entry. Despite a two hour delay reeving a new main halyard she rounded the Rock first, some three hours ahead of *Zwerver*, and finished first, with the big American schooner *Constellation* second, and the Dutch boat third. Up to that point it had been a tough race, with 32 retirements out of the 95-strong fleet. But then the wind died, and the new British hope, *Quiver III*, which until then had been easily ahead on corrected time, was becalmed off the Lizard. This cost her the race but she won Class II with the Class III

prize going to the Swedish *Belmore*.

The Onion Patch Trophy
The idea of a series like the Admiral's Cup, raced for by national teams, now began to have wider appeal and after the 1962 Bermuda race the Royal Bermuda Yacht Club presented the Onion Patch Trophy to be raced for the first time in 1964. Three teams representing the US, Bermuda and Argentina raced in this first series, which consisted of two short Olympic courses, the well established 175-mile Astor Trophy race and the Bermuda race. The Americans won this first series, though the Bermuda race itself was won by a non-team boat, *Burgoo*, the smallest yacht taking part.

The first China Sea race 1962
A long-distance race in the China Sea was also started in 1962 which in 1970 became the long distance race in the China Sea series. The China Sea race sprang from a visit to Manila by the Hong Kong yawl, *Morasum*, in the early 1960s. As a result, the Royal Hong Kong Yacht Club and the Manila Yacht Club decided to sponsor jointly a biennial race with the course being the 633-mile passage be-

▼ *By 1961, when his 73-foot plywood ketch, Stormvogel, made her debut by taking line honours in the Fastnet, her owner Kees Bruynzeel had moved to South Africa.*

tween the two places, with the finish off Corregidor Island, some 30 miles from Manila.

The entry list of five yachts was thoroughly international. The eventual winner, a 40-foot yawl called *Reverie*, came from the RHKYC but was sailed by a Swede, C F von Sydow. *Morasum*, sailed by an American, S. Baldwin, was second while third place was taken by a 37-foot sloop, *Tolo*, sailed by a Swiss. The other two yachts were a 36-foot Japanese sloop and a 40-foot yawl from the Philippines.

Canadian West Coast races

In Western Canada, yachtsmen also decided it was time they had their own series. In 1960, a short race of some 200 miles had been run from the Columbia River lightship to Port Angeles. In 1962 it had been extended to 366 miles, with the start at Neah Bay and the finish at Port Angeles via the lightship.

The reaction to races being held in such rugged waters was not favourable. Only four yachts competed in the 1960 race – *Sea Fever* won – and she was the only yacht to finish in the 1962 race, the rest being forced to retire.

In 1964, NORPAC, as it came to be called, was changed to a cruise, and thereafter it developed along the lines of the New York Yacht Club cruise in which a series of short races are held which take the fleet from port to port. In due course, however, the West Coast Race, sponsored by the British Columbia Royal Naval Sailing Association, was inaugurated and this has now become the Canadian West Coast's main medium-distance event. The course is from Victoria, along the whole length of Vancouver Island to Triangle Island, north of Cape Scott and back again, a distance of 536 miles. By 1983 it was drawing a large number of entries which included a division for short-handed yachts.

The Southern Cross Cup

Halfway across the world, the 1962 season ended with the Sydney-Hobart which, five years later was to become the main event in yet another international team series with the Southern Cross Cup as the prize. This series has succeeded – it originally consisted of four races but a fifth was added in 1983 – because by the late 1960s the Sydney-Hobart had already become established as one of the great ocean racing classics, a view spread by men like Huey Long who took *Ondine* down to compete in it in 1962, the first American to

▲ *Reverie, owned by a Swede, C F von Sydow of the Royal Hong Kong Yacht Club, was the winner of the first China Sea race.*

sail to Australia specifically for the race.

As usual it blew hard, but for a change it blew in the right direction, and after a few hours beating at the start it was a full-speed reach to Hobart, though the wind died away near the finish.

Ondine and the larger Fife-designed *Astor* sailed neck and neck all the way, with, Vic Meyer's *Solo* close behind. Creeping up the Derwent to the finishing line, *Ondine* just managed to ease ahead and took line honours in the record time of 3d,3hrs,46mins. It was a tight finish but not as tight as the one in 1982 when Bob Bell's *Condor of Bermuda* snatched line honours from Jack Rooklyn's *Apollo* by half a boatlength which amounted to a mere seven seconds, the closest finish in the race's history.

The success of *Ondine*

Along with *Stormvogel* and Jim Kilroy's *Kialoa*, *Ondine* was one of the new breed of ocean racers. At 57 feet overall, she was the first all aluminium yacht ever built. But it was not her construction that was so revolutionary so much as the manner in which she was campaigned. Of course, yachts had been getting around for years: Australians crossed the Pacific to enter the Transpac; Americans sailed down to Buenos Aires for the triennial BA-Rio, and across the Atlantic; and Europeans regularly entered the Bermuda race. But *Ondine* and her crew put international racing on an altogether different level. Never before had a yacht been raced with quite the same intensity, for Huey Long drove both

boat and crew with the same vigour and determination that had taken him to the top of the commercial shipping business.

Huey Long is one of those legendary figures in the sport. He rarely took the wheel even during the height of his yachts' successes and he never normally stood a watch. But his ability to know the right sails to have set was quite uncanny. Designer Bill Tripp told how he was steering during one dawn watch in moderate weather when Long appeared on deck to say the wrong spinnaker was set. He was right, but Tripp never could fathom how Long had been able to know this.

But if *Ondine's* success was derived from the total dedication of her owner and crew to winning she was also a portent that the happy-go-lucky days of ocean racing were at an end if getting there first and staying first was all that mattered. 'There's no joy in Mudville in this boat,' commented one crew member after a later Transatlantic race. 'The laughs come afterwards on shore, but she gets there fast.' Winning was what mattered, the fun could wait.

After the Sydney-Hobart *Ondine* returned in time to take part in the second Miami-Montego Bay, in which she picked up her class prize and came second overall. Then she joined that year's Atlantic event – to the Eddystone – and won it, took part in the Fastnet, where she did not show, and ended three seasons of racing which had taken her all over the world by coming second on corrected time to the French *Eloise II* in the biennial Plymouth-La Rochelle race.

Success of Sydney-Brisbane (Mooloolaba)

In Australia, 1963 ended with the Halvorsen brothers' *Freya* winning the Sydney-Hobart race, the first of three straight victories, and it was followed in 1964 by two new long distance races around the Australian coast and the inauguration of a much longer one from New Zealand to Noumea.

The 580-miler from Queenscliff to Port Lincoln in South Australia failed like the one to Sydney. But the 500-miler from Sydney to Brisbane – in 1973 the finish was moved to Mooloolaba just north of Brisbane – was much more successful. The course is a testing one against the Australian east coast current and boats have to hug the land. There were only seven starters in the first race and eight the following year – both races were won by the Swanson-designed and owned *Cadence*, which also won the 1966 Sydney-Hobart –

but by 1982 the numbers had risen to 55. In 1984 it was one of the three races which provided points for the South Pacific Offshore Championship, won by *Scamp A* from IOR Class IIIA. The other two races were the well-established Brisbane - Gladstone race and a new 306-miler, from Gladstone to Hamilton Island which attracted 44 starters.

Auckland (Whangarei)-Noumea

The Australian race to Noumea, inaugurated in 1953, never really took off until the 1970s. It was run again in 1957 with a small fleet, and had to be cancelled in 1966 through lack of interest. But the New Zealand race fared much better. Organised by the Onerahi Yacht Club in conjunction with the *Cercle Nautique Caledonien*, the first race in 1964 attracted a large fleet of 36 local yachts. It had a charmed passage, with a 20-knot easterly taking it close hauled up the coast and then giving it a glorious spinnaker run to the finish. Only the slower entries got caught in a calm near the finish forcing two to retire. The Colin Wild-designed ketch, *Tara*, won line honours in 5d,58mins,8secs, but on corrected time the 36-foot Herreshoff-designed ketch, *Tarua*, took first prize. The race was held again in 1967, and then became a quadrennial fixture, which it still is. However, it was run in 1978 and not 1979 to avoid clashing with New Zealand's other long distance race, the Auckland-Suva, which was made biennial after 1977.

The 1964 OSTAR

The most widely publicised race of the year took place on the other side of the world when 15 single-handers put their yachts across the line for the start of the second Observer Single-Handed Transatlantic Race, or OSTAR as it came to be known.

Although the previous race had not sparked off the imagination of the press, it had certainly made an impression on a good many experienced yachtsmen who, like Hasler, had become disillusioned by traditional ocean racing. One of the objects of the race was to encourage the development of suitable boats, gear, supplies and techniques for single-handed ocean crossings, and this second race showed that the contestants were fully aware of it.

To begin with, three multi-hulls were entered, and this provoked a good deal of controversy. Doubts as to their seaworthin-

ess were expressed, and it was not until some of their achievements in cruising and racing had been highlighted in the yachting press that the Royal Western Yacht Club relented and let them race.

Apart from the three multihulls there were 12 mono-hulls, each carefully rigged and equipped to the tastes and desires of their skippers. *Jester* was at the starting line once more and the influence of her curious rig could be seen elsewhere in the fleet with the schooner *Ilala* carrying Chinese lugsails on both her masts. The largest yacht in the race was a specially built, hard chine ketch called *Pen Duick II* sailed by a young French naval officer, Eric Tabarly. Though she was 45 feet long her light displacement meant that she did not need a large sail area to drive her at maximum speed, and Tabarly said he did not think she was the optimum length possible for the race. In this he was soon proved to be only too right.

The favourite to win was again Francis Chichester in the second largest yacht, *Gipsy Moth III*, but Chichester himself had doubts and regarded the young Frenchman as a dark horse. 'I think I can hear him galloping through the night,' he radioed back at one point in the race, 'if my senses tell me right I can make him out about 120 miles to the north.'

Chichester's instincts were quite correct and on 15th June, Tabarly was spotted by a plane 350 miles from the finish. He crossed the finishing line on 19th June having completed the crossing in the remarkably fast time of 27d,3hrs,56mins, and this despite his self-steering gear having packed up a third of the way across. Chichester came in three days later, and Valentine Howells, another 1960 entry, came third.

Tabarly was made a *Chevalier* of the *Legion d'Honneur* by President de Gaulle and became a national hero. He was also given a memorable accolade by the redoubtable Francis Chichester. 'He's a cracking good sailor,' the Englishman commented, ' a hell of a chap and tough as old boots'.

First Canadian Transpac 1965

For some time the Canadians had been trying to promote long distance racing from the West Coast, and in 1963 the idea of a North

▼ *Huey Long's 57-foot, Tripp-designed Ondine first appeared in 1960. She performed well in that year's Bermuda race and Long went on to campaign her worldwide. She was placed in 60 per cent of the races in which she entered.*

Pacific race was born in the mind of John G. Innes, a member of the Royal Vancouver Yacht Club and the skipper of the 36-foot sloop, *Long Gone*. In 1965 the idea came to fruition and *Long Gone* was joined by *Velaris* and the Royal Victoria Yacht Club's *Noreana of Wight* in a 2380-mile race from Neah Bay to the island of Maui in Hawaii, the route that the explorer George Vancouver had taken 150 years earlier. *Long Gone* won in an elapsed time of 15d,16hrs,29mins, and interest in the race was such that the Royal Vancouver Yacht Club, in co-operation with the Royal Lahaina Yacht Club at Maui, decided to sponsor an official race in 1968. It is now well-established as the Canadian Transpac.

First Long Beach-La Paz race 1965
The second new Pacific race in 1965 was the 960-miler from Long Beach Harbor to La Paz in Mexico, which became a biennial fixture and is still raced. The sport had grown to such an extent that, like the Bermuda race from 1964 onwards, this inaugural race was by invitation only. In moderate breezes that kept blowing for the whole race, Baldwin M. Baldwin's *Audacious* took line honours in 6d,11hrs,9mins, though on corrected time the race went to a GRP production L-36 sloop called *Viva*, a typical representative of the new type of mass-produced ocean racer. Whether the man who gave the idea for the race to the Long Beach Yacht Club, Charles Sweet, entirely approved of her victory is doubtful. For though designs like the L-36 were really the saviour of the sport before it priced itself out of existence, there was also a reaction against them. Sweet himself later founded the Wooden Hull Owners Association, a group of yachtsmen who believed that 'if God had wanted boats to be built of fiberglass, He would have planted fiberglass trees'!

The Cal-40
That year's Transpac showed just how much the production boats were beginning to dominate ocean racing. All the big Class A 'goldplaters' like *Stormvogel*, *Ticonderoga*, *Ondine* and Jim Kilroy's new *Kialoa II* were there as were *Contessa II* and *Chita II*, the first Japanese yachts to enter a major international

▲ Long Gone, *the winner of the first Canadian Transpac, was a 36-foot sloop designed by Bill Lapworth and owned by John Innes.*

event; but though *Ticonderoga* and *Stormvogel* fought one of the closest line honours battles ever seen in a Transpac – *Ticonderoga* won by a thousand yards after 2225 miles of racing – first and second places overall were taken by two Class C Cal-40 production boats called *Psyche* and *Hanalei*.

The Cal-40 was the brainchild of Bill Lapworth who had designed and raced the 1959 Transpac winner, *Nalu II*, to victory. In 1963, he produced the design of the Cal-24 for the new firm of Jensen Marine and later he designed the equally successful Cal-20. Then came the Cal-40, a yacht which made his name famous around the world. His L-36 Class, which included *Nalu II* and *Viva*, had become the biggest one-design class of ocean racers but their popularity was nothing compared to the Cal-40. This boat was what every racing man had dreamed about. The mass-moulded GRP hull made it reasonably priced and its speed was quite phenomenal. In fact, it was the Cal-40s that brought to ocean racing the excitement of being able to surf and they managed to sail up to their rating in nearly all conditions. *Conquistador*, the second of the stock line, had won the SORC the previous year; *Psyche's* Transpac win was the first of three wins in a row by Cal-40s; and when they won the 1966 SORC and that

year's Bermuda race, as well as many other events, printed cards were passed amongst yachtsmen on the lawn of the Royal Bermuda Yacht Club which stated they were for membership of an association 'to help stamp out Cal-40s'!

Admiral's Cup 1965
In Europe, interest was centred on the Admiral's Cup which attracted teams from Sweden, Holland, France, the US, Eire, and Australia. The last two were newcomers, and the Australians in particular made quite an impact. 'The Australian challenge was a revelation in the northern hemisphere,' commented Paul Antrobus, a crew member on Ron Amey's succession of *Noryemas*. 'The crews got down to three weeks of intensive sailing practice, the likes of which had never been seen in the British fleet.'

This professionalism nearly paid off and only 14 points divided the Australian team from the British at the start of the Fastnet. They thought the great blue-water classic a pretty tame affair compared with the Sydney-Hobart race, and indeed it was a light weather race that produced only one nasty squall when the largest yachts were close to the Rock. But though there were no prolonged gales there was quite enough wind for the massive French yawl, *Gitana IV*, owned by Baron de Rothschild, to smash the previous course record, held by the German yacht *Nordwind* since 1939, by more than 11 hours.

Although *Gitana IV* took line honours, the Fastnet Cup went to a boat at the other end of the spectrum. Bristling with new ideas, *Rabbit*, a Class III 34-foot sloop, was a radical boat and one very much of her time. She was both small – she was only the second Class III yacht ever to win the Fastnet – and of very light displacement.

A talented amateur designer from America, Carter had constructed a yacht which reduced windage to a minimum. All standing rigging fittings, for instance, were inside the aero-dynamically designed mast, as was all the running rigging. Carter was unusual in that he preferred to design to the RORC and not the CCA Rule, considering the former less restrictive on hull design and was less frequently changed than the CCA Rule. He also felt that the courses in Europe were far more challenging than American ones.

The emergence of *Firebrand*

Although she only finished 19th overall in the 1965 Fastnet and 8th in Class 11, Dennis Miller's *Firebrand* certainly deserved her place in the winning British Admiral's Cup team and in many ways she typified the advances that had been taking place in rigging and the changes in British attitudes. Miller, whose partnership with Derek Boyer had been amicably wound up because Miller felt *Clarion of Wight* – their 1963 Fastnet winner – needed superseding, decided it was time to break new ground. Up to that time British yachtsmen had been inclined to feel that you could not win for Britain if you were not sailing a British designed boat. Miller had no such patriotic feelings. Instead, he went to the man who was designing the fastest boats, and that man was still Olin Stephens. The end result was *Firebrand*, and her appearance, in the opinion of Rod Stephens, was a turning point for ocean racing in Britain.

Ted Hood

Miller also turned to an American, Ted Hood, for his sails. Hood had shown, by providing such winning yachts as *Ondine* and Bill Snaith's new Derecktor-designed and built yawl, *Figaro*, with their sails, that he could produce the best in the world. Part of the reason for his success was that he wove his own cloth

using narrow 18-inch panels against the 36-inch normally used. This tight-weave method minimised stretch and was the most effective method of keeping a sail in shape.

Hood was the first sailmaker to produce a successful masthead genoa, but this could only be properly employed on a rig that could hold taut under the tremendous pressure of the huge headsails. Wooden masts and wire rigging had been unable to keep the forestay tight, essential if a headsail was to be set properly. Metal masts and then the introduction of rod rigging in the 1960s overcame this problem. Miller used both on *Firebrand*, and this advance accelerated the trend, started by Illingworth, of smaller mainsails and larger headsails, a trend encouraged by the rating rules.

The One Ton Cup 1965
1965 saw the introduction of the One Ton Cup. First raced for in the previous century, it was revived by Jean Peytel of the *Cercle de la Voile de Paris*. The trophy was to be raced for by yachts that were all identically rated

◄ Firebrand, *the successful British yacht which was designed by Olin Stephens.*

▼ *The start of the inaugural Long Beach – La Paz race*

under the RORC Rule. The name of the cup, incidentally, has no connection with a yacht's tonnage now, though originally it did.

Peytel had long been campaigning to introduce ocean racing into the Olympic Games and by reviving the Cup he hoped to further this aim. Though he did not succeed in this respect, the One Ton Cup was an instant success amongst ocean racers at the time. Level rating racing was especially popular in France, and in 1967 the Half Ton Cup was created by the *Cercle de la Voile de Paris* and the La Rochelle Yacht Club. The latter club also started the Quarter Ton Cup the following year. Later, world championships for two-tonners, three-quarter tonners, and mini-ton yachts were also introduced, and enthusiasm for the half-tonner in France led to long distance races like the single-handed *Course de L'Aurore* (now *Le Figaro*), sailed in the Atlantic approaches, and the double-handed *Triangle du Soleil*, sailed in the Mediterranean, being specially created for them.

Recently, level-rating racing has been on the wane, especially amongst the larger classes, while one-design racing has become more popular.

Level-rating racing was, and is, highly competitive. Though mostly conducted over short offshore courses, this type of racing became the focus for experimentation in design

▲ *Sailmaker Ted Hood is one of the most notable offshore racing helmsmen of the last 20 years. He has raced his succession of* Robins *to many victories.*

and boat handling, and its effect on ocean racing generally was profound. 'The truth is,' wrote one yachting journalist, when commenting on the dislike of some old-timers for

this type of racing and the kind of yacht it produced, 'that we are getting near to genuine *racing* over something longer than an afternoon's club course.' Had everyone really been cruising up to that time, he asked, while they had been *calling* it ocean racing?

This was exaggerating the case, but this new awareness that the sport could be brought to the same pitch as dinghy racing slowly filtered through to the consciousness of all ocean racing men during the 1960s, and it brought about some vital changes. But level-rating racing was not the only influence for change: international competition, the explosion of interest in the sport at the turn of the decade, and the entry of big money via firms who saw a new way to promote their products, all helped to create a metamorphosis in the sport.

▲   *The 73-foot S & S-designed* Kialoa II *was one of the maxis which was campaigned worldwide during the 1960s.*

▶   *Baron de Rothschild's* Gitana IV *smashed the Fastnet course record by more than 11 hours when she took part in the 1965 race.*

Racing in the Baltic 1966

The One Ton Cup helped make Copenhagen the centre of yachting attraction in the northern hemisphere during 1966, for the second world championships were held there after a Danish One Tonner *Diana III* had won the previous year. It was also the centenary of the Royal Danish Yacht Club, and the climax of their regatta was the Skaw race, extended that year to 360 miles. Two feeder

GITANA IV

BEKEN

races were run for the regatta, one from Bermuda and another from Harwich. In addition to these long distance events shorter ones were organised from Travemund, Flensburg, Marstrand and Hankø. Everyone seemed to be heading for the Baltic in 1966 and 100 yachtsmen from at least 14 nations sat down to dinner at Helsingør after the prize giving!

The Onion Patch Series 1966
Preceding the Transatlantic race from Bermuda to Copenhagen was the second Onion Patch series and teams from Bermuda, Britain, Argentina, Germany and the US competed. The big event of the series was, of course, the Bermuda race, and in 1966 it was decided to handicap the competitors by a new method. The benefits of the computer age were applied to the sport in an effort to obtain a more equitable system of handicapping than had been achieved by the old means. It meant feeding information by telex to a computer in New York, and the delays which this caused did not increase the new system's popularity, nor did the fact that the winner, the Cal-40, *Thunderbird*, belonged to the President of IBM. However, when *Thunderbird's* time was calculated by the old system she still won, and by a larger margin.

Though an American yacht won the Bermuda race, the Onion Patch series was taken by the British whose team of three was amongst a record fleet of 47 to start the Transatlantic race to Copenhagen.

The series is still raced but has not the importance of other international series. Twelve teams raced in 1982, but only five in 1984.

The 1966 Transatlantic
The Transatlantic race was a rough one in 1966, with the start taking place in a howling north-easterly and under an overcast sky. Someone commented that only the flying fish made it look any different from a typical English race! The weather moderated later, but a number of yachts, including Eric Tabarly in *Pen Duick II*, were forced to retire after losing their rudders, while others who fell out simply felt they had had enough. Later, the wind switched and there were days of wild spinnaker rides though all but the leaders were caught in light weather near the finish.

Three-quarters of the entries were American and they took nearly all the silverware. The line honours winner, *Ticonderoga*, made the fastest crossing since *Atlantic*,

▲ Thunderbird *added to the innumerable victories notched up by Bill Lapworth's Cal-40s when she won the 1966 Bermuda race.*

finishing in 15d,23hrs,46mins. She averaged 8.8 knots and blew out one sail after another in the process. But she could not save her time and Class A and the overall prize went to *Ondine*, now firmly established as one of the great yachts of all time. An equally celebrated yacht, Dick Nye's *Carina*, took Class B; Ted Turner's Cal-40, *Vamp X*, which had already picked up that year's St Petersburg-Ft Lauderdale race and then the SORC by a convincing 57 points, won Class C; and yet another American, Tyge Rothe won Class D in *Kirsten*. Not only did the Americans win all

four classes but they took second and third places in all but Class D, where second and were taken by Stig Koningson's Swedish boat, *Belmore*, and Norman Rydge's *Lorita Maria* from Australia. None of the British Onion Patch team distinguished themselves, except that after 3500 miles of racing all three crossed the line within 50 yards of each other!

The Skaw race 1966

After being first across the line in the Trans-atlantic race, *Ticonderoga* repeated her success by taking line honours in the Skaw in an elapsed time of 47hrs,5mins, a time which won her the King of Denmark's Cup from another American yacht, *Audacious*, and Herr Krupp's *Germania VI* which had been second to finish in the Transatlantic. Since Robert Johnson had taken over the great ketch in 1963, *Ticonderoga* had sailed some 50 000 miles in races around the US and Europe. This put her not only in the same category as *Ondine* but also the well travelled *Stormvogel* which had cleaned up line honours in the 1965 Sydney-Hobart before moving up to Hong Kong to do the same in the 1966 China Sea race.

The Skaw that year was no place for a yacht to be. A force nine westerly gale hit the huge fleet of 149 during the first night, ripping it to pieces and building up big, steep seas. From all accounts it seems very lucky that there were no fatalities for as many as 20 yachts were dismasted, and one entry, racing the shorter 200-mile course for the smaller classes, was wrecked on the Swedish coast. No less than 96 yachts were forced to retire with the smallest class on the long course, Class III, taking the worst of the hammering with over 80 per cent failing to finish.

The Round-Britain race 1966

Although interest was centred on the Baltic in 1966, two new races were also inaugurated in Europe that year. One was an RORC race to Spain over a new course from Yarmouth to Lequeitio, but the other was something entirely different: the first Round-Britain race since 1887. But this second circumnavigation was very different from the first. For one thing it was a double-handed race — the first of its kind — and it was just the sort of race to appeal to the new breed of ocean racing yachtsman who was not attracted to the increasingly time-consuming and exacting art of traditional ocean racing.

The idea for the Round-Britain race was 'Blondie' Hasler's and the Royal Western Yacht Club again took the plunge and agreed to organise it. The race was open to both mono- and multi-hulls exceeding 24 feet overall.

Unlike the 1887 Jubilee race, which was raced anti-clockwise non-stop, the 1966 race was clockwise and broken into five stages to ensure the crews were properly rested. The first port was Crosshaven, the second Castlebay on the Isle of Barra, the third Lerwick, and the fourth Harwich. The first yacht home was to win the Round-Britain Trophy and £1000, with the *Genesta* Trophy being awarded to the first boat on corrected time.

The fleet of 17 which started from Plymouth on 2nd July was a mixed one and consisted of six sloops, four catamarans, five trimarans and a Polynesian double outrigger called *Tiki Roa*. Unusual as this last entry was, Hasler's experimental sloop, *Sumner*, looked even odder. In a race which ran the gamut so far as the weather was concerned the multihulls showed their superiority to an astonishing degree. This was the first time that these yachts were not only allowed to race with monohulls — as in the 1964 OSTAR — but actually encouraged to do so, and this showed considerable foresight on the part of the organisers. The multihulls took both the prizes and dominated each of the five legs of the race.

The race was won by the scratch boat, a 42-foot trimaran called *Toria*, sailed by her designer, Derek Kelsall, who had been a 1964 OSTAR entry. Averaging 6.9 knots over the 1940-mile course, Kelsall covered the distance in 19d,17hrs,23mins, some 16 hours less than the second yacht, a catamaran called *Snow Goose*. The third yacht to finish was another catamaran, *Iroquois*, and she saved her time on the rest of the fleet to win the *Genesta* Trophy. The first monohull finished seventh.

▼ *The 72-foot, L Francis Herreshoff-designed ketch,* Ticonderoga, *was an old-timer which held many course records in her time. Her 1940 Miami-Nassau record remained unbroken for 26 years.*

Racing in the US 1967

Interest in ocean racing with multihulls was also on the increase in the US with five competing in the second multihull Transpac and the inauguration the following year, 1967, of the biennial multihull Bermuda race. Starting at Sheepshead Bay, New York (later changed to Newport) the first to finish was the 35-foot trimaran *Trilogy* in an elapsed time of 5d,20hrs,7mins, but on corrected time the race was won by the Arthur Piver-designed 25-foot trimaran, *Amistad*.

The most interesting American long-distance races in 1967 were the well established fixtures. *Chubasco* won a tough St Petersburg-Ft Lauderdale race in which three of her rivals were dismasted and nine others forced to retire. However, the effect of the weather on the Annapolis-Newport race was even more drastic. A north-east gale struck the 91-strong fleet on the nose as it rounded the Chesapeake light tower sending no less than 34 yachts running for shelter. 'The roughest and toughest in the history of any major offshore event in this country,' was how one commentator described it. Very different to the usual struggle against light breezes to get out of Chesapeake Bay with a pleasant downwind run to follow. Six yachts were dismasted and one later ran aground and broke up, though all her crew were rescued.

The 1967 Miami-Montego Bay race

Equally sensational was the 1967 Miami-Montego Bay race, hailed by some as the greatest of the decade. It 'offered everything skippers can ask for in ocean racing,' remarked one commentator: a weather leg across the Gulf Stream to Great Isaac, reaching legs through the Hole in the Wall between Great Abaco and Eleuthera islands, numerous "holes" which everybody fell into sooner or later before arriving at the Windward Passage, and, finally, one of the most demanding, exciting spinnaker runs down the Caribbean that such veteran skippers as George Moffett and Thor Ramsing had ever experienced.

'It involved more than 250 miles of surfing in 30-40 knot winds and shorter, more difficult waves than the rollers yachtsmen generally experience in the Transatlantic or Honolulu race.'

◄   *Toria, seen here at the start of the first modern Round-Britain race*

These were just the kind of conditions in which the 28-year-old up-and-coming yachtsman from Texas, Ted Turner, revelled and during the final night's spinnaker run he decided he was either going to win the race or dismast his new yacht, *Vamoose*, in the attempt.

So hard did Turner drive his Derecktor-designed 40-foot Class B sloop that he finished only eight hours behind the much bigger *Ticonderoga*, saving his time and winning the race from another Class B yacht, *Otseketa*. Despite having the reputation for being one of the best ocean races in the world, the popularity of the Miami-Montego Bay race declined until, in 1981, it was abandoned altogether. In 1983 a handicap class was added and this revived the event sufficiently for it to attract 12 starters. It was won by Bob Bell's super-maxi, *Condor of Bermuda*, which later that year won the Fastnet race in the record time of 71hrs,02mins,10s.

The sucess of the 1983 race encouraged the sponsors to make it an annual fixture, but unfortunately the 1984 race only brought four yachts to the start line. Nevertheless, it was a dramatic race, for two of the entries, *Brigadoon III* and *Cachasa*, were taken into custody by a gunboat while sailing in Cuban territorial waters. After being held for 34 hours both yachts were released, and they resumed racing. Much to their surprise the two smaller yachts in the race were still behind them. This enabled *Brigadoon III* to snatch line honours, though on corrected time *Cachasa* won the race when a 27-hour allowance was made by the organisers for the enforced stopover.

Ted Turner

Turner's performance in the Miami-Montego Bay race in 1967 was an example of the competitiveness that was soon to catapult the fast talking, aggressive Texan to defending the America's Cup and winning the first World Ocean Racing Championship. Nicknamed – among other things – 'The Mouth of the South' and 'Captain Outrageous' the millionaire businessman was brash and outspoken, but he had a will to win that few could equal. In 1964, he reckoned he spent $100 000 a year on racing, and perhaps as much as $20 000 on plane fares. Bob Derecktor, who designed some of Turner's boats and sailed with him, summed him up as follows. 'Some people put in a lot of time, some people put in a lot of money, and some put in

a lot of effort. But nobody puts in as much of all three as Turner. He has the drive. Not many want to win as badly as he does.'

The 1967 Transpac

Times they were changing and the Transpac that year, restricted to an entry of 75 yachts (though only 71 started), was proof of that if any was needed. *Ticonderoga* stayed on the East Coast that year as she was up for sale. With his biggest rival out of the way, Kees Bruynzeel staved off the rest of the opposition, which included *Kialoa II*, *Audacious* and other goldplaters, and took line honours. So determined had the Dutchman been to get in first that he had had *Stormvogel* specially fitted with a bowsprit to improve her downwind performance. But he could not save his time and the race was won on corrected time by a 22-year-old skipper in a Cal-40 called *Holiday Too*.

'I can recall when the Transpac was a race for wooden ships and iron men,' quipped one veteran afterwards. 'later it became a test for iron ships and wooden men. Now it seems to be a race for fiberglass boats and kids.'

Australia takes Admiral's Cup 1967

Changes were taking place in Europe too and at the start of the Fastnet race that year the Australian Admiral's Cup team were 19 points ahead. All three of their yachts finished among the first 18, quite good enough for them to take the trophy back to Sydney.

The newest boat in the Australian team was *Mercedes III*, designed, owned and sailed by Ted Kaufman. *Mercedes III* was seen as a radical boat and later Kaufman described the reaction of the British. 'They regarded it as a stripped out boat, which it wasn't. A guy came up and asked how we tied the boat up as there were no cleats. I told him there were plenty of winches to tie something to, but that wasn't traditional . . . We were new and we did things that according to tradition we had no right to do.'

However, Dennis Miller, whose *Firebrand* was again a member of the Admiral's Cup team, was not stuck in the rut of tradition. Influenced, as everyone was, by the radical underwater split configuration of some of the fast new One Tonners, the previous year Miller had had his boat fitted with a separate skeg and rudder to try and further increase *Firebrand's* speed. This new kind of keel design cut down on a boat's wetted sur-

face, and it soon became obligatory on all new ocean racers.

Not satisfied with just getting the most out of his boat, Miller broke up the traditional two-watch system by decreeing that when a sail needed changing he wanted the whole crew on deck. From then on those off watch snatched what sleep they could when they could.

Pen Duick III

Though the Australians showed they were now in the same league as the Americans and Europeans, they had to wait a year or two to actually win the Fastnet. In 1967 it went to the French yachting hero, Eric Tabarly, sailing *Pen Duick III*.

This remarkable new yacht had been designed primarily for the 1968 OSTAR, but she rated extremely favourably under the RORC Rule and spent the 1967 season winning most of the RORC events and ended up heading the Class I championship table. Described as a wishbone ketch, she had two masts of identical height between which was set a sail on a wishbone gaff. This sail was rated as a foresail and was not penalised under the Rule, and her mainsail was extremely small. This meant that no less than 25 per cent of her sail area was free and this made her rating very low indeed.

The first Southern Cross Series 1967

After her success in the Fastnet, *Pen Duick III* was shipped down to the stormy waters of the Tasman for the Sydney-Hobart race and

▲ *In 1967 Australia captured the Admiral's Cup for the first time. Mercedes III, designed and raced by Ted Kaufman, was in the Australian team that year and in 1969.*

the new Southern Cross series. That first year only New Zealand sent a team from overseas, but the main Australian states each fielded one. The Sydney-Hobart gave the Cup to the team from New South Wales. They beat the New Zealanders by 312 points to 268 despite the race being won brilliantly on corrected time by *Rainbow II*, a One Tonner sailed by a young New Zealander called Chris Bouzaid who earlier in the year had raced the same boat to victory in the second Whangarei-Noumea fixture.

At one time, though, it looked as if the race would go to Tabarly. He had managed to keep his lead half way through the race, but near the finish luck deserted him when a calm and adverse tides forced him to anchor for nearly an hour at the mouth of the Derwent. Eventually, he picked up a breeze and still managed to take line honours ahead of *Fidelis*, a converted harbour racer from New Zealand which had been first home the previous year. But Bouzaid was close behind. He had driven his boat so hard she had broached 25 times on the last day, but it won him the race by 58 minutes on corrected time.

The TransTasman resurrected 1968
Following this first Southern Cross series, the TransTasman was resurrected as a means of getting New Zealand yachts back home. It is now run after every Southern Cross series from Hobart to Auckland, a distance of 1517 miles. The one exception to this was when, in 1969, it was run from Hobart to Wellington, a distance of 1320 miles, to celebrate the 50th Jubilee of the Royal Port Nicholson Yacht Club.

Single-handed around the world
For the less orthodox participants in the sport, the single-handed Transatlantic race became established after 1964 and created a number of spin-offs like the Round-Britain race and later the *course de L'Aurore*, and the solo TransTasman and Transpac races. But the biggest challenge in this kind of racing had not yet been suggested. Then in 1967 Francis Chichester completed a single-handed circumnavigation. Alec Rose, also a 1964 OSTAR competitor, tried to make a race of it with him. But he was dogged by ill-luck and forced to make a separate circumnavigation, which he completed in July 1968. From the courage and determination of these two men the idea of a single-handed round-the-world race was born.

▲ Built in 1967 in aluminium, Pen Duick III *had several rigs but started life as a wishbone ketch. Under the RORC Rule of the time the wishbone sail was not penalised.*

The Pace Quickens

1968–73

BY THE END OF 1967 at least four yachtsmen had taken note of Chichester's feat and had decided to better it by sailing non-stop around the world (Chichester had stopped at Sydney).

Commander Bill King built specially for his circumnavigation, and went to designer Angus Primrose and to 'Blondie' Hasler for his yacht's construction and design. In January 1968 he was announcing that he had newspaper sponsors.

A 28-year-old Merchant Navy officer called Robin Knox-Johnston also became fired with enthusiasm for the idea of a non-stop circumnavigation, and began to look for sponsors to build him a suitable boat. When none was forthcoming he made up his mind to go in his 32-foot ketch, *Suhaili*, which he had had built in the Far East in 1963, and which he had sailed to England in.

The third man to become obsessed with the idea was an ex-SAS captain called John Ridgway, who was already well known as one of the two men who had rowed across the Atlantic in 1966. He had little sailing experience and looked upon the voyage mainly as a survival exercise.

Lastly, there was a Frenchman called Bernard Moitessier. Already a legendary figure in his own country, and the holder of the record for the longest non-stop voyage (14,216 miles from Tahiti to Spain via Cape Horn), Moitessier was known to be something of a mystic as well as a first class writer about the sea.

The Sunday Times Round-the-World race

While this formidable quartet were independently making their plans, *The Sunday Times*, which had backed Chichester on his circumnavigation, began to make plans to capitalise on the success of their investment. When the management discovered there were at least four men who had made up their minds to try to better Chichester's feat, they decided to sponsor a race, around the world non-stop. To make sure that everyone who intended making the circumnavigation would join this event the rules merely stipulated that competitors had to start between 1st June and 31st October 1968 and that they had to round the Cape of Good Hope, Cape Leeuwin, and Cape Horn. As it was thought that Moitessier wanted to start from Toulon it was also stipulated that a competitor could start from any port north of 40°N. However, this proviso proved unnecessary as the Frenchman later agreed to bring his yacht to Britain.

There were two prizes: the Golden Globe Trophy for the first yacht home, and £5000 for the fastest non-stop voyage. The race was announced on 17th March, and it immediately attracted additional entries: Ridgway's companion in his row across the Atlantic, Chay Blyth, decided to start; so did a Royal Naval officer, Lt-Cdr Nigel Tetley; an Italian Merchant Navy officer, Alex Carozzo; an Australian dentist, Bill Howell, though he later withdrew when his multihull failed to come up to his expectations in the 1968 OSTAR; a seasoned French yachtsman, Loick Fougeron; and an English businessman, Donald Crowhurst.

Only Ridgway got away on the first permissible date, but after encountering four days of exeptionally heavy weather in the South Atlantic his 30-foot fibreglass sloop literally began to fall apart. Wisely, he called it a day and made for Recife and shelter. In a race where a stable temperament was a prerequisite, he probably would not have been able to manage the months alone anyway, for it was reported in the press at the time that acute loneliness, and an anxiety not to let his friends and family down, had made him cry on no less than 27 consecutive days. Even Knox-Johnston, described by a psychiatrist as being 'distressingly normal', had fits of depression and anxiety, and had to give himself a strict routine to keep himself and *Suhaili* going.

Blyth was next to leave, on 8th June, but he was another early retirement, driven out of the race by a combination of gear failure and self doubt when off Tristan da Cunha. He sailed on to South Africa and then returned, with his wife aboard, to England. Two years later he established his reputation as one of Britain's finest seamen by making a solo circumnavigation east to west against the prevailing winds and currents.

Knox-Johnston left on 14th June, Moitessier on 21st August, Fougeron on the same day, King on 24th August, Tetley on 10th September, and Crowhurst on 31st October. Carozzo also officially started on 31st October but spent a week on a buoy making final preparations. The last to set sail, the Italian covered the least distance, being forced to retire when he began to vomit blood in the Bay of Biscay.

Bill King was doing well in his junk-rigged schooner, *Galway Blazer II*, and was almost in the Indian Ocean, when a rogue wave completely capsized him, snapping the foremast and springing the mainmast and carrying away his self-steering gear. Surveying the mess, King knew he had only one decison to make and that was which port he should try and make.

In the meantime, Fougeron was having a tough ride, being battered by high winds and rough seas. Then at the end of October, the day Crowhurst was starting, he ran into hurricane force winds. At times, his yacht, a gaff-rigged cutter, was driven deck deep into the waves, and when the storm eventually abated the Frenchman decided he had had enough. He made for St Helena and safety.

The first to start amongst the four remaining, Knox-Johnston was half way round the world before Christmas, and had survived some hair-raising experiences. Behind him was Moitessier in his steel yacht, *Joshua*, described as being as rugged as a trawler. She needed to be, because off the southern tip of South Africa Moitessier suffered two knockdowns in quick succession, but was able to race on. So did Tetley in his trimaran, *Victress*, though she had taken a terrible hammering and was leaking badly by the time the Englishman reached Australia. He was tempted to put in at Albany in Western Australia, but then the weather deteriorated again and he was more or less forced to continue. He was also driven on by the thought that the fourth man remaining in the race, Donald Crowhurst, was probably closing up on him in his trimaran, *Teignmouth Electron*.

But by this time Crowhurst had already opted out, not by retiring but by simply sailing around the South Atlantic until it was time to turn north and claim the £5000. He was the least experienced seaman of all the entries, and though brilliant in many ways he was also unstable and the stress of the first weeks of his voyage had been too great. He began to transmit false positions and to make up an entirely false log of his route. For over seven months he kept up this amazing deception, but it was not until he heard that thousands of people had gathered at Plymouth to give him a hero's welcome that he finally cracked up completely. No one will ever know what happened, but on 10th July 1969 his trimaran was found abandoned some 700 miles off the Brazilian coast, ghosting under mizzen only. There was no sign of Crowhurst, but ample evidence of what he had been doing and that he had decided that death was the only answer to his problems.

This bizarre tragedy was not the only example of the appalling strain that long distance single-handed racing puts on yachtsmen participating in this ultimate form of competition. Moitessier, approaching Cape Horn and with a good chance of taking both prizes, came to the decision that he had had enough of so-called civilization. 'I have no desire to return to Europe with all its false Gods,' he wrote in his log, 'It is difficult to defend oneself against them. They eat your liver and suck your marrow and brutalise you in the end . . . To leave Europe and then go back again is senseless. Like leaving from nowhere to re-

▲ *Merchant Navy officer Robin Knox-Johnston was the first to perform the incredible feat of sailing non-stop around the world, in his 32-foot teak-hulled ketch, Suhaili.*

turn to nowhere. I will return there one day but I think as a tourist, not to live . . . I know that life is a battle, but in modern Europe this battle is idiotic. Make money, make money — to do what? To change your car when it is still going well, to dress "decently".' He rounded the Horn, but then kept sailing east instead of turning north. 'I continue non-stop because I am happy at sea,' he recorded, 'and perhaps because I want to save my soul.' He went one and a half times round the world, and then

stopped at Tahiti.

By the time it was known that Moitessier had dropped out, Knox-Johnston was only a few weeks from finishing, and he arrived at Plymouth to a rapturous welcome on 22nd April 1969 after 313 days at sea.

But what about Tetley? The English naval officer passed Cape Horn the day before the news about Moitessier broke on 19th March, but he still assumed Crowhurst was hot on his heels. Once in the Atlantic again he began driving his trimaran hard, far harder than was prudent. The deck sprang in several places and hull and float frames were broken, but still Tetley pressed on. Then at midnight on 21st May, after pushing too hard through a storm off the Azores, a float snapped and smashed into the centre hull of the trimaran. Tetley was below asleep at the time and he only managed to send out a distress signal and climb into his liferaft before *Victress* sank just 1200 miles from the finishing line. He was picked up safely.

With Tetley out of the race Knox-Johnston was the only man to finish, and he collected both the Golden Globe Trophy and the £5000 – though when he heard about Crowhurst he immediately donated the cash to an appeal fund for the dead man's family. Of Crowhurst's deception plans Knox-Johnston said simply: 'None of us should judge him too harshly.'

The idea of this round-the-world race had been received with less than enthusiasm by the yachting press when it had been announced – one labelled it as no more than an advertising stunt – and even when it was over it did not elicit much comment from them, though the winner was hailed as a hero by the general press. Perhaps the reason for their reticence was that sponsorship was gaining ground in the sport and in some yachting circles this was regarded as an unnecessary evil. To a few it still is.

Sponsorship and the 1968 OSTAR

But the economic facts of life meant that the money required to build and race the kind of yacht that could win races like OSTAR was already getting beyond the reach of any individual's pocket. Before the 1968 OSTAR Leslie Williams, who was to sail the 53-foot sloop, *Spirit of Cutty Sark*, into fourth place,

◄ Joshua, *wrote Moitessier in his book* Cape Horn à la Voile, *was 'solid, simple, sure – and fast on all points of sailing.' Moitessier liked to meditate on the deck of* Joshua.

stated that in his opinion the only British yachts that stood a chance in the race were the ones that had been sponsored. He was proved right for the winner, Geoffrey Williams, was sponsored by Lipton Teas who put up the money for his Robert Clark-designed 56-foot ketch, *Sir Thomas Lipton*.

Williams' search for a sponsor, his detailed planning for the race and his rigorous training for physical and psychological fitness all showed the increasing complexity of tackling an event which had originally been intended as the simplest possible form of competition. The design of the yachts themselves was becoming equally complex. In 1968, there were 34 starters from nine different countries. Many were specially designed for the race. A good example was *Voortrekker*, sailed by South African Bruce Dalling and financed by the Springbok Ocean Racing Trust, set up specifically for the event. One of

the lightest 50-foot offshore racing yachts ever built, she had a very high sail area to displacement ratio, but her ketch rig broke it up so that it could be handled by one man. Below, the accommodation was what one magazine described as an exercise in ruthlessness: there was a galley, chart table, two berths and nothing else, literally nothing.

Sir Thomas Lipton was equally sparse and Williams' specifications for her were a lesson in austerity, but ones that bred speed and ease of handling. He required 'the minimum freeboard necessary to stop water coming over green, and its high ballast ratio and uncluttered decks would give me a clear and stable working platform ... no auxiliary engine, no WC, no wash basin, no hanging lockers, no standing headroom, and its berths are made up of Pirelli webbing stretched across aluminium tubes.' The result was a thoroughbred design of great beauty.

Both these yachts started hot favourites as did Tabarly's *Pen Duick IV*, one of the 13 multihulls which were entered for the race. Tabarly, having decided that *Pen Duick III* was not suitable for this event, had constructed this huge 67-foot schooner trimaran at the very last minute. 'She is immediately a winner,' wrote one expert. 'There can be no other boat to compare with her on absolute terms. She is instantly attractive; stark. The genuinely exquisite and robust construction and workmanship is striking. The boat is made of A64MC light alloy, an aluminium alloy named Duralinox, and built to the very highest possible standards of workmanship by Chantiers de la Perrierre, Lorient, in Brittany.' With a beam of 35 feet *Pen Duick IV* was wider than the length of some of the smaller entries.

▼ *Teignmouth Electron's* cabin when she was found drifting in the South Atlantic.

Besides Tabarly, there were eight other French entries, illustrating France's determination to dominate this type of ocean racing. Only the British, with 14 entries, had more, but there were three each from Germany and the US, the former entering the first woman OSTAR competitor, Edith Baumann, while the latter provided the most unusual craft, a 40-foot proa* called *Cheers*, designed by Dick Newick and sailed by Tom Follet.

The start of the 1968 OSTAR, on 1st June, was in such light airs that some of the competitors were forced to row away from the line! Tabarly, however, soon edged his way into the lead, but within 36 hours a disaster occurred, just the kind of incident that the critics of the race had long feared might happen. Tabarly had gone below to make a cup of tea when his trimaran ran smack into an anchored freighter at 15 knots. He returned to Plymouth for repairs and started out again, but finally had to retire when he found the boat when travelling at speed was shaking its steering gear to pieces.

Other withdrawals followed. Edith Baumann's trimaran, *Koala III*, began to break up and so did Jean de Kat's *Yaksha*, several yachts were dismasted, and before the race was completed there had been 16 retirements.

At the end of the first week, *Voortrekker* was leading on the direct route, with Geoffrey Williams in *Sir Thomas Lipton*, Leslie Williams in *Spirit of Cutty Sark*, and Bill Howell in his multihull, *Golden Cockerel*, close behind. To the south, Follet was going well in his proa having already covered a thousand miles. Then, at the beginning of the second week, a deep depression moved over the area and soon these leaders were being lashed by storm force winds, forcing all of them except *Sir Thomas Lipton* to heave to.

Williams was able to keep going by using a computer in London which fed him vital weather information. This helped him to choose the best course as he progressed across the Atlantic, and enabled him to avoid the worst of the storm. Perhaps the Frenchman Alain Gliksman had a chance of catching him but then he had to retire to Newfoundland with rudder trouble, and Williams crossed the finishing line first in a record time of 25d,20hrs,33mins. Both Dalling, who finished second, and Follet, who had come up from the south to snatch third place, also broke Tabarly's 1964 record, but the last boat to finish, *Jester*, now owned by Michael Richey, took over 57 days to cover the course.

The pace quickens

Though these single-handed events tended to overshadow the other more conventional races of the next few years, the traditional ocean racing calendar was full of fixtures that showed that the tempo of expansion in the sport was beginning to quicken.

In the South Atlantic, 1968 had begun with the triennial BA-Rio race attracting 32 starters while the Transatlantic race later in the year, run as a feeder race for the centenary celebrations of the *Norddeutscher Regatta Verein*, had 33 entrants, including ones from Poland and Austria, the first time these

*Proa is Polynesian for outrigger canoe, an inadequate description of this 40-foot schooner which sported two unequal sized hulls. In order to keep the one outrigger to leeward, *Cheers* was tacked by swinging her booms through 180° so that what had been the bow became the stern.

◄ *Nigel Tetley's* Victress. *Only 1200 miles from the end of the 30 000-mile voyage she began to break up in a storm and Tetley had to abandon her.*

90

nations had been represented in an international fixture. Huey Long in his new *Ondine II* took line honours and the overall prize in the former, the first non-South American yacht ever to win the BA-Rio, and then went on to take line honours in the Bermuda race and the Transatlantic that followed it. (Furthermore, he took them again in the 1969 Transatlantic from Bermuda to Cork, winning in the phenomenally fast time of 12d,21hrs, 54mins.)

It was a good year for the Canadians. Perry Connolly's 40-foot sloop, *Red Jacket*, won the St Petersburg-Ft Lauderdale and he became the first Canadian — and only the third foreign yacht — ever to win the SORC. Later in the season the first official Canadian Transpac was run with a fleet of 14 and was won by Bill Killam's *Porpoise III*.

Besides these well established events, new races were started from Ft Lauderdale to Charleston, from Galveston to Vera Cruz, from Colombia to Kingston, Jamaica (the TransCaribbean), while in Europe the 604-mile Middle Sea race round Sicily was inaugurated by the Royal Malta Yacht Club.

WORC

This vast and still expanding number of long distance ocean races world-wide attracted a new idea, one designed to appeal to the more competitive globe-trotting yachtsmen who every year sailed further and further afield for the best the sport could offer. The idea was for a supra-national competition that involved all the classic races, and when the St Petersburg Yacht Club in Florida announced it would sponsor the first World Ocean Racing Championship (WORC) in 1968 it received a good deal of support. In order to qualify, an owner had to sail his yacht in two mandatory races, the St Petersburg-Ft Lauderdale and the Miami-Montego Bay, and five optional ones out of a list of 16 which included events like the Fastnet, the Skaw, the China Sea race, and the Sydney-Hobart. This could be done over a three-year time span, but hull and owner had to remain the same, though rig and rating could vary. The same race could be sailed more than once but only the best result would count for championship points. If more than five of the optional races were sailed, the best five finishes counted.

▶ *When Tabarly decided that* Pen Duick III *was unsuitable for the 1968 OSTAR he had* Pen Duick IV *built in a few months.*

Maybe it was this new championship that brought a record fleet of 75 to the line for the ninth St Petersburg-Ft Lauderdale race. It was a rough, tough thrash which caused injuries and gear damage, but it gave Ted Turner's converted 12-metre, *American Eagle*, maximum points. Often, the winner of this long-distance race turns out to be the winner of the SORC, but in 1969 the new Bob Derecktor-designed 46-foot aluminium yawl, *Salty Tiger*, headed the list at the end of the six-race series — though she had not won one of them!

As one competitor noted, the quality and quantity of the gear on the SORC yachts was outstanding and the series was still living up to its reputation as a 'great towing tank' where new ideas and designs were tested against the toughest, fastest, most professionally sailed yachts in the world. That year saw a profusion of such refinements as rod rigging, internal halyards, tapered spars, as well as the very latest fittings and navigational equipment.

The other mandatory event for the WORC, the 811-mile Miami-Montego Bay fixture, attracted a fleet of 23 top boats such as *Salty Tiger* and Bob Johnson's replace-

▲ Sir Thomas Lipton, *designed by Robert Clark, was sponsored by Lipton Teas for the 1968 OSTAR. Sailed by Geoffrey Williams she had an on-board computer to help Williams assess the weather.*

◄ *One of West Germany's most successful ocean racers up to the 1970s, Hamburg VII, at the start of the 1968 Transatlantic race from Bermuda to Travemunde. She won class B.*

ment for *Ticonderoga,* the 73-foot ketch, *Windward Passage,* designed by the English ex-patriot Alan Gurney.

Windward Passage

Johnson was one of the few skippers who had taken part in all five Miami-Montego Bay races. He liked the course so much he named his new yacht after a part of it, the stretch of water between Cuba and Haiti, which had proved so often to be one of the toughest legs of the race. *Windward Passage* proved she was a very fast yacht for when she took

line honours in 4d,10hrs,22mins, she not only shaved over 12 hours off the record set by *Ticonderoga* in 1965, but established a new course record for the second time that season having already set a new record in the Miami-Nassau race.

Later in 1969 Johnson was involved in a controversial disqualification when he took part in that year's Transpac which turned out to be a heavy weather race that created carnage amongst the fleet. A remarkable race which developed into a battle for line honours took place between *Windward Passage* and another 75-foot ketch, *Blackfin.* The two yachts switched leads no less than three times before *Windward. Passage* crossed the line first in the record breaking time of 9d,9hrs,24mins, just 35 minutes ahead of her rival which also broke the old record. But then the result of a protest at the start was announced and *Windward Passage* was given

a two-hour penalty. *Blackfin* was now announced as the line honours winner, her time being slated as the new record, with the overall prize going to the Class C *Argonaut*.

At the end of 1969 *Windward Passage* was able to exact her revenge when she and *Blackfin* both took part in the third Long Beach-La Paz race, a 960-miler usually sailed in balmy weather. On this occasion, however, the 32 boats had a rail-down beat in a 30-knot south-easterly which brought with it heavy rain and a lot of discomfort for crews used to a pleasant sunny trip to Mexico. The two big ketches again had a close race, with *Windward Passage* taking line honours in 6d,21hrs,53mins, beating *Blackfin* by 1hr,9mins – and this time no protest took victory from her.

Two years later *Windward Passage* had another run of successes. Besides taking line honours in the first Cal Coastal she broke her own record in the Miami-Montego Bay race by more than 30 hours before entering the Transpac to even the score after the 1969 debacle. She did it, too, not only finishing first in a record time of 9d,9hrs,6mins, but also winning the race and her class outright, the only Class A yacht ever to have taken all three prizes (*Dorade*, in Class B, had achieved it in 1936). It was a poignant victory, for Bob Johnson had sworn never to race in the Transpac again after the 1969 decision had gone against him. But he had died soon afterwards and his sons, Mark and, later, Fritz, took over the helm, and Mark dedicated his 1971 victory to the memory of his father.

In over a decade of campaigning her the two brothers established *Windward Passage* as one of the great ocean racers of all time. In 1981 they sold her to Atlanta businessman

▲ The 73-foot Ondine II *was an immediate success all over the world. Here she is seen taking line honours in the 1968 Sydney-Hobart.*

▶ The most spectacular finish ever? Certainly one of the most unusual. The 78-foot Canadian ketch, Mir, *was dismasted near the finishing line during the 1969 Transpac. Her crew cleared the wreckage and then sailed her across the line – stern first!*

William Johnson (no relation) who gave her a sloop rig and raced her with great success. In 1982 and 1983, for instance, she collected line honours in five races and seven wins on corrected time.

Ocean racing in Japan

The traditional side of the sport received a boost with the WORC, as did the less orthodox side with the introduction of the first single-handed Transpac, from San Francisco

to Jogashima Island, Japan, a distance of 4536 miles.

Occupation after the Second World War introduced the Japanese to ocean racing. The Cruising Club of Japan was started in 1948 with the encouragement and participation of Americans stationed in the country, and in 1951 the first Oshima race of 90 miles was run with a fleet of six yachts. In 1954, the CCJ was reorganised as the Nippon Ocean Racing Club and the RORC rating rule was adopted. A number of long-distance ocean races were established over the next decades. They included the Okinawa-Tokyo race of 830 miles, the Hachijo Island race, the Sendai-Hakodate race, the Tokyo-Sendai race, and the 600-mile Ogaswara-Tokyo race, inaugurated in 1979; but the Solo Transpac, run in conjunction with the Slocum Society, was the first Japanese-organised international event.

First solo Transpac race 1969
The race attracted five starters: two Frenchmen, one German, one Belgian and one American. Eric Tabarly was at the start line in his new monohull *Pen Duick V*, specially designed for the race, as was another young Frenchman, soon to make a name for himself, Jean-Yves Terlain, who was sailing a 30-foot Arpège Class sloop. The race started on 19th March 1969 with a fleet of more than 200 spectator boats watching the five yachts sail under the Golden Gate bridge and out into the Pacific. The Belgian, Rene Hauwaert, soon had to turn back when he was dismasted, but after repairs he started again on 11th April. The American, Jerry Cartwright, got as far as Honolulu but had to retire with an ear infection. First to finish was Eric Tabarly who completed the course in 39d,15hrs,44mins, a good 11 days ahead of Terlain, and 13 days before the German, Klaus Hehner.

The first single-handed TransTasman 1970
A year later, on 11th April 1970, solo long-distance racing came to Australasian waters when the inaugural single-handed TransTasman race started from New Plymouth, New Zealand in rough seas and a 30-knot southwesterly wind. Seven yachts crossed the line on this 1300-mile race to Mooloolaba, Queensland, and the Californian, Marvin Glenn, took line honours in the fast time of 9d,5hrs,7mins. The handicap prize went to a New Zealander, Don Boyes-Barnes, who sailed his 35-foot plywood sloop, *Tom Bow-line*, into second place, some 27 hours behind Glenn. It was held again in 1974 and 1978 but then came a ban on solo racing in Australian waters.

Into the 1970s
The start of the new decade saw the stranglehold which the smaller yachts had traditionally maintained on the SORC well and truly broken by the boats which had so dominated line honours the previous year. The St Petersburg-Ft Lauderdale saw the first clash between *Windward Passage* and *Ondine II*. The former took line honours, but on corrected time the race went to another Class A yacht, *Equation*. However, overall Ted Turner's converted 12-metre, *American Eagle*, scored top points in the series, the first yacht over 50 feet to have won the SORC since 1957.

The two big Pacific events in 1970 – the 3571-mile San Pedro to Tahiti race and the Canadian Transpac (won by *Graybeard*) – were also won by Class A yachts. Although the Tahiti race had been established as long ago as 1925 it had been held only intermittently since then. The first race from San Pedro had been in 1956, but that race, and the others held in 1961, 1964, and 1968, had never attracted more than seven starters. Nevertheless, after the 1968 race, the organisers, the Transpacific Yacht Club, had decided to make the race a biennial fixture, making it at the time the longest regularly scheduled event in the world. This doubled the number of entries and attracted such competitive yachts as *Blackfin* and *Pen Duick III*. *Blackfin* took line honours, but victory on corrected time went to *Widgeon* which finished fifth.

The double-handed Round-Britain race 1970
In Europe, the calendar was full of long-distance events including a 400-miler during Gdansk Bay Week in Poland, the inauguration of the 750-mile Baltic Sea Cup by the Russians, as well as the Aegean and Ionian Rallies, started in 1964 and 1969 respectively. But the one that attracted the most attention was the second double-handed Round-Britain race. The first race had attracted a lot of publicity, and the entry list for the 1970 event was a long one. It was headed by the 71-foot ketch, *Ocean Spirit*, at that time the largest fibreglass yacht in the world. Crewed by Robin Knox-Johnston and Leslie Williams *Ocean Spirit* represented a tough challenge both to her crew who had to handle her and to those sailing in smaller boats. The best suited to do this were a number of fast and very unusual multihulls. Derek Kelsall, who had won line honours in the first race, was sailing one, a schooner proa called *Sidewinder*. Another was *Trixia*, an experimental boat with many unusual features. Amongst the monohulls was *Slithy Tove*, described as a wildly unconventional 48-foot hard chine sloop which, with her excessively narrow hull, looked very fast indeed. There were 25 starters and they made up as mixed a bag as has ever been seen at the start of an ocean race.

The first yacht into Crosshaven after a 230-mile beat in light airs was *Trumpeter*, a 44-foot trimaran sailed by American Phil Weld, followed closely by *Ocean Spirit*. Kelsall decided *Sidewinder* was unfit to continue and retired as did the British multihull designer Rod Macalpine-Downie in his catamaran, *Warlord*.

The wind freshened on the second leg to Castle Bay and *Slithy Tove* arrived only three hours and a bit after *Ocean Spirit*, now the fleet leader. On the third leg a strong north-west wind and heavy seas gave the bigger boat an advantage, and *Slithy Tove*, being driven hard in pursuit, sprang a leak and was forced to retire. *Trumpeter*, well up with the leaders, began to take in water in all three of her hulls and had to put in for repairs.

However, the conditions suited the much heavier multihull, *Apache Sundancer*, and if she had not lost the use of her only suitable headsail she could well have finished the leg very close behind *Ocean Spirit*. As it was she ended the leg 15 hours after the big monohull. This should have given Knox-Johnston and Williams a commanding lead but they had incurred a technical penalty before the race and needed at least a 12-hour lead to be sure of winning.

By the end of the leg, however, *Ocean Spirit* had managed to open the lead to 20 hours from her nearest rival, *Snow Goose*, which had taken over second place from *Apache Sundancer*. She retained her lead over the last leg making it a race for second place between *Snow Goose*, *Apache Sundancer*, and *Trumpeter*. As these three sailed south they met a south-westerly gale. *Snow Goose* ran for shelter but *Apache Sundancer*

▶ Windward Passage, *one of the most successful and enduring of modern ocean racers, seen here during the 1969 Sydney-Hobart. She is still racing.*

kept going. However, she met exceptionally rough seas off the Isle of Wight and she capsized and began to break up. Her crew took to the liferaft and were rescued. When the storm abated *Snow Goose* beat the larger *Trumpeter* into second place.

A new popularity

By 1971, the great upsurge in ocean racing in all its forms was reflected in its increasing popular appeal. In France, for instance, increasing interest in the sport was reflected by the formation of the *Union Nationale pour la Course du Large* (UNCL). This organisation, the equivalent of the RORC and CCA, was formed from the *Union Nationale des Croiseurs* and *Le Groupe des Croiseurs Legers*, the French equivalent of JOG and the American MORA, to help expand the sport and it actively encouraged yacht clubs to run ocean races. This, in fact, had already started to happen. The Cannes Yacht Club for instance, had organised a 350-mile race from Nice to Cagliari in 1969, and the following year had joined with the Yacht Club Italiano to sponsor a much longer event, from Cannes to Minorca and then on to Bonifacio, a distance of 515 miles. Others, in conjunction with commercial sponsors, soon followed suit, especially in organising single- and double-handed long-distance races, events which were to become something of a speciality with the French following their successes during the 1970s in OSTAR.

In Britain, increasing interest in the sport manifested itself in a different way. Up to 1969 ocean racing to the British public was as obscure a pastime as, say, polo. Certainly the press had treated Chichester and Knox-Johnston as heroes, but their feats did not bring ocean racing into the limelight in Britain to the same degree as Tabarly's had managed to do in France.

But then Mr Edward Heath, leader of the Conservative opposition party in the British parliament, bought a 34-foot fibreglass sloop, one of a new class recently developed by Sparkman & Stephens from one of their One Ton Cup designs, and ocean racing in Britain received its biggest publicity boost ever.

Up to that time Heath had been a dinghy sailor, but he was a quick learner and, not surprisingly, an extremely able organiser. *Morning Cloud* was runner up in her RORC Class in 1969, and had achieved a respectable seventh in class in that year's Fastnet, as well

as heading her class championship list in the East Anglian series.

Morning Cloud's Hobart win

After the Fastnet, the first British team to enter the Southern Cross series had to be chosen, and some care was taken to pick the right yachts. Max Aitken's Class I *Crusade* — which had come second overall in the Fastnet to Dick Carter's revolutionary *Red Rooster* by a marginal, and disputed, 68 seconds — was chosen as the big boat in case of heavy weather; Arthur Slater's latest *Prospect of Whitby* was named as the middle-sized boat; and the choice for the smallest member of the team lay between *Morning Cloud* and another S & S 34, *Morning After*. *Morning After* had done better in the season's earlier races, but *Morning Cloud* had been improving so rapidly that the choice was a difficult one. In the end the selection plumped for *Morning After*, and sent *Morning Cloud* as reserve.

With a leading politician in the team, there proved to be little difficulty in finding a firm to finance the shipping of the boats and an airline to fly the crews to their destination. And the RORC, which had not previously been involved in sponsorship, accepted the necessity of it without a qualm, and for a time less was

◀ *Ocean racing in Japan was started in the early 1950s. Here is the start of the inaugural Okinawa-Tokyo race, an 830-miler which is sailed in even-numbered years.*

Ted Heath was only known as a politician until he led the British Admiral's Cup team to victory in 1971.
▼

heard about the deleterious effect it would have on the sport. In fact, it only became a real bone of contention when sponsors began to demand more for their money by requiring the names of their products, and their logos, to be displayed on sponsored yachts, or for yachts to be named after the firm financing them. Both forms of advertising is forbidden under clause 26 of the International Yacht Racing Union rules, which bans advertising on a yacht's hull or sails.

In the 1969 Southern Cross series, Syd Fischer's remarkable *Ragamuffin* was the star early on, winning outright the three shorter races which preceded the Sydney-Hobart race. But in that blue riband event she could only manage 17th overall in a tough race won by none other than *Morning Cloud*, which had kept well offshore. It was just as well for the defending New South Wales team that Ted Heath had not been in the British team, and in the final count they retained the Cup, despite *Crusade* taking line honours in the Sydney-Hobart.

Heath's Hobart win boosted British interest in the sport. By 1971 he was Prime Minister, and when he was chosen that year to lead the British Admiral's Cup team, ocean racing began to mean something to people who had never even heard of it before. The 1971 Fastnet was won by *Ragamuffin*, but Britain won back the Admiral's Cup, and the newspapers and television were full of it.

Ocean racing in South Africa

The upsurge in popularity of the sport was not just confined to those countries where it was already well established, and in South Africa an altogether new race was started at the beginning of 1971 when 65 yachts from 15 countries began the first Cape Town to Rio race, an event described as a race between the two most spectacular cities in the world.

The weather off the coast of South Africa is notorious for its violent winds and big seas, and the lack of suitable shelter for yachts along much of the coastline is an added deterrent to those keen on ocean racing. Up to 1971, therefore, long-distance races were non-existent except for the 460-mile Agulhas fixture, which had been inaugurated in 1969 when it was won by the 1968 OSTAR entry, *Voortrekker*. The race had developed from the much shorter 180-mile Simons Bay-Mossel Bay fixture which had been first run in 1955 when Frank Morgan from Tasmania had challenged a local yachtsman, Ivor Jamison, to a 'real' ocean race. The Agulhas race is now a well established fixture in the South African yachting calendar and is raced biennially. Apart from the Agulhas fixture South Africa's chief offshore event is the race from Laurenço Marques to Durban for the Vasco da Gama Trophy.

▼ *In 1968 Australian Syd Fischer decided to break into big-time ocean racing and had S & S design* Ragamuffin *built for him. Among her many victories was the 1971 Fastnet.*

Cape Town to Rio 1971

The Cape-Rio race was, of course, on quite a different scale to the Agulhas race and it put South Africa firmly on the yatching map, attracting top ocean racing men like Robin Knox-Johnston, sailing *Ocean Spirit*, Eric Tabarly, sailing *Pen Duick III*, and Kees Bruynzeel, based in South Africa for many years now, sailing *Stormy*, his replacement for the veteran *Stormvogel*.

The start, on 16th January, was gusty. The yachts were seen off by a vast crowd of spectators, and as the wind strengthened the casualties began. *Stormkop's* bulkheads split; *Jacaranda* lost her rudder; *Guia* stripped the spokes of her wheel; *Stormy* had her rudder cables severed; *Sprinter*, sailed by an all-girl crew, got water sucked into the engine; and *Mam'selle's* centreboard broke loose. *Guia*, *Jacaranda* and *Sprinter* returned to Cape Town, made repairs and restarted. The others pressed on and made good the damage as best they could.

The optimum course was 300 miles longer than the shortest route, but it offered a steady west-going current, which varied between half a knot and one and a half knots, and trade winds two-thirds of the way. Most of the fleet chose this route and were heading north-west when the South Atlantic high decided to shift with them. After a week a few altered course to a more westerly direction, and this paid off as most of the others ran out of wind. One of these, a South African Van der Stadt-designed 43-footer called *Albatross II* now took the lead despite having damaged her mast early on. She was ahead not only on corrected time but boat-for-boat, quite an achievement for a Class III yacht. Gradually, however, the bigger boats that had taken the more northerly course overtook her and for the last 200 miles they were boosted towards the line by a fair current and a steady onshore breeze. *Ocean Spirit* was first to finish and she surfed across the line in grand style, having covered the 3500-mile course in 23d,42mins. *Albatross II* finished two and a half days later, but on corrected time won by 40hrs,43mins.

Such a lengthy race always produces dramas and the inaugural Cape-Rio event was no exception. The South African 30-footer, *Pioneer*, was hit by a whale a

▶ *Kees Bruynzeel's replacement for* Stormvogel *was* Stormy, *seen here off the South African coast. Bruynzeel sailed her to victory in the 1973 Cape-Rio race when he was 73-years-old.*

thousand miles out. It ripped off her fin keel and she sank in 16 minutes without her crew's SOS being heard. They all got away in the liferaft and were lucky enough to be picked up 17 hours later by a freighter. The race also produced a tie for third place in Class III.

New events on the US West Coast 1971
The other South Atlantic race that year was the BA-Rio, won by a Brazilian Class I entry called *Pluft* despite *Ondine II* setting a new course record of 7d,9hrs,30mins. But the main action in 1971, outside Europe, took place off the US West Coast – where three new long-distance events were added to the four already established – and in Australian waters.

The first of the new Pacific races, was the 1130-miler from Marina del Rey in California to Puerto Vallarta in Mexico. The problem with all the races to Mexico up to that time was the lack of wind off Baja, California – an area commonly called the 'parking lot' as the larger yachts were normally forced to wait there while the smaller ones caught them up – and this new fixture, which is still run today, suffered from it just as much as the others. In the light conditions three yachts retired and on corrected time the prize went to one of the smaller yachts, the Class C *Aquarius*. She had already cleaned up the Ensenada earlier in the year and before the end of it was to make it a hat trick by winning the long haul from Long Beach to La Paz.

In the same year, the Newport Harbor Yacht Club organised a race which was to stop just short of the 'parking lot'. They chose Cabo San Lucas, 790 miles from Newport, as the finishing line. The nearness of both the La Paz and Acapulco fixtures limited the fleet to six that first year, when it was won by the smallest boat, *Kahili*, but it has survived as a biennial fixture.

Despite the lack of wind, the Mexican races were popular and 1971 saw the first feeder race for them, from San Francisco to Newport, a distance of 385 miles. This first Californian coastal race – or Cal Coastal as it came to be called – attracted 30 starters. It was won by a Britton Chance-designed 50-footer, *Warrior*, which beat *Windward Passage* into second place overall though the latter took line honours.

New Zealand win the Southern Cross Cup 1971
The year ended with New Zealand achieving an outstanding win in the Southern Cross series against seven teams which included one from Britain and one from the US. Before the Hobart race Britain led New South Wales by three points with the New Zealanders just one point behind the Australians. A record fleet of 79 started in a fickle breeze which had most of the entries drifting across the line. But later the wind freshened and at one time it looked as if *Kialoa II* might break the course record, but a calm patch caught the leaders and she, with them, was stopped dead.

While the boats in front were struggling to move at all, the smaller ones, including the New Zealanders in their one-tonners, *Pathfinder, Runaway* and *Wai-Aniwa*, were running down towards Hobart in a 25-knot breeze under spinnakers. *Kialoa II* was still first to finish, nine hours outside the record set by Huey Long in 1962, but on corrected time *Pathfinder* was first overall, *Runaway* second and *Wai-Aniwa* third. All three finished within 1hr,14mins of each other, a truly remarkable result.

This win was undoubtably due to the intensive effort the New Zealanders had put into building, tuning and crewing their yachts for the One Ton cup championships which had taken place in New Zealand the previous year. The fiercely competitive atmosphere of these championships had forged tough attitudes and a dedication which later paid dividends.

By now, however, such total single-mindedness to the task in hand was more the norm than the exception. For those at the top – and for those determined to get there – the sport had become as serious a business as any other. It was a full-time occupation and crews dedicated their lives to it. Paul Antrobus explains it clearly when he wrote about how and why Owen Aisher's son, Robin, entered ocean racing when he built his Admiral's Cup contender, *Frigate*, for the 1973 series. 'As far as Aisher was concerned, his only reason for taking up ocean racing was the challenge of winning a place in the Admiral's Cup team. That was the prime objective for the boat. If that objective was achieved, then helping the team win was the next. In building *Frigate* there was no consideration beyond this. She would be redundant after the series and there was no business investment involved. The designer, Dick Carter, was told to worry about nothing other than winning.

'Crew selection, training and racing of the boat were equally intense. On board life was spartan and often extremely wet. Everything was planned to help the boat go faster. Before the race, sails were packed in tight bricks which were shifted around the boat to alter trim or add weight to windward. After they had been used, it was impossible to repack them into bricks on board, so, particularly in heavy weather, the inside of the boat was gradually filled up with a mass of wet sails, among which the crew often found themselves sleeping rather than in the bunks.

'On a beat to windward, any crew below was woken up on each tack and moved to windward bunks. If on deck, they sat birds-on-a-branch style, facing outwards with their feet dangling over the weather side – although with their torsos in the strictly legal position *inside* the lifelines. There was no time to enjoy this business of sailing.'

The second WORC
The beginning of 1972 saw the end of the first WORC, and the second, sponsored by *Yachting* magazine, was begun with that year's St Petersburg-Ft Lauderdale race. Almost until the time limit expired Pat Haggerty with *Bay Bea* had been in the lead in the first WORC event. But then Ted Turner in *American Eagle* turned in a sparkling performance to come second overall in the optional 1517-mile TransTasman race from Hobart to Auckland and pipped Haggerty at the post by a mere two points.

Turner's performance during the three-year period had been outstanding. It included wins in the 1969 and 1971 St Petersburg-Ft Lauderdale race (only one counted) and the 1969 Annapolis-Newport fixture; in the 1969 and 1971 Fastnets (only one counted); and third in the 1969 Transatlantic. He began the second WORC with a bang, too, winning line honours and first overall in the 1972 Sydney-Hobart, up to that time the only yacht besides *Rani* ever to have taken the elusive double.

The 1972 Bermuda race
The Bermuda race was one of the roughest ever, and for the first time in its 66-year history the classic was won by a foreign entry. The north-east quadrant of a large tropical depression buffeted the fleet so severely that

▶ *Brazilian Admiral's Cupper,* Pluft, *broaching wildly in the Solent in 1971. She won the BA-Rio earlier that year.*

102

it is remembered to this day. Several yachts were dismasted and others badly damaged. One had 800 eggs stowed below in preparation for the Transatlantic race. By the time she arrived in Bermuda her bilges were one large omelette. The British Admiral's Cupper, *Noryema*, was one of those that chased a dip in the Gulf Stream well to the east of the rhumb line, though it went right against the normal tactics for the race. When the storm blew up and the wind switched she was in such a good position she won on corrected time.

The 1972 OSTAR

While the Bermuda entrants were being lashed by heavy winds on one side of the Atlantic the 1972 OSTAR got under way in much milder conditions on the other. The starters had risen from 35 to 55 and they included such extremes as David Blagdon's tiny 19-foot *Willing Griffin* up to the massive schooner, *Vendredi Treize*, sailed by Frenchman Jean-Yves Terlain. The number of multihulls had dropped, from 40 per cent of the entries in 1968 to 15 per cent in 1972, but they performed much better, taking first, third, fifth and sixth place.

The OSTAR committee also ran into troubled waters over sponsorship of some of the yachts. Though the race was free of many of the rules and regulations that governed conventional ocean racing, blatant advertising was prohibited. Yet when yachts appeared which were named after the firms that sponsored them it was not always so easy to know where to draw the line. One French yachtswoman turned up with a yacht named *Pieter Stuyvesant* and she was told to change it. She explained that the name was to commemorate the famous mayor of New York, not to advertise a well known brand of cigarette. The committee was unimpressed and the yacht's name had to be changed to PS!

A dozen countries were represented in the race, including entries from the eastern block (Poland and Czechoslovakia), but apart from Terlain wearing a shiny crash helmet, everyone's eyes at the start were on Sir Francis Chichester in his new *Gipsy Moth V* and a young Frenchman called Alain Colas who was sailing *Pen Duick IV*. He had bought the famous multihull from Tabarly two years previously and had established a formidible reputation by circumnavigating the globe singlehanded in her in the record time of 66 days and at the same time creating a new record of 305 miles for the distance run in 24 hours. A university lecturer, whose sunny temperament was in marked contrast to the rather taciturn Tabarly, Colas had made a lot of modifications to his new acquisition and she was now a proven success. 'She's no longer the wild cat that Tabarly handed over to me,' he commented, and alluded to her affectionately as his 'floating tennis court'.*

*Tabarly did not compete in the 1972 OSTAR as he had entered the Tahiti race instead, and won it in *Pen Duick III*.

◄ *The New Zealand team of one tonners won the 1971 Southern Cross Cup. Seen here are two of them: Wai-Anina (left), which clinched the New Zealand victory by winning the Sydney-Hobart, and Pathfinder.*

▶ *American Eagle sails through Sydney Heads at the start of the 1972 Sydney-Hobart watched by a huge crowd, on land and afloat.*

The start on 17th June nearly brought immediate disaster with the vast *Vendredi Treize* coming within an ace of colliding with *Gipsy Moth V*, but eventually everyone got safely into the Atlantic though Chichester nearly ran ashore at Penlee Point. It was obvious to everyone that the old warrior was not well and that his powerful new boat was too much for a 70-year-old man to handle alone. Within a week he had been forced to retire, and he died later that year, mourned as one of the greatest seamen Britain had ever produced.

While the drama of bringing Chichester safely back to port was being played out, Colas, now about halfway across, saw Terlain ahead of him. This spurred him on to coax some extra speed out of his tri and he eventually managed to pass the huge schooner. This put him in the lead and it was one which he never lost. He finished the race in 20d,13hrs,15mins, knocking five and a half days off Geoffrey Williams' 1968 record. Terlain arrived second, 16 hours later. In fact, the French swept the board as Jean-Marie Vidal took third place in *Cap 33* and a French girl, Marie-Claude Fauroux, became the first girl ever to finish an OSTAR.

'Around the State' 1972

Unlike the OSTAR, the inaugural 'Around the State' race around Hawaii banned multihulls, though from 1974 onwards they had their own class. This 755-mile event started on 5th August off Waikiki in what must be one of the most perfect settings in the world for an ocean race. An 8-10 knot breeze put *Silversword* (ex-*Widgeon*) into an early lead from the small fleet of eight other yachts, but she and the other leaders were later slowed when the blustery North-East Trades were blocked by the volcanic peaks of Mauna Kea and Mauna Loa as they approached Ka Lae, the southernmost point of the US. This enabled the smaller entries to catch up and, unofficially, the race began again.

Once out of the lee of the two peaks the yachts were buffeted by 30-knot winds and

10-foot waves, and one was forced to retire with a broken rudder. At Cape Kumukahi, Hawaii's easternmost tip of land, *Ricochet* had taken over the lead, with *Silversword* close behind. The two leaders maintained their positions for nearly 100 miles before *Silversword* surged ahead through wind squalls that sometimes exceeded 30 knots and which caused gear damage on nearly every boat. 18 miles from Kaui, *Ricochet's* rudder snapped, and *Silversword* went on to take line honours in 5d,18hrs,29mins, but on corrected time the race was won by the much smaller *Nalu III*, a Cal-33 from Waikiki. The race was voted a success and became an annual event until 1978 when it became the long-distance race in the very popular biennial Pan-Am Clipper series.

The Rio Circuit

With the sport becoming so popular everywhere it is not surprising that 1972 produced a new series in South America. The Argentinians had long provided hot competition for the British and the Americans and in 1969 the Brazilians began to get government backing for ocean racing which soon brought them to the forefront of the sport. *Pluft's* win in the 1971 BA-Rio race was an early indication of their potential, and the same year a Brazilian team was sent to compete for the Admiral's Cup. Then in 1972 they sent a team to the Onion Patch series and the Brazilian *Saga* topped the list of individual performances, beating world-class yachts like *Charisma* and *Yankee Girl*.

The Brazilians' growing interest and skill in ocean racing was affirmed later the same year when the Italia Cup was donated by them as a trophy to be raced for by teams from other countries in the four-race Rio Circuit off the Brazilian coast which had been inaugurated in 1970. Modelled after the Admiral's Cup and the Onion Patch, it consisted of two short races, a 200-miler and the 430-mile Santana race, from Santos to Rio via Cabo Frio. This last event was sailed in winds which sometimes touched 50 knots. Despite two knockdowns, Jesse Phillips' *Charisma*, with Ted Turner at the wheel, led the fleet until fog closed in near the Cape and at this point *Saga* edged ahead and took line honours. On corrected time the race went to *Fjord VI*, designed and sailed by German Frers Sr, who, with his sons, also designed the other top two boats in the circuit, *Atrevido* and *Recluta*.

▲ *The end of the line for the great old man of ocean racing: Sir Francis Chichester being escorted home when his yacht was crippled after the start of the 1972 OSTAR.*

The second Cape-Rio race 1973

Rio was also the host port for the second Cape-Rio race which started in January 1973. The fleet of 43 was smaller than for the previous time but the quality of the entries was higher. The weather, as before, posed the biggest tactical problem, but this time the mid-Atlantic high remained stationary and the most successful yachts, with the new mark, Trinidade Island, to round, skirted well to the north of it. *Ondine II*, however, cut much too close to its centre, became becalmed and was forced to retire. But *Stormy*, with her septuagenarian owner, Kees Bruynzeel, aboard, was one of those which kept well to the north and by doing so finished first and clipped two days off the record by finishing in a time of 21d,12hrs,15mins.

Bruynzeel's performance was even more remarkable than his yacht's. He had been in at the start of ocean racing in the 1930s, and had been a consistent winner during the post-war years. His previous yacht, *Stormvogel*, had notched up the equivalent mileage of sailing ten times round the world in her long ocean racing career. Now, at the age of 73, after three heart attacks, Bruynzeel still insisted on racing, and for the Cape-Rio race his after-cabin was turned into an intensive care unit complete with nurse – and, so the rumour had it, a coffin. But he survived the race and lived on for several years.

New Races in Australia

No new long-distance races were introduced in the US or Europe in 1973, but in Australia the sport had become so popular that it even penetrated to the far north with the Darwin Sailing Club inaugurating a race from Darwin to Dili, a distance of 500 miles across the Arafura and Timor Seas to Portuguese Timor. There were only six entries, four of those were multihulls. Such was the interest in the race the following year, however, one local yachtsman was keen enough to buy a brand new Hood-23 and tow it 2700 miles from Sydney to Darwin for the start!

At the opposite end of the vast continent the final months of 1972 had also seen the inauguration of two long distance events: the Melbourne-Hobart West Coaster and the South Solitary Island race.

The 480-miler from Melbourne to Hobart via Tasmania's rugged west coast was organised by the Ocean Racing Club of Victoria (previously called the Cruising Yacht Club of Victoria) and the Derwent Sailing Squadron, and was run at the same time as the Sydney-Hobart. This caused some ill-feeling, but the new race did not detract from the old one and nowadays both act as feeder races for the 'King of the Derwent' event organised by the Tasmanian club. This fixture is itself part of the Sovereign series of three races: the 'Cock of the Bay' race from St Kilda to Mornington, the West Coaster, and the 'King of the Derwent'.

Before the first race there were dire warnings about sailing down the weather-exposed coastline of Tasmania, but in the event the mixed fleet of cruising boats and lesser known racers had little trouble. *Wendy II* took an early lead but was soon overtaken by the Warwick Hood-designed *Mary Blair* which held it to the end and took line honours in 64hrs,19mins. On corrected time, however, the race went to the veteran Victorian 30-foot sloop, *Ailsa*.

Further up the coast at Sydney, the first South Solitary Island race also started on Boxing Day. The object of this 500-miler was not only to give local yachtsmen some good racing but to get them back home in time for New Year's Eve, hence the nearly circular course from Sydney up to the island just north of Coffs Harbour, with the finish at Pittwater. It was also one of the three ocean races which qualified for points in the new Ampol Tasman Sea Trophy, which also included the Montagu Island and the Sydney-Mooloolaba races. Despite this, there was only a modest fleet of eight at the start with the race on handicap going to Australia's reigning half ton champion, *Plum Crazy*.

The Admiral's Cup 1973

In Europe, the major attraction in 1973 was the Admiral's Cup series, which over the years had established itself as the most prestigious event of its kind in the world. In 1973, teams from 16 countries were represented. To illustrate just how competitive it had become, no less than 32 owners competed in the British trials for the three places in the team, and 24 of them built new boats. The continuing dominance of the Americans was revealed with the veteran Sparkman & Stephens designing 23 of them.

The boom in the sport, combined with the introduction of the International Offshore Rule in 1971, had created an insatiable demand for new design ideas. But major design improvements like the split configuration underbodies of the late 1960s, were the exception not the rule, and an 'advance' in design or equipment now sometimes turned out to be anything but that. Occasionally, it turned out to be nothing more than a costly mistake. Arthur Slater, for example, tried out a radical alteration to the rigging of his latest S & S design in an attempt to obtain a lower rating without loss of sail area. The experiment failed and for the first time since 1967 the British team was without a *Prospect of Whitby*. Another flop was Sir Max Aitken's radical Britton Chance-designed centreboarder, *Perseverence*.

Despite the intense competition for a team place, the British could not retain the Admiral's Cup in 1973 and it was won for the first time by a non-British speaking country, West Germany, whose top yacht, *Saudade*, turned in a brilliant performance. She came fourth in the Channel race, won both inshore events, and then finished tenth in her class in the Fastnet.

But though the Germans won the Cup – a feat they repeated in 1983 – the Fastnet itself was a triumph for the South Americans, with the Brazilian Admiral's Cupper, *Saga*, finishing first overall and the Argentinian *Recluta III* second. A fire-engine red beauty owned by Carlos Corna, *Recluta III* caused quite a stir at Cowes and heralded the appearance of a new design talent in German Frers Jr, who later went on to produce gold-platers like the 1974 SORC winner, *Scaramouche*, Ted Turner's *Tenacious*, and the Australian Admiral's Cupper, *Bumblebee 3*.

A decline in numbers

During the previous five years the traditional side of ocean racing had grown enormously, spurred on by increasing public interest, the proliferation of inexpensive, fast, mass-produced designs, and a healthy economic climate. But just as it reached a new peak, numbers began to decline. Starters in RORC races in 1967 had totalled 851, and in later Admiral's Cup years this had grown steadily until 1973 when they numbered 1350, a figure which has yet to be topped. But the following year, with the advent of the first oil crisis and with recession in the wings, the number dropped back to 819.

But though the numbers in some of the top competitions now began to decline – a situation perhaps at least partly created by the cut-throat quality of the sport at this level and by the worsening economic situation – the kind of imaginative racing introduced by OSTAR and the first single-handed Round-the-World race continued to expand to an astonishing degree during the next decade.

▲ In 1973 the West German team of Saudade, (seen here), Rubin and Carina III, won the Admiral's Cup, the first non-English speaking nation to do so. The Germans won again in 1983.

◄ Table Mountain is a dramatic backdrop for the start of the 1973 Cape-Rio race. In 1976 the finish was moved to Punta del Este.

Swuzzle
Bubble, Toil
and Trouble

IT HAS BEEN possible to review the story of ocean racing up to the 1970s by interweaving the development of the traditional side of the sport with the rapidly expanding single- and short-handed racing. After all, one stemmed from the other.

In 1973, however, inter-ocean racing began and the newer branches of the sport begun to grow away from the traditional side. For the sake of clarity, therefore, recent developments in traditional ocean racing, and the story of the rapid expansion of the new forms of the sport, have been given separate chapters.

This chapter is an attempt to explain the influence of IOR and of sponsorship on the traditional side of ocean racing as we know it today. It is not always a happy story, but the tenacity and enthusiasm with which the sport is still pursued leaves no doubt that it has a secure and exciting future.

The IOR introduced

The International Offshore Rule had been a long time coming. Ever since the CCA had abandoned the current RORC rule in the early 1930s, sporadic efforts had been made to combine the two, but without success. But as the sport began to grow so the pressure increased for an international rule which would govern the design and handicapping of all ocean racers. Eventually, one was agreed and implemented on 1st January 1971, the governing of it being placed in the hands of a new body, the Offshore Racing Council (ORC).

As could be expected in the age of computers, the new rule was extremely complicated and the administration of it not cheap. Both these factors were early causes of complaint.

Although the rule first began to operate in 1971, it took some time for it to come into operation on a worldwide basis. MkI was never used. After MkII was announced in 1971, the Americans urged changes which brought about MkIII, and later MkIII(a). MkIII(a) originally dealt with age allowances for older yachts and was tacked on to MkIII, but did not replace it. Nowadays, both are used to compute the rating of a yacht, whether old or new, and the lowest result is used.

Refinements to the rule were made continually and were added through the years though the rule became increasinbgly stable after 1978. There have been no changes of any significance since 1981, showing that at last the rule is working well.

But throughout the 1970s, with the rule constantly altering, designers and owners found themselves with yachts which were superseded almost before they were launched, and before various loopholes were closed in the rule a whole generation of ultra-light racers appeared whose seaworthiness was open to question.

The effect of all the uncertainty, combined with the difficulties in making the changes to the rule politically acceptable to national yachting authorities and the succession of oil crises which threw the world economy into deep recession, is not hard to imagine. In fact, it is miraculous that such an expensive sport has not suffered more than it has, at least at grass roots level.

At the top level, however, competition increased. And the men involved in it became sharper, more professional and more dedicated than ever. Numbers fell slightly but the yachts became larger not smaller, the rise of the 'Maxi' and then the 'super-Maxi' being the most extravagant phenomena of the sport in recent years.

Growth of sponsorship and Rule 26

But though owners were willing to pay what was necessary to have a top boat and crew, sponsorship became increasingly needed during the 1970s to maintain the events in which they wanted to compete. In Britain, for instance, Champagne Mumm will be sponsoring the Admiral's Cup throughout the 1980s, while Hitachi have now tagged their name onto the Sydney-Hobart classic, and Lufthansa onto the China Sea race series. In New Zealand, John Fair, President of the New Zealand Yachting Federation, stated bluntly that if there is to be true international racing, financial help is going to have to be provided for local yachtsmen, and that such help is unlikely to be forthcoming in New Zealand without contravening Rule 26.

Teams from several countries have failed to turn up for a series – Hong Kong for the 1982 Pan-Am Clipper Cup series is one example – because a sponsor could not be found for them, and though no series has yet been cancelled through lack of funds, it could happen. In order to make sure this does not happen Rule 26 is now sometimes waived by local administrators for special long distance events – the 1982 Sydney-Rio race is a recent example – but there is a strongly entrenched opinion, both in the US and Europe, that its abolition would open the floodgates, resulting in a complete takeover of the sport by commercial interests.

The professional approach
Sponsorship, the IOR, and the state of the world economy, has sharply polarised traditional ocean racing into the pros and the rest of us, and the pros are very professional indeed. The owners have the money, and very often the skill, to campaign their boats regardless of cost, and the best of them attract top-notch crews to whom racing is a way of life.

'The most sought after owners are those who really understand what the crews need,' wrote yachting journalist Bob Fisher in *Yachts and Yachting* in 1981. 'The best sails and equipment are a prerequisite; with those a good crew believe that they can get a moderate hull to the front of the fleet – a "dog" however is quite a different matter. A hull so condemned will drop in value to about a tenth of its original cost overnight, and no one who values his reputation will be seen anywhere near it again. Not even minor surgery to the hull and a paint job will attract the heavies.

'Given the right formula the top owner will then place considerable responsibility on his paid skipper – a member of the IBNA (International Boat Niggers' Association) – and the pay that the skipper receives will be commensurate with running a £250 000 business, for that is what an Admiral's Cup campaign is. The rest of the crew will be chosen by the owner and skipper working together. They will both have their preferences, but the essential that guides them is that they will all get on together.

'The successful owner will be the one whom crews will seek out. Not only should he be successful on the water; he has got to be successful in his career – overnight flash-in-the-pans don't get the ear of the serious crews – and if he is a "personality" he is likely to raise the profile of the boat and thus engender greater aura for the crew, in which they can be reflected. All these factors are part of the price which owners have to pay. Owners create respect among the crews if they do not tolerate wastage, but niggardly penny-pinching is not acceptable.

'There is now considerable specialisation among crewmen. And it isn't a case of helmsmen and others; bow-men, foredeck, mast-men, grinders and trimmers all have their own personal skills, while the navigators have that mumbo jumbo that is all their very own. Trimmers are often supplied from the sail loft – that will be one part of the deal that the owner and skipper will demand before they commit themselves to the particular sail-maker. This explains why there are so many sailors working as Sail Consultants around the lofts these days.

'The rest of the crew may come as a unit. Like a band of wandering minstrels, these close-knit groups of friends can be found at the major regattas all over the world. For the price of a few air tickets and the promise of some excellent sailing aboard a potential race-winner, the real heavies will give their all. They are easily identified. Sun tanned, with their hair naturally bleached, sporting as like as not a Californian style moustache, they have turk's heads around their wrists and well-used Topsiders on their feet. Ashore their badge of office is the crew shirt of one of the more famous boats on the International circuit. They drink lager (the colder the better) while remembering the rum drinks that they had in the Caribbean, and they smoke only exotic cheroots. Britain's climate they can do without, but not the Admiral's Cup.'

Space-age technology
The yachts that these rarified characters race are out-and-out machines, tuned like concert pianos, filled with electronic gadgetry, and built in the most exotic materials which makes them weigh a fraction of their predecessors. In the 1960s, masts were stayed to hold them rigid. The 1970s changed all that: when the fractional (non-masthead) rig returned, masts were bent like bows by hydraulic pumps, a tricky and delicate operation. So tricky that on one yacht – the Canadian Admiral's Cupper, *Evergreen* – no less than nine dials are needed to show the tensions of various parts of the rigging!

The advance in sail cloth and design has been equally dramatic. Kevlar, a yarn, and Mylar, a plastic film, are both du Pont trade names that have increased strength and reduced stretch, though the prohibitive cost and low-fatigue resistance of the former led to it being partially banned by the ORC. This ban was later rescinded.

However, the number and cut of sails in the locker of a goldplater has proliferated beyond the pockets of all but the richest and most dedicated yachtsman. Bloopers, ghosters, big boys, flankers, blast reachers, to name just a few, were joined in 1982 by the staysail-spinnaker, and no doubt there are others on the way which will get that last inch of pace out of a yacht.

Against this background of design confusion, economic retrenchment, controversial sponsorship problems, and big advances in yacht technology, it was not surprising that by 1974 most ocean racing fleets had been reduced in numbers. But this did not stop the inauguration of new events like the 638-miler from Nassau to Kingston – now a biennial fixture – nor the continuation of ones already well-established.

Sydney-Noumea resurrected
In Australia the worsening economic climate did not prevent the Sydney-Noumea race, not run since 1957, being held to celebrate the bicentenary of the discovery of New Caledonia by Captain Cook. Thirteen yachts raced in 60 knots of wind and torrential rain. Two of the main contenders for line honours – the concrete-built *Helsal*, known affectionately as the 'floating footpath', and *Apollo*, owned by Jack Rooklyn – were both forced to retire with structural problems while well ahead of the fleet. This left the 60-foot double-ended sloop from Victoria, *Banjo Paterson*, in the lead and she finished first in 8d,5hrs,32mins, though on corrected time the race went to the steel built *Tui Manu*.

The success of this race made the Australians now realise that they liked racing out into the Pacific after all. As a result, the Sydney-Noumea was run again in 1977, and then became a quadrennial fixture. A race to Suva from Sydney was also inaugurated in 1976 and this is now quadrennial as well.

Racing Down Under
At the end of 1974 the Australian Admiral's Cupper, *Love and War*, a sistership of *Saudade*, won the Sydney-Hobart. The fleet received its usual dose of Tasman weather with two gales sweeping through it and causing a lot of damage. Another Australian entry, *Bumblebee 3*, was a hot favourite to win, but she began what was to be a very successful career by grounding on some rocks in Sydney Harbour, and later she tangled with a whale off Twofold Bay. But she still managed to take second place overall.

Syd Fischer's new *Ragamuffin*, another favourite, was not so lucky and had to retire on the third day with rigging failure. *Ondine II* took line honours, but could not crack the record time of 3d,1hr,32mins set by *Helsal*

▲ *The 72-foot Australian sloop, Helsal, was constructed of ferrocement. Nicknamed the "floating footpath", she broke the Sydney-Hobart course record in 1973.*

the previous year. However, *Helsal* did not hold onto it for long as another record breaker, Jim Kilroy's *Kialoa III* came along in 1975 and covered the course in 2d,14hrs,32mins, and set a record that still stands. Two years later *Kialoa III* took line honours again, and saved her time, putting her amongst the select few – *Rani* in 1945, *American Eagle* in 1972 and *Ceramco New Zealand* in 1980 – to take double honours.

Top designer Lexcen

The new *Ragamuffin* had been designed by Bob Miller (he later changed his name to Ben Lexcen), a top Australian designer whose in-

ternational reputation in ocean racing had been made* when he produced two of the 1973 Admiral's Cup team *Apollo II* and *Ginkgo*, for Bob Bond and Gary Bogard.

Miller had been an early critic of the IOR. 'Sometimes I look at pictures of yachts of the 1890s,' he remarked in 1971, 'and wonder whether yacht design has advanced at anything like the pace of the materials of our boats', and he added that IOR designs looked like boxes and were 'really bitchy' downwind. But with *Apollo II* and *Ginkgo* he produced

*Lexcen will now of course be best remembered as the designer of *Australia II*, which won the America's Cup in 1983.

designs that were both easily driven and capable of high speeds downwind.

In 1974, he was asked by the flamboyant, cigar-chomping Rooklyn to design a bigger boat for him, and the result was *Ballyhoo* (now *Mistress Quickly*), a 72-foot maxi which snatched line honours in the 1975 Sydney-Mooloolaba race before going on to take both line honours and the overall prize in the Brisbane-Gladstone, a remarkable performance for such a highly rated boat. Even more impressive was *Helsal*'s run the following year when she shattered the existing record times in both the Sydney-Mooloolaba and Brisbane-Gladstone events, before going on to take line honours and the overall prize in a new 500-miler up Australia's east coast, from Gladstone to Cairns.

Racing under MkIII(a)
At the beginning of 1976 IOR MkIII(a) came into effect and the organisers of the SORC – which had been won the previous year by the remarkable Ted Hood in *Robin Too II* – reacted to it by dividing the fleet into two. Division I, for boats over two years old, went to *Saudade*, now under American ownership, while Division II, reserved for the new hotshots, was won by the Peterson-designed *Williwaw*.

The CCA went further than the SORC organisers and showed its doubts about the type of boat the IOR was encouraging by modifying the rule for the Bermuda race in order to help the more traditional, narrower and shallower design over the new, beamier, and deeper-drafted yachts the rule was producing.

It was a windward race that year in which, as in 1972, it paid to keep east of the rhumb line, and the fleet was so strung out by the time the line honours winner, *Tempest*, crossed the finishing line that it would not have mattered what handicap system had been used. The winner was the 1969-built *Running Tide*, campaigned since 1972 by Al Van Metre.

Running Tide was the first Class A yacht to win the Bermuda race since *Nina* in 1962. But she broke the drought for the big boats simply because the Class B *Bumblebee 3*, continuing her run of bad luck, cut a mark and had to return to round it. The detour took 35 minutes and she lost the race by seven. However, she still managed second place overall and first in her class, beating top boats like *Salty Goose*, *Scaramouche*, *Charisma* and *Tenacious*.

Copa Mil Millas
The same year, 1976, the first Chilean long-distance race was established when the *Copa Mil Millas* – thousand mile cup – was run in the Pacific. The race was in three legs, from Valparaiso to Isla Robinson Crusoe, a distance of 350 miles; from Robinson Crusoe Island to Talcahuano, again a distance of 350 miles; and

▲ *The 45-foot Australian Admiral's Cupper, Ginkgo, seen here in the Solent, established Bob Miller's reputation as a designer when she was launched in 1972. Better known as Ben Lexcen, he designed Australia II.*

finally a 250-mile sail from Talcahuano north up the mainland coast to Algarrobo just south of Valparaiso. This quadrennial fixture attracts mostly local yachts though occasionally there are British and American entries.

Middle Sea race lengthened
In 1977, nine years after it was first raced, the Middle Sea race was extended to 630 miles, making it at that time the longest regularly held traditional ocean race in Europe. Nowadays it is only 606 miles.

During the 1970s the popularity of this race had increased by leaps and bounds. In the early 1970s the British had even organised feeder races to Gibraltar and then on to Malta for it, and it was also made one of the optional races for the WORC, which encouraged those who raced the international circuit to include it in their itinerary.

Originally intended to be a biennial to alternate with the Fastnet, on which it was modelled, the success of the first Middle Sea race turned it into an annual event, with the

RORC including it in its programme. The fascination of the course for yachtsmen is easy to understand, for the scenery is dramatic. Stromboli, an active volcano, and the sheer cliffs of Lampedusa, Gozo, and Pantelleria, act as turning marks. The sea is a dark blue and so translucent that dolphins can be seen 15 metres down.

Light displacement problems
The rumbles of discontent about the IOR as the middle 1970s came and went refused to subside. In 1977, it caused a direct confrontation between Australia and New Zealand when the Cruising Yacht Club of Australia (CYCA), the organisers of the Sydney-Hobart, insisted that the new self-righting test decreed by the ORC would be applied to the Hobart fleet before its official introduction date of 1st January 1978. The test had been introduced to counter the trend towards light-weight flyers with inboard ballast and lifting keels, which were liable to broach to and be knocked right down.

The New Zealanders, with their long tradition of light displacement harbour yachts, were at the forefront of this new development, and they felt that the ORC, dominated as it was by the nations of northern hemisphere, did not fully appreciate that it was this tradition, and not any overt wish to find loopholes in the IOR, that had been at the root of the introduction by them of this type of yacht.*

The upshot of the clash was that New Zealand officials threatened to withdraw their Southern Cross team of *Swuzzle Bubble*, *Jenny H* and *Smir-Noff-Agen* unless the CYCA's decision was rescinded. As New Zealand was the defending country this put the series in jeopardy and the Australians reconsidered their options. The ORC self-righting test consisted of hanging a pre-calculated weight on the truck of a yacht's mast and seeing if it came upright after it had been laid on its side. But it was also possible to apply a similar test mathematically, through a computer, and this was what was eventually agreed upon. 'The *Swuzzle Bubble* puzzle

*When it is remembered that New Zealand has more sailmakers per head of population than any other country in the world, and that by the end of 1979 their world-class designers like Ron Holland, Bruce Farr, Laurie Davidson and Paul Whiting had, between them, amassed 14 Ton Cup championship titles, it can be understood that New Zealand had, and has, an influence on ocean racing quite disproportionate to its size.

solved,' announced one headline gleefully, and indeed all those that were computer tested passed and raced.

The weather, however, had its own method of sorting out which boat was sea-worthy by producing an 18-hour, 50-knot gale on the second day which had 58 out of the fleet of 130 deciding that Hobart was not for them that year. The ultra-light half-tonners like *Swuzzle Bubble* did not come out of it well. Although this type composed only five per cent of the fleet they were re-sponsible for 50 per cent of retirements caused by hull damage. Of the seven entries in this category only one, *Jenny H*, finished – though she, too, had suffered structural dam-age.

Despite the retirement of the other two members of the team, the points gained by *Jenny H* were enough for New Zealand to retain the Cup they had won from Britain in 1975 for they had built up a huge lead in the earlier races. They won again in 1983.

The Transpac and the ULDBs

Earlier the same year, 1977, the Americans, too, had had to face the problem of these new ultra-light displacement boats (ULDBs), like the ones developed by the designer Bill Lee for the very different sailing conditions that dominate the Transpac.

A Lee-designed ULDB called *Chutzpah* had taken the overall Transpac prize in both 1973 and 1975 and it became apparent that this type had a grip on the race which, despite the organisers modifying the IOR formula to reflect the downwind nature of the race, was going to be hard to break. So when the news got about that the 'Wizard of Santa Cruz', as Bill Lee was sometimes called, was building the 'ultimate sled', the decision was made to run the 1977 race in two divisions, one for the heavy displacement yachts and one for the ULDBs.

It was a very fast Transpac indeed that year with the first five boats smashing *Wind-ward Passage*'s 1971 record. As predicted,

Bill Lee's 'ultimate sled', the 67-foot *Merlin* which weighed only 20 000lb, took line hon-ours in 8d,11hrs,1min, a feat she repeated in 1981. She also saved her time to come in first in the ULDB division, with the other division being won by *Kialoa III*.

Her success in 1977 and 1981 meant that *Merlin* was so severely rated for the 1983 race that only drastic changes, which included a shorter boom and spinnaker pole, and having four quarter-ton lead pigs bolted to her gunwhales, enabled her to qualify at all. However, with the capacity still to sail in bursts at 29 knots, she was a candidate for line honours. But it was a Holland 67, *Charley*, that swept the board by clocking up several 300-miles-a-day runs to beat *Merlin* by two hours, though the Class C *Bravura* won on corrected time.

Charley is a real representative of ocean

▼ *The New Zealand 40-foot, Holland-designed half-tonner,* Swuzzle Bubble, *was the centre of much con-troversy when she was a member of her country's Southern Cross team in 1977.*

racing in the 1980s, for she has aboard a computer so sophisticated that the crew can examine their speed through the water in relation to their competitors and an automatic direction finder that locks on to each opponent to verify its claimed position.

World Ocean Racing Championship

The second WORC, which finished in 1975, was won by Wally Stenhouse in his 49-foot S & S-designed *Aura*, and the third, which finished in January 1978, was taken by Jim Kilroy who had a runaway victory in *Kialoa III*. The format of the WORC now changed. It was limited to five races over a two-year period: the St Petersburg-Ft Lauderdale, Bermuda, Fastnet, Sydney-Hobart, and Transpac. This was to ensure that competitors met each other more frequently than they had when there had been a much larger choice of events. The best of three of them counted for the championship.

Burt Keenan, in *Acadia*, topped the list in 1980, by winning the 1978 Bermuda race and coming fourth in the 1978 St Petersburg-Ft Lauderdale, and eighth in the 1979 Fastnet. Then the format was changed again. This time it was to make it more inviting for Pacific yachtsmen, so it included the St Petersburg-Ft Lauderdale, Bermuda, Around Hawaii, Sydney-Hobart, Transpac and Fastnet fixtures, with the best three results counting. It was won by an American East Coast yachtsman, Chuck Kirsh, in his latest *Scaramouche*.

Revolt against IOR

On the East Coast of America the IOR was causing problems too. Such was the discontent with it that the CCA decided to run the 1978 Bermuda race under a new handicap system as well as under IOR.

Ever since the earliest days of ocean racing there had been different handicapping systems in different parts of the world, though the blue ribband races had always been run under either RORC or CCA rules. At one time there were as many as 20 different rating systems in the US alone, though the one now most commonly used worldwide for the non-IOR divisions in a race is the Performance Handicap Racing Factor (PHRF), which originated in southern California where it was known as the Pacific Handicap Racing Fleet.

Unlike IOR, which is a formula, PHRF is an arbitrary handicap assigned to a particular yacht after its performance capabilities have been assessed by a local committee. The handicap is expressed in seconds per miles which has to be subtracted from the yacht's elapsed time. By 1977, this system was more and more popular in the US, and the number of IOR-rated boats was dropping. In the 1977 Ensenada race, for instance, 75 per cent of the 600 starters were rerated under PHRF. It is a continuing trend, with the IOR fleet world-wide dropping to under 10 000 at the end of 1983.*

With this in mind, it is not so surprising that when a club like the CCA found that IOR was unpopular it decided to switch to a more favoured form of handicapping. It therefore

*In 1984 the British and French introduced the Channel Handicap, for less competitive racing. Though it is in no sense a rival to IOR it will be interesting to see how popular it becomes.

decided to adopt the Measurement Handicap System (MHS), a new method devised by the Massachusetts Institute of Technology, which was able to predict a boat's performance in any sailing conditions. This analysis was then converted to a conventional time allowance by using a factor that estimates the weather expected on the course for a given event. This factor was worked out in great detail and it included reviewing weather reports of past races over a particular course. However, MHS did not take over completely because the Onion Patch series was, of course, raced under IOR. In 1978, 90 boats competed under IOR and 72 under MHS, with the traditional Bermuda Trophy being awarded to an

▼ *The 67-foot, Lee-designed, ultra-light displacement, boat, Merlin, which established a new Transpac course record in 1977.*

MHS boat – it was a pre-war Class F yawl, *Babe* – while the IOR entries raced for a new trophy, a gold model of *Tamerlane*, the first Bermuda winner in 1906. This went to Burt Keenan's *Acadia*, a 51-foot Frers design from New Orleans and star of the 1978 SORC.

The Bermuda race in the 1980s
For the 1980 Bermuda race all except the Onion Patch competitors raced under MHS, but IOR rated boats were awarded prizes within their particular class for IOR performance. Again the winner, *Holger Danske*, was an old boat which had been built in the early 1960s with no thought whatever as to how she would rate! Although cruised a great deal, she had hardly raced at all, but she won convincingly.

In 1982, the organising clubs compromised between IOR and MHS, with the overall prize going to the yacht beating the next placed boat in its division by the largest margin. Seventy-seven boats sailed in the IOR division, 101 under MHS, with ten-year-old S & S-design, *Brigadoon III*, winning the MHS overall prize, and an even older yacht, Dick Nye's *Carina* (built 1969) taking the IOR prize. For the first time in its history the race was delayed for two days by a tropical storm. But for many it will probably be best remembered for the performance of *Nirvana* which cracked the course record by more than five hours when she finished in 62hrs,29mins, the first boat ever to have averaged more than ten knots.

The CCA, concerned about the fragility of modern rigging, and the narrow escape the fleet had had from being caught in the 1982 tropical storm, issued a strong statement about the conditions for racing in 1984.

'The hulls and rigging of some recent yachts designed to the current rules may be marginally acceptable for coastal racing where rescue facilities are readily available. The risk to the same yachts in ultimate offshore conditions beyond the range of assistance is unacceptable in the view of the race sponsors. Many masts and a few hulls have failed recently. In the absence of adoption and application of mast and hull scantlings by the rule-making bodies, the sponsoring clubs will withdraw the invitation of any skipper and any yacht that has lost a mast from 1

◄ Kialoa III, *Jim Kilroy's* replacement for Kialoa II. *The new yacht was just as successful and included amongst her many trophies was the 1978 WORC.*

June 1983, to the start of the Bermuda race on 22 June 1984. Any boat or captain who has lost a mast from the period of 18 June 1982 to 1 June 1983 will be required to establish that steps have been taken to correct the causes of rig failure in detail before being considered for eligibility for an invitation.'

This seemed as much a shot across the bows of the rule makers as of any unfortunate skipper who lost his mast. In the event only one yacht lost hers, though two others retired because of structural failures, in a race which after a perfect start was plagued by squalls, lumpy seas, headwinds of 30 knots or more, and then calms. The prizes were awarded as they had been in 1982 with the MHS prize, the Lighthouse Trophy, going to the Class B *Pamir*, while the IOR division was won by a Frers 51, *Retaliation*, from Class A.

Team racing and the Champagne Mumm World Cup
Although there was a decline in the number of teams competing in the Onion Patch series in 1978 – won by the Canadian province of Ontario team – it was the year when, with the inauguration of the Sardinia Cup and the Pan-Am Clipper Cup series, increasing interest began to be shown in team racing.

To foster this interest, Champagne Mumm introduced in 1981 a World Cup for an international team racing championship. Points were awarded to national three-boat teams taking part in the 1981 Southern Cross Cup, the 1982 Sardinia Cup, the 1983 SORC, and the 1983 Admiral's Cup, the idea being to encourage Admirals-Cup type racing on a worldwide basis. In the first series the winning country was the one with the most points after adding the scores of the best yacht sailing for each country in each of the events, the best three results being taken into account. Different yachts were allowed to represent a country at the different events, but the winning country had to field a team in at least three of the four events. The first winners were the Americans. The rules for the 1983-85 series are more or less the same except that a fifth event, the 1984 Pan-Am Clipper Cup, has been added to the other events.

Sardinia Cup
The Sardinia Cup is a four-race series based at Porto Cervo in Sardinia, a yachting centre which has been developed by the Aga Khan. The idea is that it should be the Admiral's Cup

of the Mediterranean, and in its first year in 1978 it attracted 12 national teams, including ones from Costa Rica and Monaco, both making their debut in big-time racing. The Americans, represented by *Acadia, Williwaw* and *Mandrake*, were the favourites to win, but it was the Italian team of two-tonners that scored the highest points. Their Peterson-designed *Yena* and *Didaquinta*, and the Kaufman-designed *Vanina II*, won all four races which included a 380-miler out to the Iles Porquerolles off Hyères and back. The number of races was increased to five in 1980, and it is now a well-established biennial event though the racing in 1982, won by the Italians, was disappointing.

However, the racing in 1984 was much better, with 16 three-boat teams involved in some highly competitive racing. The long offshore race to the Iles Porquerolles and back took place in heavy weather which gusted to Force 10 at times and caused many retirements, though towards the end of the race the wind died right away. The Irish *Nitissima* built up a huge lead early on and never lost it, but the series was won, by a mere half-point, by the highly successful West German team of *Pinta, Container*, and *Rubin*.

The Germans' win was the culmination of a two-year campaign which illustrates just how dedicated you have to be in the 1980s to come out on top. Willi Illbruck, the captain of the German Sardinia Cup team, had *Pinta* built in 1983. She was a sistership of Udo Schutz's *Container* and in the early part of 1983 they both tuned up together in readiness for that year's Admiral's Cup. *Pinta* was chosen as one of the German team for that event and Illbruck selected as the team captain, made sure his yacht was one of the first to arrive in the Solent for tuning. The Germans won, but instead of sitting back and enjoying his success Illbruck took *Pinta*, accompanied by *Container*, to the highly competitive SORC, one of the very few Europeans to do so. This paid dividends, for both *Pinta* and a new *Container* dominated the German trials for their Sardinia Cup team, and again Illbruck led them to victory.

Pan-Am Clipper Cup
The idea for the Pan-Am Clipper Cup series came from an Australian, Dick Gooch, who saw that without international competition to stimulate the Around Hawaii race it would die through lack of participation. Local yachtsmen had done the race several times and

were looking for something new.

Gooch approached Pan-Am who agreed to sponsor the five-race series, and both club and national teams were allowed to enter. For the first series there were two teams from Australia, the US, and New Zealand, and one from Japan, plus several club teams, amounting to 42 boats in all. By 1982 this number had nearly doubled and this second series showed how new yachting nations could enter top competitions and acquit themselves with honour. The Japanese have shown for some years that they have some fine yachtsmen but in the 1982 Pan-Am Clipper series they also showed they could produce a yacht and a crew that could beat the best. *Tobiume*, the winner of the King Kamehameha Trophy for the highest scoring individual yacht, was totally Japanese in design, construction, and equipment, and was the first Japanese yacht to win a major international event. The Pan-Am Cup itself was won by the American Blue team. The series highlighted the continuing controversy about sponsorship and the erosion of Rule 26 because the Australian team, sponsored by Dunhill, had called themselves Dunhill-Australia. Naming a yacht after a sponsor is banned, but naming a team after one is apparently not. As yachting writer Guy Gurney pointed out, if the idea caught on the Admiral's Cup series could be contested by teams from Suntory-Japan, Gauloises-France, Guinness-Ireland, and if the economic climate got much worse, perhaps Coca Cola-USA!

The 1984 series was dominated by the super-maxis, though none were included in any of the 11 teams sailing for the Pan-Am Clipper Cup. Several of them took part: *Boomerang, Kialoa IV, Sorcery, Condor of Bermuda, Nirvana, Ragamuffin* (ex-*Bumblebee IV*) and *Winterhawk* (ex-*Ceramco New Zealand*), The King Kamehameha Trophy went to *Boomerang* with *Kialoa IV* in second place, while the Pan-Am Clipper Cup went to the American White team.

Rule 26 problems

The sponsorship problem had been a thorn in the side of yachting authorities for some years already, and when there was a crackdown on those breaching Rule 26 in Australia and New Zealand in 1977, the result was often less than satisfactory.

A New Zealand boat, *Mr Jump*, was ordered to be renamed because its name was that of its knitwear sponsor's trade mark. So the skipper added an 'A' onto the end of the name - but made sure it was painted in a different and much more subdued colour. In Australia, one owner simply changed his yacht's name to her sail number, *B195*, while Jim Hardy, one of Australia's yachting establishment and now knighted for his services to the sport, was also obliged to change the name of his yacht. At first he simply covered it, but later changed it to *Nyamba*, an aboriginal word meaning something very rude indeed. It was all rather silly, but no one quite knew what to do about it. Then in March 1985 a new Rule 26 came into effect which acknowledged that sponsorship and advertising was now a necessary part of modern ocean racing though not all the restrictions were lifted.

Atlantic Round

Besides the Pan-Am Clipper Cup and Sardinian Cup series, the Atlantic Round was introduced in 1978 to both encourage new long-distance races and the participation by more American yachtsmen to European fixtures. Sponsored primarily by the main Scandinavian clubs, and by the CCA and the Royal

◀ ▶ *Two yachts which have won the World Ocean Racing Championships: the S & S-designed* Aura, *owned by Wally Stenhouse, won it in 1975; and Burt Keenan's* Acadia *in 1980.*

Bermuda Yacht Club, races were organised across the Atlantic to link with races from Gosport to Cuxhaven, Copenhagen to Helsinki, the Round Gotland, the Skaw, Cowes to Bayona, and some shorter Mediterranean events, before returning to the US via the Caribbean which, with events like Antigua Week and the 800-mile St Maartens Tradewind race – started in the early 1970s – was becoming more and more the favourite spot for those who liked ocean racing in warm and exotic climes.

Cape-Rio becomes Cape-Punte del Este

The first major race in 1979 was the Cape-Punte del Este which replaced the Cape-Rio which had not been held since 1976. The Brazilians had never been too keen on the race, if only because of its starting place, and a week before the start of the third race they had made it clear they did not want the race to end at Rio. They had eventually relented but in 1979 the race was given a new finish, at Punta del Este in Uruguay. Line honours were taken by a maxi boat called *Kwa Heri* but on corrected time the race went to a One Tonner, *Weet-bix*, designed by Angelo Lavranos and skippered by South African Bobby Bongers. The race was held again over the same course in 1982 when line honours were taken by *Rampant II* and the corrected prize by *Suidoos*.

Williwaw wins 1979 SORC

For the first time in several years the SORC reverted in 1979 to having an overall winner. The St Petersburg-Ft Lauderdale, now the most hotly contested long distance race in the US, was won by Ted Hood in one of his earlier *Robins*, now generously rerated under IOR MkIII(a), with the 1977 SORC and Fastnet winner, *Imp*, second, and Seymore Sinett's latest *Williwaw* third. However, *Williwaw* won the series, giving Sinett his third SORC title in four years (1975, 1978, and 1979). It was also the year which saw the first race to Cuba for 19 years, from Key West to Verdero; Ted Turner winning the Miami-Montego Bay race in *Tenacious*, the first man ever to win it thrice; the inauguration in Australia of the annually run Golden Fleece Around Tasmania race; and the phenomenal success of Frenchman Jean-Louis Fabry in winning the RORC Class III championships in his 1973-built *Revolution* having already won the Class II championships three times before his boat was rerated into Class III because of her age.

Fastnet and other tragedies

But 1979 will stick in everyone's memory as the year of the Fastnet tragedy when the biggest-ever fleet of 303 was caught in a vicious storm which led to 17 deaths. The race has already been covered extensively by books and articles and there is no need to repeat what happened here. But it was a grim reminder that in any sport where man comes into conflict with nature he does not always triumph. This book has not dwelt on the losses at sea while racing, but it is perhaps timely at this point to list just some of the tragedies that have taken place in conventional ocean racing, since the Second World War, if only as a reminder that the Fastnet was not unique.

In 1952, a fleet of 20 taking part in the 175-mile Wellington to Lyttleton race in New Zealand got caught in the notorious Cook Strait by a 50 knot southerly gale. Only one yacht, *Tawhiri*, finished and when a final count was made two yachts and ten men were missing. In 1964 a severe gale struck the Santander-La Trinité fleet. A French yacht, *Marie Galante*, tried to make for port but foundered in heavy seas near the Cordouan Bank. The skipper, entangled with the yacht's rigging, went down with his boat, and two members of the crew were drowned. Another competitor, *Aloa*, was swamped

while lying a-hull, and then capsized, drowning the skipper. A third yacht, *L'Esquirol*, was driven ashore but the crew survived. During a 75-mile Marseille Week race in 1977, a Mauric-designed One Tonner, *Airel*, was lost in heavy weather with all seven of her crew. Two years later there were two fatalities in the 1979 SORC, and in the 1980 TransTasman from Hobart to Auckland the New Zealand designer, Paul Whiting, was lost at sea along with his crew while racing his one-tonner, *Smackwater Jack*.

The latest losses occurred in 1983, all of them in the Antipodes. In Australia two Junior Offshore Group yachts were overwhelmed during an overnight race off Sydney and four men were drowned. Then some of the competitors in the eighth biennial Auckland-Suva race were cruising home after the race when a storm, not unexpected, struck and caused havoc. The New Zealand Clipper Cup representative, *Southern Raider*, radioed that she was sinking just north of Norfolk Island after being rolled three times by 40-foot waves. A search was started and a container ship was able to come alongside, but one of the crew was crushed when he missed his footing. The yacht sank soon afterwards. Other distress calls were received and answered, but the worst tragedy occurred when another competitor, *Lionheart*, attempted to enter Whangaroa Harbour in darkness and a 60-knot wind. She hit the huge Cone Rock situated four miles outside the harbour entrance and broke up immediately. All but one of the crew of eight was drowned.

SORC disqualifications

If the cut-throat quality of modern ocean racing obliges yachtsmen to sail their boats to their limits, and sometimes beyond them, it also imposes stresses which occasionally have the most undesirable consequences, as the 1981 SORC showed.

It was a series full of drama. To start with the St Petersburg-Ft Lauderdale, won by Ted Hood for the fourth time, was a tough race, so tough that six yachts were dismasted and two ran aground, luckily without loss of life. But the real drama came when five yachts were remeasured after protests lodged by competitors. Three were found to have insignificant variations from their certified ratings. But two, *Acadia* and *Williwaw*, both new

▼ *The Italian Peterson-designed* Dida Quinta *was top boat in the inaugural Sardinia Cup series.*

boats, which had finished second and third overall and had been chosen for the American Admiral's Cup team on the strength of their performance at the SORC, were found to have substantial variations. *Acadia* was found to rate 31.3 not 29.9, and *Williwaw* 38.1 not 37.1. Both were removed from the Admiral's Cup team and later an investigation was started.

But the upsets did not end there for when the series winner, *Louisiana Crude*, was sold to Sweden after the Circuit she was found to have hull irregularities which resulted in her IOR certificate being invalidated. This in turn stopped her from being rescored along with the other measured boats, and when a valid certificate was not presented by the deadline given by the SORC organisers she was dropped from the new list. The rescoring now put *Intuition* first, with *Acadia* dropping to third place and *Williwaw* to sixth. Subsequently, the inquiry instituted by the United States Racing Union into the reasons for the inaccurate ratings ruled that *Acadia* and *Williwaw* should be removed from the scoring altogether. Keenan was banned from sailing for one year and Sinett for two. Sinett took the matter to court, saying that his ban was tantamount to being called a cheat, but the judge ruled against him commenting that if he infringed the rules he must expect to be penalised, but that his ban did not condemn him as a cheat.

Summing up the USYRU's judgement against Keenan – which specifically absolved him from cheating – Bob Bavier said that it was his personal regret 'that there were people who *did* cheat in the last SORC and, in the absence of anyone protesting or of firm evidence, those individuals have gotten off scot free. It behoves all of us to help the Union to police the sport, and it is now crystal clear that it also behoves all yacht owners to know their responsibilites under the rules and to beware if they don't live up to them.'

Incredibly, when the 1982 SORC came round, the highly successful British Admiral's Cupper, *Victory*, third overall in the series and its Class C winner, was disqualified when it was found that her rating, too, was inaccurate, climbing from 33.1, her Admiral's Cup figure, to 34.5. This posed some awkward questions, not the least of them being the validity of Britain's win in the 1981 Admiral's Cup series. On rescoring, however, it was found that Britain would still have won by more than 70 points.

There was also a vital difference between the reason for *Victory*'s incorrect rating and that of *Williwaw* and *Acadia*. Almost the total rating difference between the American boats, as raced, and as remeasured, was because weight had been removed from them after measurement. In *Victory*'s case it was her out-of-the-water hull measurements which were badly awry, and the case resulted in the resignation of the RORC's rating secretary.

These incidents, along with the one in 1983 when three Australian yachtsmen were disqualified from racing for periods of up to two years for alleged measurement irregularities, must leave the average ocean racing enthusiast wondering about the adequacy of IOR and the ability of the authorities to cope with the problems it has caused. Equally, it is up to each yachtsman to abide scrupulously by the rules, however complicated they may be and to report any infractions of them.

▲ *Pinta, a Judel and Vrolijk 42-footer, which led the German team to victory in the 1983 Admiral's Cup and 1984 Sardinia Cup.*

Without the full co-operation of its participants no sport can flourish satisfactorily.

New designers
After all the drama in 1981 and 1982 the next SORCs passed off without incident. *Scarlett O'Hara* won the series in 1983 and *Diva*, the top Admiral's Cupper in 1983, in 1984. Apart from the increasing competition, the main difference between the SORC in the 1970s and the 1980s has been the enormous increase in the number of top designers. In 1980, for instance, six different ones gained top honours in the six classes; and six more won second or third places in those classes. The dominance of Sparkman & Stephens, so marked right up to 1975, was definitely on the wane after that year as young men like Ron Holland and Bruce Farr from New Zea-

land, German Frers Jr from Argentina, Ben Lexcen and Scott Kaufman from Australia, Doug Peterson, Gary Mull and Britton Chance from the US, and Ed Dubois from Britain, began to dominate the scene. By 1983, 25 different designers were represented at the SORC, German Frers and Doug Peterson being the most prolific with 14 designs each.

The future

It is hard to guess how the traditional side of the sport will develop. Probably the polarisation between the Grand Prix circuit yachtsmen and the rest of the ocean racing fraternity will continue to widen and will have to be accepted by the authorities in such matters as Rule 26 and the banning of exotic materials.

As for new fixtures, there certainly seems to be no lack of one-off events and new ones are being inaugurated all the time. In 1981, for instance, there was a one-off race from Fremantle to Bali, won by *Siska II* in six and a half days while 1982 saw a race from Sydney to Rio, won by *Buccaneer* in 39d,7hrs,34mins, and a French organised race, a 5000-miler from La Rochelle to Gulfport, Mississippi, won by an innovative multihull design, *Charente Maritime*. Then in 1983 there were races from Salvador to Rio, and from Fremantle to Dampier. In 1984 two new major ocean races were inaugurated in Australia alone: a 1600 miler from Sydney to Vanuatu and a 620 miler from Esperance to Fremantle. The 1986 Sydney-Hobart will be linked to this latter event by a race from Hobart across the Great Australian Bight to Esperance, enabling the top ocean racers to race all the way to Fremantle to arrive for the America's Cup races early in 1987. There is also now a Round-Spain race and at the end of 1984 Spain's Deep Sea Navigators' Association organised a race from Benalmadena on the Costa del Sol to Santa Domingo to celebrate the voyage of Christopher Columbus.

These one-off fixtures seem to be increasingly popular and will, perhaps, inhibit the inauguration of any new regularly run

◄   *Tobiume was the first Japanese yacht to win a major prize when she topped the individual scoring list in the 1982 Pan-Am Clipper Cup series.*

▶   *Bob Bell's super-maxi, Condor of Bermuda II, which established a new course record for the Fastnet in 1983.*

events, though a new biennial started by the RORC, to Antigua via Gran Canaria, has had a successful start.

Perhaps, too, there will be increased interest in those more unusual races, like the Cobb Sea Mount race run during the early 1970s off Canada's west coast, where a submerged mountain was used as a turning mark; or the British Three Peaks race in which separate crews use their skills at mountain climbing and sailing; or the Worrell 1000-mile Hobie 16 race from Ft Lauderdale to Virginia Beach in which shore-based teams keep the small multihulls flying down the coast between eight mandatory check points; or the French *Tour de France à Voile*, where one-design yachts are raced by two teams of crews in stages between Dunkirk and Menton, entries being transported between the Atlantic and the Mediterranean by lorry.

However it develops, and in whichever direction, the traditional side of ocean racing has the enthusiasm and support of many thousands worldwide, and always will have, so long as men and women enjoy sailing in open water.

◄ *Rolly Tasker's 72-foot maxi, Siska II, was an Australian entry in the Parmelia race. She had a fine racing record in Australian waters which included line honours in the one-off Fremantle-Bali race.*

► *Seventeen yachtsmen were lost in the storm which hit the 1979 Fastnet. It could have been more had it not been for the bravery and resourcefulness of the Royal Navy's Air-Sea rescue helicopters.*

Around Alone

FOR MANY OCEAN racing men recession, inflation, sponsorship and the IOR brought about a revolution in style and attitude during the early 1970s – and a good deal of disillusionment.

'Yacht profiles have gone from low and slim to high and fat,' wrote Jeff Hammond in 1974, 'rigs are higher and keels are lower, mains are smaller and headsails bigger, new sails have evolved each year, fifteen different headstay systems are now available, whereas three years ago there were two, and decks have gone from the place where people sat to a complex sheeting platform equipped with as much track as the Penn Central switching yard. The success of boat designs is now measured in terms of weeks instead of years. One major yachting personality has suggested making boats out of foam and throwing them away after each race. Since 1970 not only has the rule and the shape of boats changed, but the level of competition has changed, the approach has changed, and, most important – the basic concept of ocean racing has changed. For many people ocean racing, as they knew it all their lives, is dead.'

Two years later designer Charley Morgan said bluntly: 'I don't care too much about ocean racing any more. Modern ocean racing is too damn expensive . . . a lot of the charm is out of the sport', and in 1978 Bruce Farr, the brilliant New Zealand designer who had created some of the fastest light displacement ocean racers in the world, turned to designing cruising boats. He was, he said, tired of the 'torment' of the endless changing of ratings and rules by the chairbound commodores of international yachting, and he was tired of designing winning boats for clients who considered their yachts obsolete a couple of years later. But he has now returned to designing ocean racers and has set up an office in Philadelphia.

In many ways ocean racing was merely conforming to the style demanded by a rigorous economic climate and the demands of sponsors and the media. Golf and tennis had gone that way already and there was no reason why ocean racing should not follow. The exciting and newsworthy short-handed events, the crewed inter-ocean races that had developed from Chichester's circumnavigation and the single-handed round-the-world race were, in many ways, reflecting the increasing commercialism of ocean racing.

The first Whitbread Round-the-World race 1973

The first of these latter events was a crewed round-the-world race sponsored by a British brewery company, Whitbread, which started on the 8th September 1973. The race was to follow the course of the old clipper ships, much as Chichester had done, but this time it was to be done in four legs: Portsmouth-Cape Town (6900 miles), Cape Town-Sydney (6500 miles), Sydney-Rio (8370 miles), and Rio-Portsmouth (5560 miles).

This was quite a different challenge to even the longest traditional ocean race, and one which demanded a very special approach and a special kind of yacht.

As it happened, the changeover to the IOR had imposed a maximum rating limit instead of the old overall length restriction, and this was all the encouragement yachtsmen and their sponsors needed to build large yachts for this exciting new event. Entries were received from France, Italy, Germany, Mexico, Britain and Poland, and totalled seventeen yachts.

Britain's main hope lay with a new 'maxi', as they came to be called, named *Great Britain II*. Constructed in GRP and 78 feet long, she was designed by Alan Gurney and was a development of his remarkably fast 'super dinghy' *Windward Passage*. She was skippered by Chay Blyth and crewed by tough paratroopers. Two other British yachts were also in the running: *Second Life*, a sister ship of Knox-Johnston's successful *Ocean Spirit*, and a new aluminium ketch, *Burton Cutter*, sailed by Leslie Williams. Challenging these contenders was Eric Tabarly sailing *Pen Duick VI*, a black aluminium ketch ballasted with wasted uranium and with titanium rigging. This space-age craft looked extremely fast and as wasted uranium had almost twice the specific gravity of lead she had a distinct advantage over her rivals.*

Both *GBII* and *Burton Cutter* started well, the former averaging 170 miles a day during the first week and during one seven-day period the latter covered 1780 miles. Though *Burton Cutter* was the first to arrive at Cape Town she was leaking badly and was in any case not sufficiently tuned for such a long race. She dropped out of the second and third legs and rejoined for the final one.

Another serious rival to *GBII* was Tabarly in *Pen Duick VI*, but he too had trouble

*wasted uranium was later banned as ballast

▲ *Chay Blyth at the helm of* GBII *during the inaugural Whitbread Round-the-World race.*

early on when he lost his mast and had to put into Rio to wait for a replacement. The winner of the first leg, on corrected time, was a British entry, *Adventure*, which had been entered by the Royal Navy.

The storms and high seas of the Southern Ocean made the second leg far tougher. *Adventure* reported 50-foot waves 'continual winds of gale force or more, blizzards of driving snow, and driving freezing rain' and in one incident the helmsman on *British Soldier* was thrown so violently against the steel wheel that it was bent. Under such appalling conditions it was not surprising that some of the entries ran into serious trouble. 1800 miles west of Tasmania *Sayula II*, the Mexican entry, was picked up by a freak wave and almost capsized. The chaos was indescribable, but only one man was injured. Luckily, those on deck had their safety harnesses attached. Two were washed overboard but managed to get back aboard.

Not so lucky was the skipper of the French yacht, *33-Export*, Dominic Guillet. He and two others were washed overboard when the guardrail collapsed. The wire to which Guillet's harness was attached broke and he was lost. The other crew were rescued. More or less the same thing happened to Paul Waterhouse, a British crewman on board *Tauranga* and he, too, was lost. Gear damage was extensive. One of the two Polish entries, *Otago*, lost part of her mast; Chay Blyth aboard *GBII* lost his mizzenmast and one of his crew broke an arm; and *Grand Louis* broke her main boom.

Tabarly, however, was having a miraculous race. Averaging around 10 knots he pushed his boat to the limit to catch up on lost time. He arrived first in Sydney, though on corrected time the second leg was won by *Sayula II*, with *Grand Louis* second and another French boat, *Kriter*, third.

Tabarly knew he would have to continue racing at the same breakneck speed if he was to stand any chance of winning but his hopes were dashed when, soon after starting the third leg, he was dismasted again and this time he was forced to retire. *GBII* surged into the lead but her success was soon marred. While running at 12 knots or so a man was lost overboard, and could not be recovered. It was a grim moment, but they raced on and finished the leg first, though *Sayula II* still held the lead on corrected time.

The start for the fourth and final leg was staggered so that all the yachts could arrive at the finish more or less at the same time, but several were delayed by calms. *GBII* was first to finish again, completing her circumnavigation in 144d,10hrs,31mins, easily beating the average times of the clipper ships that had sailed the same route the previous century.

But Blyth could not save his time on the Mexican yacht, *Sayula II*, and when she sailed in, sixth, she was declared the winner.

This inaugural round-the-world race proved that yachts of modern construction could withstand the tremendous pressures of being raced hard over great distances and through some of the roughest waters in the world. Despite the sad loss of life, it spawned a whole series of new long-distance events which were commercially sponsored and ably publicised. The Whitbread race itself has become a quadrennial fixture, and has grown in numbers and prestige.

The Whitbread race was not the only event to deviate designers from turning out yachts that best exploited the IOR, for 1974 saw the appearance of several new yachts specially designed and constructed for the double- and single-handed races scheduled over the following years.

Round Britain race 1974
The first of these fixtures, the third Round-Britain race, attracted 61 starters, and included some new multihulls like *FT*, *Gulf Streamer*, and the huge 70-foot catamaran, *British Oxygen*, designed by Macalpine-Downie. Built for Robin Knox-Johnston and Gerry Boxall, this monster notched 26 knots on some of her pre-race trials and beat the second boat home, *Three Cheers*, by over an hour to set up a new record for the course of 10d,4hrs,26mins. Though the race was won on handicap by a monohull, *Chough of Parkstone*, it was really an overwhelming victory for the multihulls. The largest yacht in the race, *Burton Cutter*, was the first monohull to finish but could manage no better than sixth place. Phil Weld finished third in *Gulf Streamer*, Alain Colas was fourth in *Manureva* (ex-*Pen Duick IV*,) and Nick Keig fifth in *Three Legs of Mann*.

Popularity of multihulls
Despite the innate superiority of multihulls in single- and short-handed racing they never seem to have broken through in the traditional side of the sport when raced over the courses of well-established classics. Only 11 took part in the 1973 Multihull Bermuda race and this dropped to seven two years later. The Multihull Transpac was equally poorly patronised, with five in the 1972 race and six in 1974 and when the Multihull Offshore Cruising and Racing Association (MOCRA) ran the first multihull Fastnet in 1979 only one trimaran, *Buck's Fizz*, started. She was caught in the storm and lost with all her crew.

Compared with the same races held for monohulls these numbers were derisory. Even when a Whitbread multihull inter-ocean race was organised by the RNSA to coincide with the last leg of the 1975 Atlantic Triangle event, only one entry, Chay Blyth, turned up and the fixture was cancelled.

Nevertheless, the superiority of the multihull in less orthodox ocean racing was soon to become unquestioned and on the traditional side it continued to have its adherents, with the French holding the largest multihull regatta in the world each year in the Mediterranean. In Australia, too, multihull races were popular, especially in Queensland

◀ *The Mexican* Sayula II, *winner of the first Whitbread Round-the-World race on corrected time.*

where the Brisbane-Gladstone multihull race became well established. In 1976, the Queensland Multihull Yacht Club inaugurated a multihull offshore series which, by 1980, had been expanded to five races, including one of 530 miles from Sydney to Mooloolaba. However, doubts continued to be expressed about the seaworthiness of multihulls and in 1982 the Australian Yachting Federation placed a virtual ban on them, as well as on solo racing, while an urgent review on safety requirements was carried out.

▶ *The huge catamaran,* British Oxygen, *which Robin Knox-Johnston entered for the 1974 Round, Britain race. She was later renamed* Kriter III *and sank during the 1976 OSTAR.*

▼ *FT, a 35-foot trimaran, was designed by Derek Kelsall for the 1974 Round-Britain race. She finished 22nd on corrected time.*

The Azores and back 1975

Not many multihulls joined the single-handed race from Falmouth to the Azores and Back (AZAB), one of the several new long-distance events in 1975 really to establish the trend towards very much longer races. Even so, they dominated the event with *Three Legs of Mann*, sailed by Nick Keig, winning both legs by a convincing margin. Second place was taken by the French trimaran, *Capitaine Cook*, skippered by Eugene Riguedel. Keig travelled so fast that he beat the race committee to the finish of the first leg and when the Multihull Offshore Cruising and Racing Association (MOCRA) ran their own race later that year over the same course, the line honours winner, *Triple Arrow*, took almost twice Keig's time.

But Keig's victory did little to reassure those who questioned the seaworthiness of multihulls, for the starboard float of his tri nearly broke away from the hull during the second leg, and at one point he actually abandoned the race for a time as he feared it would shear off. However, he changed his mind and nursed his boat home to a remarkable win. 'I was convinced all the way home that she would come apart.' Keig confessed after the race.

The 2500-mile event attracted 49 entries, which were restricted to 38 feet overall and had to complete a 300-mile qualifying cruise. Although the weather dished out its fair share of storms only a few boats retired, and the event proved a satisfactory introduction to long-distance solo racing for Clare Francis who soon became well known when she competed in the 1976 OSTAR and the second Whitbread race.

Japanese Pacific races 1975

On the other side of the world the Nippon Ocean Racing Club extended its activities by organising two long-distance races to Okinawa. The crewed event — a 3000-miler from Hawaii which was won by Jake Wood's *Sorcery* which also took line honours in 22d,10hrs,46mins — was a one-off affair, but the solo race from San Francisco had been held in 1969 and was run again in 1981. Nine entries took part in the 1975 fixture. They included the German Klaus Hebner, who'd taken part in the 1969 race, Jean-Marie Vidal from France, and David White from the US. But the winner out of the fleet of six was Hiroshi Totsuka in his 35-foot sloop, *Wing of Yamaha*, who covered the 6500 mile course

in 41d,14hrs,28mins. He was the first Japanese to win such a major event, though in 1970 Hiroaki Yoshida, sailing *Chita III*, had won the China Sea race.

The Atlantic Triangle race 1975

During the same month, November, the ambitious Atlantic Triangle race started from St Malo, with the 14 entries racing for the *Coupe Gauloises*. The first leg to Cape Town, with a compulsory stop at Tenerife, was won by Tabarly sailing *Pen Duick VI*. The French Admiral's Cupper, *Katsou*, was second and the Italian Admiral's Cupper, *Guia III* (ex-*Ginkgo*), third. Also racing were seven other French yachts, two other Italians, and one each from Britain, Belgium, and South Africa. At Cape Town they joined in the Cape-Rio race — which that year attracted a huge fleet of 128-and was won by the Costa Rican diplomat, Mottola Balestra, sailing his Carter-designed one tonner, *Chica Tica* — before completing the final leg to Portsmouth from Rio, which included another compulsory stop at the Cape Verde Islands. This too, was won by Tabarly. *Guia III* was sunk by a whale.

The *Financial Times* clipper race 1975

At 16 000 miles, a race like the Atlantic Triangle would normally have been the main attraction of the year. But the really long-distance events now held considerable attraction for sponsors, organisers, and that elite group of yachtsmen for whom ocean racing was not just a sport but a way of life and a means of earning a living; and so when a British newspaper, *The Financial Times*, declared its intention of financing another race around the world the organisers received 200 enquiries from 19 countries.

The idea behind the race was more or less the same as Sir Francis Chichester's when he raced against the clock in his 1966/67 circumnavigation to try to beat the times set by the clippers the previous century. But while Chichester had been attempting to beat the best *average* time — 100 days for each leg by his reckoning — the yachts in the *Financial Times* Clipper race were intent on cracking the *record* time of 69 days for each of the two legs, which had been established by the clipper ship, *Patriarch* in 1869/70. And, unlike the Whitbread contest, there were to be only two legs, UK-Sydney and Sydney-UK, making it even more ambitious than the earlier round-the-world-race. Though the initial re-

sponse had been strong only four yachts started in the Thames estuary on 31st August 1975.

The British entry was *GBII*, which had finished first in the 1973 Whitbread race — just six days short of *Patriarch's* record run. The French entry was *Kriter II* (ex-*Burton Cutter*) which had done well in the first leg of the 1973 race before having to drop out. The Dutch entry was a Trewes 56 steel production ketch called *The Great Escape*, and the long name of the Italian entry, *CSeRB II Busnelli*, stood for the *Cento Studi e Ricerche Busnelli* which had sponsored a smaller yacht in the 1973 event. The Australians also had an entry, the 83-foot ketch, *Anaconda II*, owned by Adelaide businessman, Josko Grubic. But she could not reach the start in time and only took part in the second leg.

The Dutch and Italian entries were not serious contenders, but the natural rivalry between the British and the French yachts saved the event from failure, and resulted in extremely close racing on the first leg. The two boats sighted each other twice, once three days out, the other time near the equator — and only 30 miles separated them when they reached Sydney. *GBII* got a lift in the South Atlantic when her radio operator picked up a signal that the South Atlantic high was moving east instead of west as expected. This enabled her to cut about 250 miles off her planned course, but *Kriter II* kept to the traditional square rigger route and fell about 240 miles behind *GBII*. However, the British boat was hit by a gale just before entering Bass Strait and was then becalmed. *Kriter II* almost caught up, but then *GBII* found some wind and surged ahead. Though she was becalmed once more, she managed to cross the line in Sydney six and a half hours ahead of the French boat. Both boats finished within 69 days and *Kriter II* won the leg on corrected time.

For the second leg Olivier de Kersauson, the skipper of *Kriter II*, kept the same crew, but *GBII*, crewed by the Services, changed hers. For the first few days it looked as if the second leg was going to be as close as the first. Five days out of Sydney, the two yachts were still within sight of one another, but then *Kriter II* lost her rudder. *GBII* stood by her for two hours but then pressed on for the Horn while the French boat returned to Sydney for repairs. She lost any chance of beating *GBII*, but after 27 days she started again and her French crew drove her so hard that she had cut five days off *GBII's* time at the Horn. Later, she was caught in the doldrums and was unable to make up any more time. The British yacht crossed the finishing line at Dover a clear winner. She accomplished the circumnavigation in the record time of 134d,5hrs,51mins, and finished on 25th February 1976. *The Great Escape* finished the same day as *Kriter II*, on the 25th March, and the Italian entry on 3rd April having spent four days at the Falkland Islands for repairs. *Anaconda II* showed her speed by finishing on 8th March, but she was an untried boat and had not been sufficiently tuned to reach her full potential.

OSTAR 1976

The clipper race had shown that though there was great interest in this kind of event, the numbers able to compete were limited if races were held too frequently. This, however, did not apply to the double- and single-handed races that now began to proliferate. The main event of 1976 was the OSTAR which attracted a huge fleet of 125. But two French long-distance events, the inaugural race from La Trinité-sur-mer to the Azores and back, and the seventh *Course en Solitaire de L'Aurore* (now *Le Figaro*), were also held in 1976, and reflected the enormous increase in interest in this form of ocean racing.

The OSTAR was now so dominated by the French that it began to be more commonly known as *Le Transat* and it had grown from a private race amongst five boats in 1960, to a multinational dollar spectacular, attracting huge crowds at the start and correspondingly huge problems for the organisers. To cope with this vast array, the fleet was split into three divisions: the unlimited division raced for the Pen Duick Trophy; those between 46 feet LWL and 65 feet LOA raced for the Gipsy Moth Trophy; and those between 28 feet LWL and 38 feet LOA raced for the Jester Trophy.

There was increasing controversy concerning the safety of the race and the size of some of the entries – particularly the vast 236-foot four-masted schooner, *Club Méditerranée*, sailed by Alain Colas. Many yachting journalists in Europe and the US condemned the race as unseamanlike. But the organisers, while hinting at changes for the 1980 race, refused to make any last minute restrictions on the grounds that limiting size or numbers at such a late stage would be unfair to those who had worked so hard to

qualify and raise the necessary finance.

Led by Alain Colas and the veteran Tabarly in *Pen Duick VI*, the French challenge was especially strong. Jean-Yves Terlain had entered again, this time sailing the large trimaran, *British Oxygen*, now renamed *Kriter III*, while his old yacht, *Vendredi Treize*, now called *ITT Oceanic*, was being raced by a fellow countryman, Yvon Fauconnier. Altogether, nearly 30 Frenchmen and women were taking part.

The British and the Americans were also strongly represented especially amongst the multihulls. The Americans included Tom Grossman, who had bought *Cap 33* after the

1972 race, and Mike Kane in his 62-foot trimaran, *Spirit of America*. But their most experienced competitor, Phil Weld, was not at the start as his tri, *Gulf Streamer*, had capsized in mid-Atlantic while crossing to England. Britain's hopes lay mainly with Mike McMullen, who had bought Tom Follet's trimaran and renamed her *Three Cheers*, and David Palmer in his 35-foot trimaran, *FT*.

Though those three countries dominated the race, there were entries from many

others including Canada, Poland, Italy, Belgium, Australia, Germany, Switzerland, New Zealand, Sweden, Holland, Czechoslovakia, and Spain, and many of the yachts were specially designed. Gerard Dijkstra's *Bestevaer*, a Dutch entry, had refinements such as a gimballed head to give the skipper greater comfort!

It was a hard race that year, and those who took the Great Circle route encountered no less than seven separate gales, some of them storm force. Fifty-one boats retired, or were sunk, or had not arrived when the 50-day time limit expired. There were two tragic incidents. Mike McMullen disappeared with his boat *Three Cheers*, and was presumed drowned; and Mike Flanagan, a Briton living in America, was not aboard his yacht *Galloping Gael* when she was found drifting in mid-Atlantic.

Broken steering was the most common cause for retirements, but there was plenty of

◄ *The Australian entry for the Financial Times clipper race,* Anaconda II, *seen here on trials off her home port, Adelaide.*

▼ *The start of the 1976 OSTAR.*

other damage. Three yachts were dismasted; one caught fire and sank; two, including *Kriter III*, broke up and sank; three were damaged by collisions, one of them later sinking; and there were numerous structural and rig failures, as well as injury and sickness amongst the skippers. And the list of damage did not confine itself to those that retired. *Club Méditerranée* had problems with her rigging and Colas was forced to put into St John's, Newfoundland for repairs. Tabarly's self-steering gear was smashed after four days at sea, and he had to spend the rest of the time at the helm. At one point he became so exhausted that he turned his boat off the wind 'to give myself time to rest and think.' For a day he brooded on his situation before eventually turning west again, just in time to beat his nearest rival, Colas, into Newport by seven hours, thereby winning the race for the second time.

Although Colas finished second in his huge vessel, it was later found that he had accepted help when leaving St John's. He was given a 58-hour penalty for this infringement, and second place went to the Canadian, Mike Birch, who had sailed his tiny tri, *Third Turtle*, into third place. He also won the Jester class,

the multihull handicap prize, and the Lizzie McMullen Trophy for the first multihull to finish. Fourth to finish, but awarded third prize, was the Polish yacht, *Spaniel*, sailed by Kazimeirz Jaworski. The winner of the Gipsy Moth Trophy was Jean-Claude Parisis in *Petrouchka* who finished sixth. High up in the place list was *Robertson's Golly* skippered by a pretty, fragile looking English girl, Clare Francis. By finishing 13th in 29 days she broke the record set by Marie-Claude Fauroux in 1972, and became an immediate favourite of the British public.

French single-handed races 1976
Along with four other OSTAR competitors – Guy Cornou, Bernard Pallard, Gustav Versluys and Gilles Vaton – Clare Francis also took part in the 1976 *Course en Solitaire de L'Aurore*, a race which is always sailed in half-tonners. Although this was the seventh time the race had been run it remained small until 1976 when the number of entries doubled to 27 single-handed sailors. A fourth leg was also added to the course, though this did not increase its total length.

The first leg was from the start at Perros-Guirec to La Baule and back; the

second from Perros-Guirec to Falmouth; the third from Falmouth to Kinsale; and the fourth from Kinsale back to Port du Crouesty. It was won for the second time by Guy Cornou in *Capitaine Cook*, with Clare Francis finishing well down the list.

The inaugural race from Trinité-sur-mer to the Azores and back, won by *Izenah* in 16d,11hrs,7mins, was a smaller affair with only 15 entries, but it was started at the right time and soon developed into a biennial fixture though it rarely attracts foreign entries.

The British Islands race 1976

Another new race in 1976, which did not fit easily into either the single- or double-handed racing nor the traditional and regularly run fixtures, was the RORC-organised British Islands race. This was held in response to the growing demand for a fully-crewed race over a long distance which did not take up too much time. The answer was a race which finished at the starting point, in this case Southsea. Some crews were eager for a non-stop race while others preferred the compulsory stops which governed the Round-Britain event so it was decided to split the event into two divisions. Division I was for those who wanted to race the 1860 miles non-stop with a minimum crew of five, while Division II was for those who wanted to stop, and they had to have a minimum crew of four. The stops for them were Crookhaven, Stornaway, and Blyth, and yachts were allowed to join in one or more of the legs even if they did not want to complete the whole race.

Fourteen entries started in Division I and nine in Division II, rather less than expected. Nevertheless, both races were hotly contested, with *More Opposition*, skippered by Robin Knox-Johnston, taking line honours in 10d,23hrs,15mins in the non-stop event, though he was pushed into third place on corrected time behind *Electron II* and *Fly-catcher*. In Division II, Rodney Hill's *Morningtown* won the first three legs to finish first, with *Contessa Catherine*, the winner of the first leg, second, and *Hindostan* third.

Double-handed around North Island New Zealand 1977

Up until 1976, most of the less orthodox ocean races had emanated from Europe –

◄ *Mike McMullen, seen here at the helm of his trimaran,* Three Cheers, *was lost at sea during the 1976 OSTAR.*

the solo Transpac and TransTasman events being notable exceptions — but in 1977 this type of racing began to spread further afield. In New Zealand, the Devonport Yacht Club sponsored a double-handed race around North Island which was divided into four legs. Started by the Duke of Edinburgh, it was raced anti-clockwise and followed the coastal route of Captain Cook's third and final voyage. Thirty-eight yachts entered for this 1250-mile race and it included some of New Zealand's best yachtsmen. Peter Blake, who had sailed with Leslie Williams in the first Whitbread race and in the Round Britain, was largely responsible for the event being organised and he, along with Graham Eder, entered the 1975 New Zealand Admiral's Cupper, Gerontius.

The first leg was so slow that it took Gerontius, the first boat home, two and a half days to complete the 160 miles from Devonport to Mangonui. Five crews got so fed up with being becalmed that they rafted their yachts together in the middle of Cook Strait and had dinner!

After a compulsory 48-hour stop Gerontius retained the lead during the remaining legs to Queen Charlotte Sound, Gisborne and Devonport, and completed the course in an elapsed time of 209hrs,54mins. But on corrected time the winner was the smallest boat in the race, Marimba, sailed by

▶ Clare Francis steered Robertson's Golly into 13th place in the 1976 OSTAR and became an immediate favourite with the British public.

▼ The Farr-designed, New Zealand Admiral's Cupper, Gerontius, sailed by Peter Blake and Graham Eder, took line honours in the inaugural double-handed race around the North Island.

Eric Wing and Dave Anderson, perfect reaching and running conditions during the last three legs having enabled the smaller entries to keep near the leaders. The race was declared a success and is now a triennial fixture.

The Bermuda One-Two 1977

In the US single- and double-handed racing had not caught on as they had done in Europe, but when American yachtsmen decided to enter this field they did so with a unique event.

Called the Bermuda One-Two, it involved sailing single-handed to Bermuda from Newport, and then back again with an additional crew member. This interesting combination had already been tried out between Galveston and St Petersburg, and the idea of a similar East Coast event drew 26 entries. A 1976 OSTAR competitor, Francis Stokes, made an amazingly quick passage in his Valiant 40, *Mooneshine*, and finished in 95hrs,27mins, one of the fastest on record for any yacht. At Bermuda he picked up another 1976 OSTAR competitor, Everett Smith, to act as his crewman and was first again on the return leg. Some of his rivals, however, did not have the same luck. One skipper was rescued from his yacht in a state of total mental collapse, while another ran his yacht onto a reef off Bermuda because the Kindley beacon had been moved without warning. However, it proved a sufficiently successful event to become a permanent fixture.

Inaugural Mini-Transat 1977

But again it was Europe that provided the main events on the less orthodox side of the sport. The most unusual was the inaugural biennial Mini-Transat, or B-Star as the first race was called. Originally conceived as a 'one-off', the idea of a poor man's OSTAR had first been aired by Bob Salmon the previous year. It was his contention that OSTAR, as with most traditional ocean racing, had got beyond the means of ordinary yachtsmen. He therefore proposed a single-handed Transatlantic race for yachts not exceeding 21 feet 3 inches LOA, with restrictions on the number of sails and electronic gadgetry.

The idea was enthusiastically taken up by yachtsmen all over Europe. The French had the largest number of entries with 13, but there were also six British, two Belgian, one German, one Yugoslav, one Pole, and one American.

The race was to be in two legs, a non-competitive one from Penzance to Tenerife in the Canaries, acting as a kind of qualifying cruise; and then the race itself, from Tenerife to Antigua, a distance of about 3000 miles.

Most of the yachts at the start line on 8th October were production boats, though some, like the Polish *Spanielek*, sailed by Kazimeirz Jaworski, and the Belgian *Nam*, had been specially built for the race. A few had had to be modified to comply with the length restriction.

Although the start was in light airs a series of storms soon battered the fleet and several were forced to return or to put into port elsewhere. One entry, Maurice Fouquet, sailing his home-built stainless steel yacht, *Nael*, simply disappeared, as did Patrick van God, a Belgian entry. A Frenchman, Daniel Gilard, sailing his Serpentaire-designed *Petit Dauphin*, was the first to arrive followed by the sole American entry, David Stookey, in his junk-rigged *Griffin*.

The trade winds were light and well to the south for the second leg. These conditions suited Gilard and during the first ten days he established a commanding lead. Once the winds increased his rivals began to catch up but Gilard crossed the line first having taken 22d,18hrs,10mins for the crossing. The Spanish entry, *Canamin*, arrived 1hr,25mins later but as the skippers had been changed during the first leg she did not qualify for an award. Bob Salmon in *Anderson Affair*

was also disqualified because he had been assisted after grounding at Antigua. Second place was awarded to *Spanielek*, and third to another French entrant, Halvard Mabire in *Haro*.

The second Whitbread Round-the-World race 1977

The big trans-oceanic event of the year, though, was the second Whitbread Round-the-World race which this time attracted 15 starters: six British, five French, two Dutch, a Swiss, an Italian, and, for the first time, an entry from the European Economic Community (EEC) – which also put together a team for the Southern Cross series later in the year. The competition was stronger than in the earlier race and duels were fought right up to the finishing lines at the end of each leg. *King's Legend*, a British entry, actually crossed tacks with the eventual winner, *Flyer*, from Holland, five days from Cape Town – after 6000 miles of hard racing!

GBII was racing again as was *Adventure* and the Italian *B & B Italia*, and Clare Francis was skippering one of the several production boats in the event, a Swan 65 called *ADC Accutrac*. But interest centred on the brand new 'super maxi', *Heath's Condor*, sailed on alternative legs by Leslie Williams and Robin Knox-Johnston, and Tabarly racing in *Pen Duick VI*.

▼ *The French have dominated the Mini-Transat from its inception. Here is the winner of the 1977 inaugural race,* Petit Dauphin, *sailed by Frenchman Daniel Gilard.*

The 'maxis' in the previous race had all been ketch rigged, but *Heath's Condor* had a single stick. One hundred feet from truck to keel, this massive spar created quite a weight problem for the designers until it was decided to use a mixture of carbon fibre and glass fibre-reinforced plastic. Carbon fibre was deemed an 'exotic' material, attracting a 3 per cent rating penalty, but tests showed that the mast's strength would be dramatically increased, windage reduced and about 400 pounds saved. Sadly, the new material did not fulfil its promise and the mast broke on the first leg. However, a new aluminium mast was flown out and nine days after the accident, *Heath's Condor* was back in the race. The breakage cost her any chance of doing well overall – in fact, she finished last on corrected time – but she took line honours on the

second and fourth legs, and finished third behind *Pen Duick VI* and *GBII* on the third.

Tabarly also ran into trouble with an 'exotic' material, in this case the spent uranium in his keel. During the first WRTWR the Offshore Rating Council (ORC), the body that controlled IOR, had amended the rating rule to exclude any material from a yacht's keel which exceeded the density of lead. Tabarly did not finish the race so the question of his eligibility to sail in it was left undecided, but during the next two years he competed in several RORC events, including the Fastnet, and was considered eligible by the RORC to do so. This anomaly was allowed to continue until 1977 when Tabarly was excluded by the Transpac race committee, and when he arrived in Auckland to compete in the final two legs of the second WRTWR the organisers

refused to confirm his eligibility to enter. However, he was allowed to race, winning the third leg on elapsed time. Still his eligibility was not confirmed and this situation created something of an outcry in the French press. Eventually, on 6th February, the race committee ruled that Tabarly was ineligible, a decision he accepted with courtesy. He was invited to sail the final leg with the rest of the fleet. At first he refused, saying that the lack of competition did not make it sufficiently interesting, but later relented and finished second behind *Heath's Condor*.

While this controversy was raging the Dutch boat *Flyer*, owned and sailed by millionaire Cornelis van Rietschoten, was establishing herself as the overall winner. On the first leg this 65-foot S & S-designed ketch – which already that year had taken line honours and the overall prize in the Atlantic race – did remarkably well, covering the 6650 miles to Cape Town in 38d,21hrs,30mins, finishing first on elapsed as well as corrected time. On the long 7400-mile leg to Auckland she kept her spinnaker flying for 30 days, but broke her main boom and finished fourth on corrected time. The third leg, predictably, produced the toughest weather and four days after rounding the Horn, *Flyer* was caught in a 70-knot, 30-degree wind shift that knocked her down and had water lapping at the main hatch. 'What did you do yourself, personally, in such a frightful storm?' someone asked van Rietschoten after *Flyer* reached Rio. 'Crossword puzzles,' the Dutchman replied.

She completed the entire course in 136d,5hrs,48mins, and beat *King's Legend*, the second boat, by over 58 hours, a remarkable achievement for this 52 year-old Dutchman who had not sailed seriously for years. But it showed that with careful planning and outstanding leadership, an amateur could still be more than a match for the sponsored professional.

However, *Flyer* might not have had such a convincing win if the French yacht, *Gauloises II*, a 57-foot ketch designed by Eric Tabarly and skippered by Eric Loizeau, had not lost her rudder in a storm while she was approaching the Roaring Forties. Rated low, *Gauloises II* finished third on corrected time in the first leg, and, after a disastrous second leg, won the third and fourth legs on corrected time. Overall, she finished sixth.

French races 1978
The Whitbread bridged 1977 and 1978, and the latter year produced a whole crop of French-organised, single- and short-handed events as well as the crewed events like the one from Trinité-sur-mer to the Azores and back, now biennial; and the Atlantic Triangle which was not run after 1978.

The annual *Course de L'Aurore*, inaugurated in 1970, attracted 37 starters, including entries from Japan, Britain, Spain and Canada. Some of the top French names like Jan de Kat, Michel Malinovski and Jean-Marie Vioal also took part. Each year the course is altered. In 1978 the first leg was from Perros-Guirec in North Brittany to Kinsale in Southern Ireland, the second leg from Kinsale to La Baule, the

third from La Baule to Laredo in Spain, and the fourth from Laredo to Quiberon, a total distance of 1300 miles with short stopovers at each staging port. As can be imagined, racing single-handed in such confined waters gave little opportunity for any of the entries to sleep. One who did went aground on the rocks at St Ives while another ran ashore and got stuck for six hours. The overall winner, both on the aggregate time for all four legs and on the points system for placings, was Gilles Le Baud sailing a prototype Jean Beret half-tonner. The race is now sponsored by the newspaper *Le Figaro* and is called by that name.

The other two French races were new. The double-handed *Triangle du Soleil*, also sailed by half-tonners, took place in the Mediterranean. It became an annual race and by the 1980s attracted as many as 30 to 40 starters. The course was from Port Camargue to Bonifacio, Bonifacio to Minorca, with a last leg back to the starting point where the fleet had to sail a short Olympic course. It is an event which mainly attracts French yachtsmen – in 1982 it was won by Hubert Follenfant – but the other new fixture, the *Route du Rhum*, has rapidly established itself as a classic of international stature.

Inaugural *Route du Rhum* 1978
After the 1976 OSTAR the organisers announced that the entry list for the 1980 event would be limited to 110, and that no yacht over 56 feet LOA or 46 feet LWL would be allowed to enter. This decision was not unexpected but the French, understandably, were furious, and some of their yachtsmen were convinced the new regulations had been introduced to break the French dominance of the event. But the truth was that the huge fleet menaced shipping, and by limiting numbers and size it was hoped that the toll on yachts and lives would be minimised. By setting class limits, the race committee was also trying, as its chairman remarked, 'to adhere to the original concept of the race – which is to defeat the ocean rather than the other competitors.'

The French, however, were deeply dissatisfied and decided to organise their own single-handed Transatlantic race, from St Malo to Guadeloupe, a distance of 3700 miles. Naturally, there was no limit on maximum size though a minimum of 26 feet LWL was imposed, more or less the same as OSTAR.

Doing things the French way meant there were huge cash prizes – 250 000 francs for the winner – no Rule 26 to worry about (it had been waived), and a special race-against-the-clock for the last 60 miles. There were no handicap prizes.

Thirty-nine starters were seen off by a vast spectator fleet – more than one journalist said it was the largest they had ever seen – and there were two collisions. Watching the world's top solo yachtsmen – Alain Colas in *Manureva*, Chay Blyth in *GBIV*, Olivier de Kersauson in *Kriter IV* and Phil Weld in *Rogue Wave* – must have been an irresistible draw. The only disappointment was that Tabarly could not compete, and his enormous foil catamaran, *Paul Ricard II*, was taken over by the famous French dinghy sailor, Marc Pajot. The eventual winner, Mike Birch, who'd done so well in the 1976 OSTAR, covered the course in 23d,6hrs,57mins. What was surprising was that his trimaran, *Olympus Photo*, which had had to be specially lengthened for the race to comply with the regulations, had been able to beat much larger rivals. Even more surprising was the closeness of the finish, with Birch and Michel Malinovski in his monohull, *Kriter V*, fighting it out neck and neck over the last miles. In the end Birch edged ahead and won by a mere 96 seconds!

Birch's dramatic victory made him a household name in France – appropriately, he had begun his solo sailing career in the 1972 *Course de L'Aurore* – but that country was soon thrown into mourning when one of its best-loved and best-known yachtsmen, Alain Colas, failed to arrive, having disappeared without trace. He had become another casualty to add to the growing list of sailors lost in multihulls.

San Francisco to Kauai 1978
In the US, a new single-handed event was inaugurated over a course from San Francisco to Kauai, Hawaii, a distance of 2196 miles. The fleet of 31 was divided into five divisions, with the smaller boats starting four days before the bigger ones. Six of the 14 in this smaller contingent soon dropped out when strong winds and big seas caused damage and exhaustion, but the larger entries fared better and only one retired. The strongest Pacific high in 50 years gave the surviving yachts winds that rarely dropped under 15 knots and sometimes topped 35. In these conditions Norton Smith, sailing an ultra-light Santa Cruz 27 called *Solitaire*, covered the course

in a quick 13d,2hrs,34mins,27secs to become both the elapsed and corrected time winner. Second to cross the finish line was Skip Allan in *Wildflower*, but he was pushed into third place overall by one of the bigger boats, *Golden Egg*, which took only 12 minutes more than the winner to complete the course. Twenty-three skippers finished, six of whom had been sailing for less than two years, and the race is now a quadrennial fixture.

The *Transat en Double* 1979

The limelight for double-handed racing turned to France once more in 1979 when a new quadrennial fixture across the Atlantic was inaugurated.

This double-handed race, the *Transat en Double*, took the 40 competitors from Lorient across the Atlantic to Bermuda which was rounded without stopping before returning to Lorient. The event, as with the *Route du Rhum*, attracted some of the world's top yachtsmen, though the majority of the entries were French, and, like the earlier race, was very closely fought. Tabarly and Pajot in *Paul Ricard II* took a route far to the

south of their other main rivals, a tactic which paid off for they were the first to round Bermuda a clear day ahead of the next yacht, *Kriter VI*, with *Tele Sept Jours*, sailed by Mike Birch, third a further four and a half hours behind. *VSD*, a Kelsall-designed foil trimaran skippered by Eugene Riguidel, lay fifth behind *Kriter V*, skippered by Michel Malinovski, but lost 13 hours when she had to put into Bermuda to replace a broken boom. This put Riguidel some 60 hours behind the leader, but he sailed a more northerly course than Tabarly on the return leg and slowly closed the gap. Thirty minutes from the line he overtook Tabarly and finished just five minutes ahead, having covered the 5782 miles in 34d,6hrs,31mins. Mike Birch was third, beating off the challenge of Malinovski yet again, this time by the margin of just over six hours.

The *Transat en Double* was, and is, not only the longest double-handed event in the world but the first ocean race where competitors were fitted with Argos satellite transmitters which allowed detailed data of a yacht's progress to be fed to the press daily. The same facility was also given to the entries

in the 1980 OSTAR.

The trio of other short-handed fixtures in 1979 all had large increases in their fleets. AZAB widened its entry list to include both single- and double-handed monohulls and multihulls. The Mini Transat – won by Norton Smith, the victor of the first San Francisco-Kauai solo Transpac – also allowed multihulls to enter, but the capsize test which the organisers rightly insisted on was so stringent none started.

The Parmelia race 1979

The crewed Parmelia race from Plymouth to Perth which took place in 1979 had entries from 28 yachts and they were divided into an IOR and an Open Division. For the IOR boats it was a pursuit race which meant that their time of starting depended on their handicap. The first past the post would be the winner. The Open Division raced in a more leisurely fashion. the organisers adopting a points sys-

▼ *The winner of the inaugural Route du Rhum,* Olympus Photo, *sailed by the Canadian Mike Birch. He immediately hit the headlines in France and was sponsored by the French TV magazine* Tele Sept Jours *in later events.*

tem which enabled yachts to start whenever they chose so long as they arrived on a given date.

The idea behind a pursuit race was that all the competitors should arrive more or less together, a contrived method of racing especially as bonus and penalty points were awarded to encourage a yacht to arrive within the appointed four-hour time band. Though it did not work on the first leg it was sufficiently successful at the finish for the huge crowd at Fremantle, the port of Perth, to give the yachtsmen an enthusiastic reception. In the IOR fleet of ten, *Independent Endeavour* arrived at Cape Town some 14 hours ahead of *Gauloises III* and 23 hours ahead of the third boat, *Siska II*, with nearly all the rest arriving over a period of six days. On the second leg the same three leaders finished within 12 hours of each other, though it took the remainder a further four days to complete the course. *Independent Endeavour*, the clear winner on both legs, won the overall prize for the IOR division and though *Siska II* dropped to third place on the second leg she finished second overall, with *Gauloises III* third. The Open division was won by a Sparkman and Stephens sloop from Western Australia, *Bluebell*.

The Nedlloyd Spice race 1980

When the Parmelia race was organised it was hoped that some of the yachts in it would choose to take part in an event organised by the Dutch for the following year. Called the Nedlloyd Spice race, it was organised by the

American solo sailor Norton Smith won the second Mini-Transat in his 21-foot American Express *at an average speed of 5½ knots.*

Spice Race Foundation which had been established after van Rietschoten's victory in the Whitbread race to keep alive Holland's interest in long distance ocean racing.

The idea of the 1980 race, which was to start at Djakarta and finish at Rotterdam, was to retrace the route of the Dutch commercial sailing ships which had plied the oceans during the previous centuries. The course also coincided with that of the British tea clippers returning from China, so it was decided that the fleet would be divided into two: those who decided to race non-stop from the Sunda Straits to the Straits of Dover in an attempt to break the record of 63 days set by a tea clipper called *Kelso* – a time not even the famous *Cutty Sark* had been able to match – and those who wanted to break the 12 500 mile race at Cape Town. However, the course of the former was so arranged that everyone could compete for the handicap prize, the Nedlloyd Trophy, a silver replica of the *Cutty Sark*.

As with the *Financial Times* clipper race five years before, initial interest was strong, but when the race started on 12th March the entry list had been whittled down to eight, only three of which, *Gauloises III*, *Seltrust Endeavour*, and Chichester's old boat, *Gipsy Moth V*, had taken part in the Parmelia race. Three of this small fleet – *Gauloises III*, van Rietschoten's *Flyer*, now renamed *Flying Wil-*

ma and skippered by van Rietschoten's navigator Gerard Dijkstra, and the giant Australian ketch, *Batavia*, built and skippered by three Dutch emigrant brothers – elected to race non-stop. The other five consisted of three Dutch yachts, *Prodent* (ex-*Williwaw*), *Lexington* and *Vetus Zanazara*, and *Gipsy Moth V*, and *Kaleo* from Singapore. Two others, *Seltrust Endeavour* and the South African *Wesbank*, joined the fleet at Cape Town.

The start was in force three to four winds and brilliant sunshine. *Flying Wilma* was first to cross the start line followed by *Gauloises III*. These two maintained their lead, but the French yacht's compass was faulty and she slowly moved south towards the high pressure area in the Indian Ocean which held both yachts becalmed for two days before the Trade Winds arrived to send them surfing on their way.

Further back *Prodent* was close to the leaders and well ahead on handicap, but sickness and gear damage had affected some of the others and *Kaleo* eventually had to put into Mauritius for repairs.

Flying Wilma's more northerly course helped her to establish a good lead over *Gauloises III* and she passed over the finishing line at Cape Town 46 hours ahead of her French rival. These two carried on and were round the notorious Cape of Good Hope before the 'Cape of Storms' produced a vicious maelstrom which had south westerly winds gusting up to 80 knots and mountainous waves sometimes topping 60 feet. This storm, which sunk one freighter and severely damaged another, wreaked havoc amongst the fleet of yachts. *Kaleo* had already been dismasted before the storm began, but it marooned her crew for five days before anyone could rescue them. The 80-foot *Batavia* was twice forced into Port Elizabeth for repairs and when *Lexington* eventually arrived at Cape Town there were hairline cracks in five of her rigging terminals and her mainsail had been ripped beyond repair.

With this storm behind them, both *Flying Wilma* and *Gauloises III* made good progress at first. But when the Dutch yacht passed St Helena she was four and a half days behind the clipper ship's record time. To save time she cut inside the traditional clipper route and began to decrease the gap. Behind her, *Gauloises III* followed suit but went much further in and at one time was within sight of the coast before being forced to tack. By doing this she closed the gap from about 480 miles to 390 miles, but *Flying Wilma* kept her lead and crossed the finishing line for the timed race some 81 hours ahead of her rival but 16hrs,3mins behind *Kelso's* record run. Her time for the complete race at Rotterdam was 65d,3hrs,25mins, good enough to also give her the handicap trophy as her closest rival for this prize, *Prodent*, had been dismasted during the second leg. *Gauloises III* was second and *Lexington* third.

UK races 1980
Britain in 1980 had yet another full racing

▶ *The start of the second leg of the Nedlloyd Spice race at Cape Town. From left to right:* Wesbank, Seltrust Endeavour, Lexington, *and* Prodent.

▼ Gauloises 3 *was an entry in both the Parmelia race and the Nedlloyd Spice race.*

season. There was a 695-mile Round Ireland race organised by the Wicklow Sailing Club. Races round Ireland had been held twice before: in 1975 when a double-handed event in three legs, organised by the Ballyholme Yacht Club, had attracted four starters; and in 1978 when a crewed non-stop pursuit race starting at Falmouth with a fleet of eight had been organised by the RORC. The 1980 race was a crewed non-stop event and it attracted 13 starters which were split into an IOR and an open handicap division. In 1982 the numbers increased to 17 and it became established as a biennial fixture and part of the RORC's programme.

The second British Islands race was run with a fleet of 13, but this time there were no stops. It was a tough race with headwinds encountered for more than half of the 1860-mile course, as well as four successive gales which hit the fleet while off the east coast. First to cross the line was Mottola Balestra's Frers-designed *Chica Tica II*, which covered the course in 12d,10hrs,42mins and also claimed the overall prize. The 1984 race was cancelled because of insufficient entries, perhaps an early victim of an increasingly overcrowded racing calendar.

OSTAR in the 1980s
Though the French ran a crewed race to Dakar from La Baule – they called it the *Course des Almadies* and it was won by Marc Pajot in a tri sloop called *Elf Aquitaine* – the main attraction in 1980 was the OSTAR.

The 110 places were snapped up quickly, and as before the French and the British predominated though the increase in American entries was marked. There were also starters from such unlikely countries as Bulgaria, Greece and Finland and for the first time a husband and wife, Rob and Naomi James, raced against one another. Ninety-one eventually came to the line and 72 finished within the 50-day limit. There were two unofficial entries. Tabarly, plagued by an old skiing injury, was forced to withdraw at the last moment and Marc Pajot again took over *Paul Ricard II*. But Pajot had not completed the qualifying cruise and was not able to race officially. Neither was Jean-Yves Terlain when he asked to be considered as a late entry, but both yachtsmen were given Argos transponders and were allowed to race alongside the rest of the fleet. 'It makes no difference,' remarked a French yachting journalist, 'if Marc is first to Newport the world

will say he won La Transat.'

But though Pajot crossed in a record breaking time of 18d,13hrs,41mins he was nevertheless some way down the final list of finishers which was headed by Phil Weld of America who finished in the remarkable time of 17d,23hrs,12mins in his scaled-down version of *Rogue Wave* – now too big to enter – called *Moxie*.

Weld's victory was a remarkable one for not only did he smash Colas' 1972 record time by a convincing two and a half days – a record which was also beaten by the first seven boats to finish – but he managed it at the age of 65.

The speed with which the race was completed by the leaders was due to a weather pattern which enabled them during the first week of northerly winds to cover almost half the course. Phil Steggal from America won the Gipsy Moth class, coming third in *Jeans Foster*, the veteran Jerry Cartwright made it a clean sweep for America when he finished first in the Jester Class in *Le First*; and Dame Naomi James took the prize for the first woman to finish, beating Clare Francis' 1976 time by completing the course in 25d,19hrs,12mins.

If the 1980 race was fast, the 1984 one was finished at an even more miraculous speed. The increasing experience of single-handed yachtsmen probably had something to do with it, but undoubtedly the design of multihulls has improved so much during the last few years that they can turn in performances that would have seemed unachievable a decade previously. However, it is not just the front runners who have improved, but the speed of the whole fleet. In the first race no yacht finished in under 30 days. By 1976 14 finished in under this time, and this had risen to 46 in 1984. No yacht finished in under 20 days until 1980, when six finished in under that time. In 1984 this number increased to 20.

What also marked the 1984 race as exceptional was that there were really two winners. The first across the line was the Frenchman, Philippe Poupon, who finished the course in his trimaran, *Fleury Michon VI*, in 16d,11hrs,55mins. This beat Weld's record by 1d,11hrs,17mins, and it was also beaten by 12 other yachts!

Poupon, however, was not declared the winner as a dramatic rescue of Philippe Jeantot by Yvon Fauconnier gave the latter the race. Jeantot was 100 miles out into the

Atlantic when his 60-foot catamaran, *Credit Agricole*, capsized. Fauconnier, sailing his trimaran, *Umupro Jardin*, saw the upturned hull about a quarter of a mile off his course and diverted to give Jeantot assistance. He took Jeantot aboard and remained alongside the capsized yacht for 16 hours until he knew help was on its way. He then put Jeantot back onto the capsized hull, went back to the race, and still managed to finish in 16d,22hrs,25mins. The organisers, quite correctly, deducted the 16 hours from his time which made him the winner by over five hours.

Increasing popularity of single- and short-handed events
The popularity of single-handed racing increased by leaps and bounds throughout the 1970s and early 1980s. Added to the solo events already described were an annual 650-miler in the Gulf of Georgia, Canada, and then in 1981 an American fixture which took single-handers round the island of Guadalupe. The same year the Japanese organised the third solo Transpac event, this time to Kobe from San Francisco, a distance of 5500 miles. It had 11 starters, a considerable increase on the earlier events and was won by Fukunari Yamada in *Taiyo* in a time of 43d,15hrs,11mins.

The expansion of short-handed events also continued. In 1983, for example, *Le Figaro*, the *Transat en Double*, the La Baule-Dakar, AZAB, and the Mini-Transat – which added a class for two-man yachts in 1983 – were held again and were joined by a new short-handed race from Plymouth to Vilamoura and back.

Organised by the Royal Western Yacht Club, the Plymouth-Vilamoura race was conceived as an event to fill the year between the more exacting 1982 Round Britain race and the 1984 OSTAR. It was won by Jeff Houlgrave and Andrew Hall in *Colt Cars GB* who beat Chay Blyth, sailing *Lonsdale Cars* (ex-*Brittany Ferries*) by 36 hours.

But the race highlighted the dangers of short-handed racing. The stragglers at the back of the fleet were hit by a severe gale and some yachts, lashed by 50-foot waves and 70-mph winds, were soon in trouble. The Polish entry, *Carmen*, was abandoned sinking 220 miles from Plymouth, and the crew had to be picked up by a ship. Then 60 miles from the Scillies another entry, *Adfin's Rival*, was overwhelmed by a giant wave and the crew were forced to take to their liferaft. They were both picked up by helicopter, but one of them had already died, of hypothermia.

Another casualty in the race was Robin Knox-Johnston's *Sea Falcon*, which was hit by a ship on the second leg. Knox-Johnston was knocked unconscious by the impact but later managed, with the help of his wife Sue, who was his crew, to sail the sinking trimaran near Corunna where they were taken in tow by a fishing boat. The yacht was later written off as a total loss.

The inaugural TWOSTAR 1981

Short-handed events have increased in popularity because of the pressure for single-handed races to be stopped. One result of this campaign was the inauguration of TWOSTAR.

At one time it looked as if the 1976 OSTAR would be the last. As an alternative the organisers had come up with the idea of a double-handed Transatlantic race. Planned before the 1976 OSTAR, it was really organised as a sop to the critics of the OSTAR and as a fallback should that event be abandoned. No one at the time seriously thought there would be any great demand for such an event, but when it was announced in 1978 the entry list of 135 was filled immediately.

The TWOSTAR attracted most of the top names in the sport and the starters were divided into six classes according to size, and the maximum length was 80 feet. The largest boat to race, however, was the 70-foot tri, *Sea Falcon*, owned by Robin Knox-Johnston. He led for the first half of the race, but was later overtaken by the eventual winner, a 65-foot tri, *Brittany Ferries GB*, sailed by Chay Blyth and Rob James; the 62-foot cat, *Elf Aquitaine*, which had won the Dakar race the previous year; and by the much smaller *Gauloises IV*, another multihull. It was another sweeping victory for the multihulls though none of the three proas which had entered finished. As with the previous year's OSTAR it was a fast race, with *Brittany Ferries GB* finishing in the remarkably fast time of 14d,13hrs,54mins.

Mini-transat in the 1980s

The third Mini-Transat was held amidst controversy about its safety and the growing expense of competing. As with the OSTAR, the race had grown away from the original concept, with expensive 'one-off' yachts being specially designed and built. And like the OSTAR, it had become something of a test tank for new ideas as well as a proving ground for production yachts. Of the maximum of 60 yachts allowed to race only 25 started and

▼ *The 70-foot* Sea Falcon *sailed by Robin Knox-Johnston took part in the 1981 TWOSTAR and the 1982 Route du Rhum, but was lost in a collision in 1983.*

The Whitbread Round-the-World-race 1981

1981 also saw the start of the third Whitbread Round-the-World-race – 'the sailor's Everest' as it was called. Specially for the event, Conny van Rietschoten, 'The Flying Dutchman', had built himself a new *Flyer*. Following the trend towards single-stickers the 76-foot Frers-designed yacht was sloop rigged as was the pre-race favourite, *Ceramco New Zealand*, skippered by Peter Blake. Twenty-six other yachts started the race from Portsmouth and the only change in the course was that the third leg was to finish at Mar del Plata instead of Rio. Of these, only the two French sloops, *Charles Heidsieck III* and *Kriter IX*, and perhaps Les Williams' new maxi, *First Co-Operative*, looked possible winners. Tabarly was racing again in *Pen Duick VI* now renamed *Euromarché*, as was Chay Blyth in *United Friendly* (ex *GB II*). The top four represented a new breed of inter-ocean racer, being lighter and faster than the generation that had raced four years previously.

It proved to be a exciting race. There were no less than nine dismastings (*Licor 43* lost hers twice) and if *Ceramco New Zealand* had not lost the top of half of hers during the first leg she could well have won on handicap for she took line honours on each of the other three legs, winning the second and final legs on handicap. It was *Flyer II*, however, which was sailed to a magnificent victory despite going into the final leg behind both *Charles Heidsieck III* and *Kriter IX* – by completing the whole course in 120d, 6hrs,34mins,14secs, smashing the previous record by an incredible 14 days, five and a half hours, a time which gave her the coveted double of line honours and the handicap prize.

Conny van Rietschoten had once again showed that with careful planning and a disciplined crew – he went as far as forbidding any shouting on board his yacht – it was possible to beat the most heavily sponsored competitor. However, after the race he put *Flyer II* up for sale, said the race had cost him a fortune, and that next time he would have to have a sponsor. During the second leg he had suffered a severe heart attack. That the 56-year-old Dutchman should talk about 'next time' at all just shows the inherent resilience and tenacity of the man.

The Whitbread has emerged as one of the world's great ocean races. What it is like to compete in such a race is hard to convey

▲ *Accidents will happen, especially at a crowded start like that of the 1980 OSTAR. American Tom Grossman's* Kriter *aboard a Spanish competitor.*

there was once again a preponderance of French boats. They took the first six places, and the winner was Jacques Peignon, sailing *Les Iles du Ponant*. His time of 32d,20hrs, 22mins was only 12 hours outside Norton Smith's time in 1979, a remarkable performance considering that the winds were light and that he was forced to take the helm most of the way.

The popularity of the Mini Transat with the French was reflected in the results of the 1983 race. It proved to be the best supported and the fastest with Stephan Poughon from France winning the solo class in *Voiles Cudennec* in 31d,15hrs,45mins and the Thelier brothers from Guadeloupe winning the two-handed class in *JCB2* in 33d,00hrs,23mins. However, the future of the race is in some doubt for the original organisers have found it has created too many demands on their time and money, and have declined to organise another. Doubtless, a sponsor will be found.

but one of Peter Blake's crew, Keith Chapman, got pretty close to it when he described one day's exhilarating ride in the Southern Ocean during the 1981 race.

'Thursday, November 5 was a day of unforgettable sailing,' he wrote in the New Zealand magazine *Sea Spray*. 'The whooping and yelling of the deck watch gradually mellowed as each surf became just another. These were the conditions for which *Ceramco* was designed and we had to make the most of them. Sleep was impossible, the speedos screaming, the sink gurgling, the noise of the foam rushing past and the movement of the stern as the helmsman swung it around to ensure a safe course. The off-watch crew were all aft, the sails piled around the chart table trying to keep the rudder in the water.

'Spells on the helm were limited and tendons in my forearms were soon complaining. Twin wheels proved a God-send as the second helmsman riding shotgun would come in to help wind the wheel into a wave or roll to ensure a safe, straight run. We would white-out as the bow wave landed beside the aft cockpit, the wind and spray blowing back across the boat and obscuring vision. The boat would hold up on a face, let go, flow down a wave to hit bottom. The crew now understood *Ceramco's* surfboat nose and flat, uplifting bow sections as she bounced across a section of flat water, planing continually.'

Route du Rhum 1982

The already crowded calendar for yachtsmen who enjoyed crewed inter-ocean or short-handed events was further filled in 1982 with the inauguration of a French-run, short-handed Trans-Mediterranean race, and re-runs of established events like the SF-Kauai Solo Transpac, the Round Britain, and the *Route du Rhum*.

It was the *Route du Rhum* which snatched all the headlines for it attracted all the top names as well as a good deal of undesirable publicity. Amongst the 51 starters, most of them multihulls, were Jean-Yves Terlain in his huge trimaran, *Gautier III*, Mike Birch in a virtually untried catamaran called *Vital*, Chay Blyth in *Brittany Ferries GB*, Rob James in his

▶ *The Farr-designed maxi, Ceramco New Zealand, under jury rig after being dismasted during the first leg of the 1981 Whitbread Round-the-World race. With a new mast she went on to win two of the last three legs.*

60-foot trimaran, *Colt Cars GB*, Knox-Johnston in *Sea Falcon*, now renamed *Olympus 3* for his French sponsor, and Eric Tabarly in *Paul Ricard II*. Tragically, it was to be Rob James' last race for later that year he was lost overboard from his yacht in the English Channel.

It was a race full of incidents and one which supported the arguments of those who feel that sponsored single-handed races are dangerous and irresponsible. With the weather forecast predicting gale-force winds, the fleet was seen off by a huge crowd of spectators, and soon the accidents began, as Cathy Hawkins recorded for *Yachts and Yachting*.

'Day one: Four spectators are reported to have fallen to their deaths from the cliffs overlooking the start, as the gun went off. Ten minutes later, the proa *Rosieres* capsized. Next, Daniel le Mere ran his catamaran *Edonil* into a spectator boat while below looking for a spinnaker. *Biotherm*, Florence Arthaud, returned to Saint Malo for a new autopilot. She restarted two days later and finsihed in 19th position.

'Day two: Eight boats had either retired or were sheltering while carrying out repairs and obtaining new equipment. Eric Tabarly was among them.

'Day three: Race leader Jean-Yves Terlain in *Gautier III* was dismasted. Marc Pajot had broken mainsail battens, Rob James had damaged his arm, and like Mike Birch who had a hand infection was truly sailing single-handed. A monohull abandoned the race and two more craft headed back with autopilot problems.

'Day four: Eric Loizeau's *Gauloises IV* had broken all her mainsail battens in an accidental gybe. Rob James in *Colt Cars GB* had broken a cap shroud. Phillipe Poupon's *Fleury Michon VI* had lost half her rudder and Alain Gabbay was reported to have been over the side in a Force 6 to straighten a bent rudder trim tab. Another swimmer was Therry Caroni who swam 60ft (20m) to recover his missing centreboard.

'Day five: Rob James abandoned the race, all *Colt Cars'* main halyards were chafed through. Chay Blyth also retired *Brittany Ferries GB* after surfing backwards at 15 knots and bending the rudder trim tab. *Vigorsol* had

◄ *The winner of the third Whitbread Round-the World race, Flyer II, a 76-foot, Frers-design sailed by Dutchman Connie van Rietschoten.*

hit the Spanish coast and was leaking. Two trimarans pulled out, one monohull headed for home and *Charente Maritime* was heading for the Madeira Islands to repair a forestay. The trimaran *BAI Brittany Ferries* collided with a trawler and carried away a hull.

'Day six: Eric Tabarly abandoned the race for good – too much ground to make up. Eugene Riguidel trailed with furling system, autopilot, mainsail and outhaul problems. He hadn't eaten or slept.

'Day seven: one monohull abandoned the race with electrical and autopilot problems, another had a leak at the rudder stock. A trimaran had electrical and mainsail batten problems, another structural problems. Robin Knox-Johnston diverted to Madeira for new batteries.

'Day eight: Patrick Morvan had a heart attack and sailed slowly for home.

'Day nine: *Jaz* and *Telegramme de Brest* called at the Azores to meet repair teams. Alain Gabbay arrived shortly after for trim tab repairs.

'Day ten: Marc Linski was taken off *Pantashop* with acute appendicitis.

'Day 11: *Rennie*, Ian Johnston, executed a carbon copy of her Round Britain Race flip with a pitchpole capsize while running under spinnaker. Olivier Moussy went to the rescue.

'Day 12: Respite. No new casualties.

'Day 17: Marc Pajot stopped at Martinique while a repair gang boarded to fix a damaged crossbeam. He continued, well in the lead, to take the FF250 000 (£23 855) first prize.

'And that was just one race!'

Despite the strong French contingent a lot of money had been put on the British. But one by one they dropped out, or behind, leaving Pajot to cross the line first.

Popularity of sailing in France

Sailing is big business in France and it has become that country's most popular recreation. In the early 1980s, Tabarly was named in a survey as being the most popular sportsman in France between 1970 and 1980. In the same survey 70 per cent of Frenchmen interviewed said they sailed, while over half said they would prefer to have a sailing boat than a second car.

Sailing is also very much a spectator sport in France and it draws huge crowds. The start of the *Route du Rhum* is probably the biggest draw. But even lesser known events attracts large numbers. The start of the thousand-mile Deauville-La Rochelle-Deauville race, for example, a multihull event, drew an estimated 100 000 in 1984.

With such a huge potential audience, it is not surprising that the large international companies find it worth their while for publicity purposes to underwrite the skills of a Pajot or a Tabarly. This in turn has created an elite, a small group of professional sailors, who can, and do, earn a fortune. And below this elite are a whole surge of young and ambitious yachtsmen who are all keen to make their names, and their fortunes, in the ever-increasing number of one-off, or regularly held, single-handed races. For instance, out of the 400 enquiries for the 1983 Mini Transat 350 came from French-speaking countries, and it is now an event almost totally dominated by the French.

Commerical sponsorship does not, of course, stop at financing the construction of yachts and supporting the men who sail them. New races are being devised all the time and huge prizes are offered. Long distance races – like the one to Dakar which was won in 1983 by *Charente Maritime* – are especially popular with sponsors and create great interest. The latest of these was the 2897-mile Transatlantic event held in 1984 to celebrate the 450th anniversary of Frenchman Jacques Cartier's first exploratory voyage up the St. Lawrence River.

TAG Transat race, 1984

This anniversary race was sponsored by a Paris based company, *Technique Avante Garde*, and it became known as the TAG Transat. It attracted a new breed of multihull, built to a new maximum size limit of 85 feet, for the prize money was huge –$110 000 Canadian. There were five of them among the 49 starters – *Royale II, Charente Maritime II, William Saurin, Formule TAG,* and *Fleury Michon VII* – and they dominated the race for the 24-hour world-speed record was beaten by one or other of them no less than three times between the start at Quebec and the finish at St Malo. The eventual winner, *Royale II*, finished in 8d,19hrs,57mins, with *Charente Maritime II* only 15 minutes behind.

▼ *The start of the 1982 Route du Rhum. Note the huge throng of spectators on the cliffs. Marc Pajot in* Elf Aquitaine *is on the left, Rob James in* Colt Cars *on the right.*

Marc Pajot

Attitudes towards sponsorship

As an example of what a firm receives for publicising its product through sponsorship, the name *Disque d'Or*, a Swiss entry in the last Whitbread race, was mentioned in the press no less than 23 000 times, including a thousand times in headlines.

Apart from France, New Zealand is perhaps the only other country that is fully aware of the advantages of sponsorship, the yachting authorities having a more relaxed attitude towards the use of it simply because of the cost of getting to and from the country for major events.

At the opposite extreme the Americans seem to have little interest in improving a brand name in this manner, and yachtsmen like Walter Green, Phil Steggall, and Tom Grossman have to look to France for support. Phil Weld, winner of the 1980 OSTAR, believes in sponsorship though he does not need it himself. This is just as well because on

the day he won the race *The Wall Street Journal* devoted its sports page to golf.

Britain is becoming much more aware of the advantages of sponsorship and when no American company showed any interest in sponsoring the second single-handed race around the world, which started on 28th August 1982, British Oxygen, now known as BOC, snapped up the opportunity.

Around alone

Of all the events that have taken place during the last few years, the BOC 'Around alone' race is the most appropriate with which to finish this chapter, for it is the ultimate challenge for the lone yachtsman.

It was the first single-handed around the world race since 1968 and it attracted 16 entrants from eight countries, though two dropped out just before the start. The rules were far more stringent than in the earlier race, with each competitor having to qualify

▲ *France's top paid sportsman, Marc Pajot, at the helm of his 62-foot trimaran, Elf Aquitaine, which was launched in 1981. 'The concept of a boat like this,' said her designer, Sylvestre Langevin, 'represents 1000 hours of study and at least 400 hours of discussion and checking on site'. She has now been replaced by Elf Aquitaine II which has a revolutionary swing rig, and came third in the 1984 OSTAR.*

with a thousand-mile, non-stop trial. And this time there were three compulsory ports of call between the start and finish at Newport, Rhode Island: Cape Town, Sydney and Rio de Janeiro.

Most of the entrants were experienced single-handed yachtsmen: men like Bertie Reed from South Africa, Desmond Hampton from Britain, Dave White, Tony Lush and Francis Stokes from the US, and Guy Bernardin and Jacques de Roux from France, who had all competed in OSTAR while Britain's Paul Rodgers and a Czech called Richard Konkolski, had already completed single-handed circumnavigations. Another entry, Australian Neville Gooson, picked up his experience on the way to the start sailing singlehanded from Sydney to Newport, covering the 11 000 miles in 79 days.

The entries were divided into two classes, Class I for yachts between 45 feet and 56 feet LOA, and Class II, between 32 feet and 44 feet LOA. The winner of each class received a $25 000 cash prize.

At the start the leader was the American, Dave White, who had conceived the idea of the race, in his 56-foot sloop, Gladiator. But along with another American competitor, Thomas Lindholm, he was an early casualty after splits opened suddenly in the yacht's main bulkhead.

The lead was then taken by Frenchman Philippe Jeantot, a 30-year-old oil rig diver, sailing a 56-foot cutter, Credit Agricole, which had been built and sponsored specially for the race by the French bank of the same name. He stayed ahead and won the first leg

of 7000 miles to Cape Town by six and a half days from the next competitor, Bertie Reed in Altech Voortrekker. Richard Broadhead was third in Perseverence of Medina and Desmond Hampton fourth in Gipsy Moth V which he had chartered from Francis Chichester's son, Giles.

At Cape Town the yachts were fitted with their Argos beacons, the satellite system which was soon to play such a dramatic part in the race. In fact, it had to be used almost immediately for Tony Lush's freedom-rigged schooner, Lady Pepperell, was pitch-poled 1500 miles out of Cape Town and began to sink. In a marvellous feat of seamanship he was rescued by fellow-American Francis Stokes in his 39-foot yacht, Mooneshine, who was about 50 miles ahead of him at the time. With a full gale blowing astern Stokes decided not to try and battle upwind. Instead, he let Lush drift down on to him, while a radio ham in South Africa gave them accurate position fixes from the satellite tracking system. After

eight hours, just before dusk, they saw each other three miles apart.

'We were very lucky,' Stokes said later, 'It would have been just as easy to miss him.'

Stokes eventually arrived in Sydney on 5 January with his passenger to take sixth place overall and second place in Class II.

During this second leg Philippe Jeantot extended his lead over Bertie Reed to eight and a half days having taken 35 days to reach Sydney. A close rival, Desmond Hampton, overslept in the Bass Strait while only 120 miles behind Jeantot, and wrecked Gipsy Moth V on Gabo Island, just 250 miles from the finish of the leg.

The remaining yachts started the third leg on 16th January 1983. It was on this leg

▼　Start of the third leg of the 1982 BOC round-the-world race from Sydney. The eventual winner, Credit Agricole (85), is on the left of the picture.

149

self – the fourth leg was completed by everyone without loss, and Jeantot stretched his winning margin over Bertie Reed to 11 days, completing the 27 000-mile course in 159d,2hrs,26mins. Behind Reed was Richard Broadhead who received a special prize for seamanship for his rescue of de Roux, with Neville Gooson fourth. Class II was won by Japanese taxi driver Yukoh Tada in his 44-foot sloop, *Koden Okera V*, with Francis Stokes, who also received a special prize for his seamanship in rescuing Tony Lush, second.

Jeantot's win was well deserved, and though he had not been among the favourites, his campaign to take the race had been carefully prepared. His sponsors had provided him with sufficient money to have a yacht designed specially for the race, which the others did not. For instance, water ballast tanks had been incorporated into the design. This allowed Jeantot to increase his yacht's righting moment by pumping in sea-water with a small diesel pump. This gave him the equivalent of a full crew lining the weather rail. When he tacked he could pump the water to the new weather side, and when he sailed downwind he could pump out the water and lighten the hull. All very ingenious and the kind of detail which wins races – especially ones of 27 000 miles.

The future
Untroubled by IOR, or, apparently, the recession, the elite world of inter-ocean and short-handed racing is booming. It is arguable that traditional ocean racing is still an amateur sport, but the inter-ocean and short-handed events mostly are not.

It is difficult to envisage a further increase in the number of events without one detracting from the other, but undoubtedly the French will continue to lead the way in inaugurating them.

that Jeantot ran into trouble. His rudder hangings had been weakened by rough weather and then the lower bearing broke when the yacht was knocked down. Jeantot consulted the yacht's designer, Guy Ribardeau Dumas, over the radio telephone and was told to keep his speed to below 15 knots or the rudder would break off. He did so, but still stayed in front, arriving in Rio de Janeiro well ahead of Bertie Reed.

This third leg proved as dramatic as the second, with New Zealander Richard McBride running aground on the Falklands and Richard Broadhead performing another remarkable rescue.

On this occasion the victim was Frenchman Jacques de Roux, Class II winner of the second leg in *Skoiern III*. He was completely rolled over while 1800 miles from land and dismasted. The yacht began to sink and de

▲ *A sad end to a great yacht.* Gipsy Moth V *was wrecked off the Australian coast during the BOC Round-the-World race in 1982.*

Roux triggered the emergency alarm on his Argos position transmitter. With no direct radio contact possible, the organisers got through to de Roux's nearest competitor, Richard Broadhead, via radio hams in Newport, New Zealand and Tahiti.

Broadhead was 300 miles ahead of de Roux when he heard what had happened, but he turned into the wind and, with the aid of Satnav backtracked for 59 hours to find de Roux's estimated position which was relayed to him from Newport. It was a miracle that he found de Roux and the Frenchman was snatched from his yacht just before it sank.

With the competing yachts down to ten – McBride was eventually able to refloat him-

▶ *One of the few new multihulls built for the TAG Transat race in 1984,* Royale II *is seen here at the start of the Route of Discovery. The race was won by Phillippe Poupon in* Fleury Michon VII.

ACKNOWLEDGMENTS

Many organisations and individuals helped me with this book. I would especially like to thank E. Alan Greene, Secretary of the Royal Ocean Racing Club, for reading the manuscript, and the following for their help in one form or another: Alexander Turnbull Library, Wellington; Auckland Institute and Musuem; Auckland Public Library; Bahamas News Bureau (Eileen Fielder); Rennie Barrett; Bermuda News Bureau (Charles Webbe); Bishop Museum, Honolulu (Betty Lou Kam); D.H. Clarke; Clyde Cruising Club (A.G. Taggart); Cruising Association of South Africa (T.G.S. Unite); Jean Louis Fabry; Sue Fielden; Hobart Mercury; Hong Kong Yachting Association (R.S.S. Hownam-Meek); Irish Yachting Association; Maine Historical Association (Margot McCain); Richard McCloskey; Middle Harbour Yacht Club; Sydney (Geoffrey B. Foster); Nippon Ocean Racing Club (K. Ogimi); Ocean Racing Club of Australia (M.R. Edwards); Ocean Racing Club of Victoria (Ken Black); Onerahi Yacht Club, Whangarei (C.M. Farley); Barry Pickthall; *Revista Mar*, Brazil (Ernani Paciornic); Hector Ross; Royal Akarana Yacht Club, Auckland (Brian Hewitt); Royal Norwegian Yacht Club; Royal Nova Scotia Yacht Squadron (George Rogers); Royal Ocean Racing Club (Janet Grosvenor); Royal Swedish Yacht Club (Ake Lundberg); Royal Vancouver Yacht Club (George A. Cran); Royal Western Yacht Club of England (Cdr L.R.R. Foster RN); Read Ruggles Jr; Sardinia Cup Press Office (Gigi Zorio); Hans-Otto Schumann; *Sea Spray*, Auckland (David Pardon); State of Hawaii (Archivist, Susan Shaner); Narelle Stewart; Bobby Symonette; Paul Titchenor; Union Nationale pour la Course au Large (UNCL); *Yachts and Yachting*; *Yachting*, Cos Cob, USA (Deborah Meisels); Yacht Club de France (Claude Breguet); and Yacht Club Italiano (Sergio Savio).

PHOTOGRAPHIC CREDITS

Page 8, From *The Great Yacht Race*, Peter Davis, London 1966; page 9, *London Illustrated News*; page 10, *London Illustrated News*; page 12, Beken; page 13, Beken; page 14, *London Illustrated News*; page 15, From *Yachting De Course A Voile*, Societé D'Editions Géographiques, Maritimes et Coloniales; page 16, *The Strand Magazine*; page 17, Morris Rosenfeld; page 18, *London Illustrated News*; page 20, (top) *Rudder Magazine* (below) *Rudder Magazine*; page 21, (top) Morris Rosenfeld (below) *London Illustrated News*; page 22, Morris Rosenfeld; page 23 (top) *Rudder Magazine* (below) State of Hawaii archives (below) State of Hawaii archives; page 24, (top) State of Hawaii archives; page 25, State of Hawaii archives page 27, Morris Rosenfeld; page 28, (top) Morris Rosenfeld (below Gunnar C Anderson; page 29, Gunnar C Anderson; page 30, RORC; page 32, Ocean Publications; page 33, Gunnar C Anderson; page 34, State of Hawaii archives; page 35, (top) Morris Rosenfeld (below) *Winning The King's Cup*, G P Putnam's & Sons London; page 36, Beken; page 37, Beken; page 38, Sparkman and Stevens; page 39, (top) Beken (below) Author; page 40, Author; page 41, Author; page 42, Morris Rosenfeld; page 43, (top) State of Hawaii archives (below) State of Hawaii; page 44, (top) State of Hawaii archives (below) *Auckland Weekly News*; page 45, Beken; page 46, *The New Zealand Freelance*; page 47, *Auckland Weekly News*; page 48, (top) *Auckland Weekly News*; (below) Auckland Public Library Photograph Collection; page 49, (left) *New Zealand Free Magazine* (right) Australian Official Photograph Collection; page 51, Beken; page 52, Beken; page 53, F J Ames; page 54, Associated News/papers Ltd; page 55, Beckner; page 56, (left) Beckner Photo Service (right) Bermuda News Bureau; page 57, Author; page 58, Beken; page 59, Author; page 60, (top) Robert H Symonette (right) Robert H Symonette; page 62, *Mercury Hobart Tasmania*; page 63, Australian News & Information Bureau Photograph; page 64, Bermuda News Bureau; page 65, Beken; page 66, Beckner Photo Service; page 67, Beckner Photo Service; page 69, *The Observer*; page 70, *The Observer*; page 71, Beken; page 72, Tigh-Na-Mara; page 73, Beken; page 74, Beken; page 75, Jim McVie Photo; page 76 (top) Bermuda News Bureau; (below) Beckner Photo Service; page 77, Ocean Publications; page 78, Beckner Photo Service; page 79, Beken; page 80, Beckner Photo Service; page 81, Bermuda News Bureau; page 82, Royal Western Yacht Club; page 84, *Yachting World*; page 85, Eileen Ramsay; page 86, Ocean Publications; page 88, (top and bottom) *Sunday Times*; page 89, *Sunday Times*; page 90, *Sunday Times*; page 91, Australian Information Service; page 92, Bermuda News Bureau; page 93, Eileen Ramsay; page 94, Australian News and Information Bureau; page 95, Gunnar C Anderson; page 97, *The Mercury* (Hobart Tasmania Australia); page 98, Ocean Publications; page 99, Ocean Publications; page 100, *Yachting World*; page 101, *The Argus*, Cape Town; page 103, Yachting World; page 104, Australian Information Service; page 105, Australian Information Service; page 106, *Sunday Times*; page 108, David Baker; page 109, Ocean Publications; page 112, Australian Information Service; page 113, Beken; page 114, *Sea Spray*; page 115, Beckner Photo Service; page 116, Gunnar C Anderson; page 118, Barry Pickthall; page 119, Ocean Publications; page 120, Sardinia Cup Office; page 121, Barry Pickthall; page 122, Phil Uhl; page 123, William Payne; page 124, A H M Patrick; page 125, Author; page 127, Author; page 128, Barry Pickthall; page 129, (top) Jonathan Eastland (below) *Observer*; page 131, Roger M Smith; page 132, Australian Information Service; page 133, *Observer*; page 134, Ocean Publications; page 135, (top) Jonathan Eastland (below) *Sea Spray*; page 136, *Yachts and Yachting*; page 137, Jonathan Eastland; page 139, Colin Jarman; page 140, *Yachts and Yachting*; page 141, (top) Barry Pickthall (below) Patrick Clayeux; page 143, Jonathan Eastland; page 144, Barry Pickthall; page 145, D Burke; page 146, Barry Pickthall; page 147, Jonathan Eastland; page 148, Barry Pickthall; page 149, Ocean Publications; page 150, Bruce Hogan; page 151, Barry Pickthall.

Index

Numbers in bold indicate black and white illustrations, the letter c indicates that subject is in colour section.